This Reckless Breed of Men

This Reckless Breed of Men

The Trappers and Fur Traders of the Southwest

Robert Glass Cleland

Introduction by Harvey L. Carter

UNIVERSITY OF NEW MEXICO PRESS
Albuquerque

Introduction

In the spring of 1950, the distinguished New York publisher Alfred A. Knopf brought out Robert Glass Cleland's *This Reckless Breed of Men*. By the fall of that year, the book had received the usual number of reviews, many of which were, at best, perfunctory. There was, however, one well worth recalling. It appeared in the *Mississippi Valley Historical Review* and was written by Louis B. Wright, then director of Folger Library.

Wright began his perceptive review by stating: "This book is an excellent example of a scholar's synthesis of an enormous body of materials . . . to produce a work at once accurate, succinct, and eminently readable." Recognizing the truth of Cleland's claim that Hiram M. Chittenden's standard history of the far western fur trade had totally neglected the Southwest, the reviewer provided his readers with a fairly full summary of the book. Impressed by Cleland's style, Wright went on to say that the book was a model of condensation, clarity, and vividness, and ended his enthusiastic review by suggesting that it be seriously considered for the Pulitzer Prize.

Robert Glass Cleland was born in 1885 at Shelbyville, Kentucky. His parents moved to Los Angeles, California, in the early 1890s and there, in 1907, Cleland was graduated from Occidental College. He spent the next five years at Princeton University, where he took a second bachelor's degree in 1909 and a doctorate in history in 1912. He then returned to Occidental College, where he taught history until 1943. In that year his wife died, and Cleland became a member of the permanent research staff of The Huntington Library in San Marino. He died in 1957.

Cleland gained early recognition for his writings on the history of California, and with the publication by Knopf in 1944 of *From Wilderness to Empire*, one of his many books, he became the acknowledged dean of the "Golden State" historians. At The Huntington Library he continued his dual role of teacher and administrator, awarding that institution's research grants and pursuing his own researches.

Cleland's avowed purpose, both in teaching and writing, was to light up the landscape of history. In 1950, when *This Reckless Breed of Men* appeared, the American Southwest during the period of the fur trade had not yet been illuminated. Cleland lighted up this spectacular and far-flung landscape so well that, after twenty-five years and a good deal of new research, his book remains the most comprehensive, reliable, and readable presentation of the subject.

It may be of some service to mention specific items in Cleland's book to which exception may be taken. On the map facing page 3, Bear River is shown flowing into Snake River, instead of doubling back, as it actually does, to discharge into Great Salt Lake. This is an error of oversight arising from the fact that the work of the mapmaker was left unchecked. On page 155, in footnote 43, the name Philip Kearny appears where Stephen Watts Kearny is intended. As both men were generals and as Philip was nephew to Stephen Watts, a confusion of the two men is not surprising. These are illustrations of factual errors, that while relatively inconsequential, are an aggravation to an author and a plague to his publisher. That there are so few errors of this nature in *This Reckless Breed of Men* is a tribute to both.

In the light of evidence now available one may comfortably disagree with the statement on page 155 that Charles Bent opposed the sale of liquor to Indians and never made use of it in his trading operations. It is reasonable to assume that the statement in David Lavender's *Bent's Fort* (1953) offers a more realistic appraisal: "Although every contemporary account of Bent, St. Vrain and Company ascribes to them an honor in Indian dealing far higher than the normal standard of the plains, they unquestionably resorted to liquor when circumstances demanded."

Referring again to the map opposite page 3, it will be observed that Cleland included the southern part of the Oregon country within his "zone of the fur trade of the southwest." It seems likely that he did so in order to allow himself the liberty of treating the operations of British fur traders stationed at Fort Vancouver. In any case, it is somewhat confusing to have the Southwest enlarged by adding a generous slice of what was and is universally regarded as the Northwest. Cleland quoted from Thomas James, *Three Years Among the Indians and Mexicans* several times, but at the same time failed to give James' trading expedition any textual space alongside the two other fully detailed expeditions to Santa Fe in 1821. This is especially to be regretted because James followed an entirely different route from that taken by anyone else.

On page 18, Cleland refers to an 1825 diary kept by William Sublette. This is now known to be the diary of William H. Ashley, so splendidly edited by the late Dale L. Morgan as *The West of William H. Ashley* (1964). Morgan not only established the authorship of the diary, but also his annotations have placed all subsequent researchers in the field heavily in his debt. In a similar way, the statement that Bent's Old Fort was begun in 1828 and completed in 1832 has become untenable. It is now definitely known that Bent's Old Fort was built during the year 1834. The frequently repeated statement, appearing on page 158, that William Bent blew up his Old Fort in 1854, cannot be given credence any longer. William Bent abandoned it in August 1849, and it was used as a stage line depot by Barlow and Sanderson well into the 1860s.

On page 158, Cleland says, "here at intervals for several years, Kit Carson was a resident hunter, supplying the [Bent's] Fort with buffalo meat." The source of this error is to be found in Dr. DeWitt C. Peters, *Life and Adventures of Kit Carson* (1858), who says that Carson was a hunter for Bent's Fort for eight years. Harvey L. Carter's *'Dear Old Kit': The Historical Christopher Carson, with a new edition of the Carson Memoirs* (1968), clearly shows that Carson was a hunter for Bent's Fort from September 1841 through April 1842, barely eight months instead of eight years.

Other less consequential instances of this sort could be cited but I prefer to point out instead an instance where Cleland was ahead of his time. In dealing with Joseph Reddeford Walker, Cleland found it hard to believe that Walker was a horse thief and conjectured that Walker's unenviable reputation had arisen from a confusion of his name with that of Walkara, the Ute chief, often called Walker, who was raiding in California during the late 1840s. Since LeRoy R. and Ann W. Hafen have shown in their *Old Spanish Trail* (1954) that Joe Walker was buying horses in California at the same time he was reputed to have been stealing them, it seems probable that Cleland's conjecture was correct.

Cleland's book inspired other scholars to follow up his research on Mountain Men. The most notable results are LeRoy R. Hafen's *Mountain Men and the Fur Trade of the Far West* (1965–72) and David J. Weber's *The Taos Trappers: The Fur Trade in the Far Southwest, 1540–1846* (1971). Hafen's monumental ten-volume work comprises nearly 300 biographical sketches of Mountain Men by 84 contributors, and represents a great advance in knowledge. In particular, note should be taken of the contributions of Janet S. LeCompte, who sketched the lives of many French trappers who penetrated the Southwest. So great was the increase of knowledge resulting from her skillful researches that future writers will certainly have to credit the French trappers with more influence than Cleland was able to perceive twenty-five years ago. Weber's study is less dramatically presented than Cleland's and does not indicate a need for revision of Cleland's carefully documented facts. It does, however, synthesize the contributions of the Spanish to the fur trade in a most satisfactory manner, and supplements Cleland's American point of view.

Above all, Cleland must be commended for the soundness of his characterization of the Mountain Men. The three popular images of the Mountain Men seem to be the heroic adventurer, the daring degenerate, and the expectant capitalist. These three popular impressions were analyzed statistically by Harvey L. Carter and Marcia C. Spencer in "Stereotypes of the Mountain Men" (*Western Historical Quarterly*, 6:17–32). They concluded that the stereotype of the "heroic adventurer was of more general application than the other two, the adventure being largely inherent in the occupation; that of the daring degenerate was of limited application during the early years of the fur trade but that it increased in validity during the closing years; that of the expectant capitalist had a high degree of validity for the leaders but a much lower application to the rank and file."

In the light of this analysis, Cleland comes through with flying colors, for it is obvious that, while he pays some attention to the business aspects of the fur trade, and while he has a good eye for quotable material with which to illustrate daring but degenerate actions, it is the aspect of heroic adventure that appeals to him most of all. Moreover, he unerringly singles out this aspect as having the greatest historical importance. To Cleland, the Mountain Men were the men who led the way. As he aptly observes in his prologue, "The feet of a nation walked in his half-obliterated trails, the course of empire followed his solitary pathways to the western sea." Robert Glass Cleland's view will probably pass the test of another twenty-five years and best express the ultimate verdict of history.

Harvey L. Carter
Professor Emeritus of History
Colorado College
Colorado Springs, Colorado

Preface

THIS BOOK is the outgrowth of an interest in the trappers and fur traders of the Southwest that began many years ago. It represents extensive research in printed and manuscript sources; a first-hand knowledge (acquired for the most part with a fly rod conveniently at hand) of many of the rivers trapped by the mountain men; and possibly some skill in joining hitherto separate and un-co-ordinated narratives into a unified and connected whole.

The purpose and scope of the book are explained in the Prologue. It does not assume to be the definitive study of the subject — such a work, indeed, chiefly because of the fragmentary and widely scattered nature of the manuscript sources, is likely never to appear — nor can it take credit for the discovery and exploitation of an entirely new field. Some twenty years ago Joseph J. Hill, of Oakland, then associate curator of the Bancroft Library of the University of California at Berkeley, published a series of valuable articles that furnished a starting-point and blazed the path for subsequent investigation of the subject. I am indebted to these articles and to Mr. Hill personally for his friendly advice and counsel.

Many libraries and historical societies have placed me under lasting obligation by their courtesy and generous co-operation. I have drawn especially upon the resources of the Bancroft Library of the University of California, the

Coe Collection of Western Americana of the library of Yale University, the Congressional Library and National Archives in Washington, the Missouri Historical Society of St. Louis, particularly upon the manuscripts in the Sublette Collection, the New Mexico State Museum in Santa Fe, the California Historical Society, and the California Pioneer Society of San Francisco. I have relied most of all upon the extensive manuscript and printed resources of the Huntington Library of San Marino.

My sincere appreciation is also due to many individuals as well as institutions. Dr. Ralph Bieber of Washington University placed his extensive knowledge of Western source material at my command and very generously lent me valuable microfilm material from the Mexican archives. Dr. Glenn Dumke, Dr. LeRoy Hafen, Curator of the Colorado Historical Society of Denver, Carl P. Russell, Superintendent of Yosemite National Park, Joseph J. Hill, and Dan S. Hammack read portions of the manuscript. Dr. Dumke, David Davies, Director of Claremont College Libraries, and Andrew Rolle were of great assistance in the collection of material. Dr. Dumke further assumed a large share of the responsibility in the preparation of the maps. I am also indebted to Miss Haydée Noya of the Huntington Library for numerous translations and transcriptions, to Carey S. Bliss and Erwin F. Morkisch of the same institution for assistance in the selection and reproduction of the illustrations, and to Mrs. Edna Fotch and Miss Norma Jones for secretarial assistance. Miss Jones and Mr. Hammack rendered great and thankless service in the reading of the proof.

Finally, to certain skeptical fishing companions I offer this book as witness to my integrity and good faith. Was I to blame if the trails of the fur traders, which the zeal of the historian alone compelled me to follow, led on occasion to shining rivers and slow meandering streams where trout as well as beaver found a congenial home?

CONTENTS

Maps

Illustrations

This Reckless Breed of Men

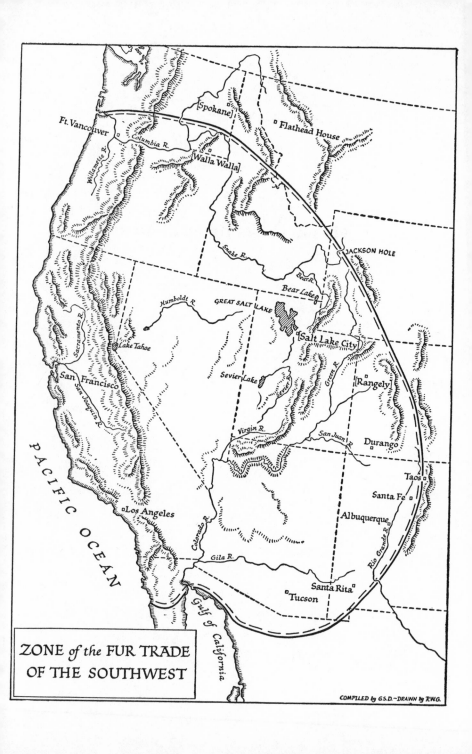

ZONE of the FUR TRADE
OF THE SOUTHWEST

COMPILED by G.S.D.–DRAWN by R.W.G.

PROLOGUE

A DECADE before the outbreak of the American Revolution most of the territory now included in the United States was still unexplored. Between the Allegheny Mountains and the Pacific, broken at long intervals by isolated settlements of French or Spanish origin, as lonely as scattered islands in a great ocean, lay a continent-wide wilderness of which the outside world had only fragmentary and often curiously distorted knowledge.

By a singular coincidence, the initial movements in the occupation of this vast region began almost simultaneously on its extreme eastern and western boundaries. The two enterprises were entirely independent of each other and represented a complete contrast in origin, character, methods, and objectives. They proceeded along wholly separate paths for nearly a generation and then came into violent and decisive conflict, a conflict that brought near-disaster to the one and gave the other dominion to the western sea.

The movement on the west began in 1769 with Spain's occupation of the province of Alta California, a valiant effort to revitalize a once virile and aggressive people and prevent a great empire from going to decay. It was a carefully planned, large-scale, generously supported undertaking. Its leaders, Don Gaspar de Portolá and the Franciscan missionary Father Junípero Serra, were supplied, at government expense, with provisions, ships, baggage trains, troops, muleteers, ammunition for presidios, furnishings for new missions, and official instructions for the conduct of the enterprise. The expedition justified these costly and extensive preparations. It provided a solid foundation for Spain's control of California and extended the King's frontier from the remote settlements of Sonora and Lower California to the strategic waters of San Francisco Bay.

Two weeks before the last contingent of this Spanish expeditionary force reached California, the second movement for the occupation of the Western wilderness had got under way. Across the continent in North Carolina four American frontiersmen led by a man named Daniel Boone left their crude log cabins on the banks of the Yadkin River and started westward "in quest of the country of Kentucky."

These backwoods settlers had neither ships, baggage train, commissary, nor bodyguard. They were clad in homespun cloth and buckskin. Coonskin caps protected their heads, and Indian moccasins lent stealth and elasticity to their walk. Their weapons were those of the forest borderlands — small-bore, long-barreled rifles, flints, hickory ramrods, powder horns, bullet pouches, short-handled axes or tomahawks, keen-edged skinning knives.

Before the solitary explorers rose the soft, tree-covered slopes of the Blue Ridge. Beyond those mountains lay a land of mystery and promise that reached to the end of the continent and touched the waters of the Great Sea. The exploration of that spreading wilderness was completed in a generation. Before the middle of the century a nation as yet unborn when Boone and his neighbors crossed the mountains was in possession of the land.

In this bold drama of exploration and expansion many types of American frontiersmen took part; but beyond the narrow fringe of border settlements in the Mississippi and Missouri valleys the fur trader played the leading role. His stage was an empire. His operations extended from the British possessions on the north to the dry tablelands of the Spanish-Mexican provinces below the Rio Grande, and from the Great Plains and the Rocky Mountains on the east to the end of the continent on the west.

The fur trader, trapper, beaver-hunter, or mountain man was a peculiar product of the American frontier. He belonged to a calling that had no counterpart. He started from frontiers at which more cautious pioneers were glad to stop. He was an adventurer to whom danger became a daily commonplace, an explorer who took tribute of the wilderness and wandered through the reaches of the outer West with all the freedom of the lonely wind. He was the predecessor of the missionary, the gold-seeker, the cattle-man, the settler, and all kindred pioneers. The feet of a nation walked his half-obliterated trails, the course of empire followed his solitary pathways to the western sea.

"It was the trader and trapper who first explored and established the routes of travel which are now, and always will be the avenues of commerce in that region," wrote Hiram Martin Chittenden. "Between 1820 and 1840 they learned almost everything of importance about the geography of the West that was to be learned and acquired a better understanding of that geography than Americans as a whole acquired for at least another generation." [1] The beaver-trappers, rather than other explorers to whom posterity gave credit, were thus, in Chittenden's estimation, " the true pathfinders of the West"; or as George Frederick Ruxton wrote more than fifty years before, "Not a hole or corner in the vast wilderness of the 'Far West' but has been ransacked by these hardy men. From the Mississippi to the mouth of the Colorado of the West, from the frozen regions of the North to the Gila in Mexico, the beaver-hunter has set his traps in every creek and stream. All this vast country, but for the daring enterprise of these men, would be even now a *terra incognita* to geographers. . . ." [2]

In all this there was a touch of irony, a measure of historical injustice. For while his contributions to national expansion were so permanent and far-reaching, the beaver-hunter himself, having played his part, was hurried unceremoniously from the scene. To all intents and purposes the trans-Mississippi fur trade began in the Northwest with the Lewis and Clark Expedition of 1804–6 and closed with the settlement of the Oregon Question forty years later. In the remainder of the West the industry rose, flourished, and declined between 1820 and 1840 — an infinitesimal interval, as history measures time, of only twenty years. Moreover, when the era of the fur trade closed, it closed forever. The mountain man, unlike the prospector, cattleman, or frontier settler, left no successor; his brief day had no tomorrows.

[1] Hiram Martin Chittenden: *The History of the American Fur Trade of the Far West* (New York, 1902), Vol. I, p. ix.

[2] George Frederick Ruxton: *Adventures in Mexico and the Rocky Mountains* (New York, 1848), p. 234.

But in his few allotted years the trapper set his impress forever upon the map of North America and the fate of the United States. He affected the destiny of nations; he changed the future of a continent; he bequeathed to later generations of Americans a tradition of heroic exploration comparable to that of the seamen of Elizabeth or the conquistadores of Spain.

The history of the fur trade of the Northwest is now a familiar tale. Many writers have described the adventures and activities of the mountain men in the valleys of the Missouri, the Yellowstone, the Snake, the Green, the Columbia, in the Wind River Mountains and Jackson's Hole, around Fort Laramie, Fort Bonneville, and Fort Hall. In that great area many of the trappers' battlegrounds, rendezvous, and trails are carefully marked by monuments of wood, bronze, or stone.

For the history of that familiar region this volume has only incidental responsibility. Its field is another segment of the West, a huge empire that lay beyond the traditional centers of the fur trade, drew little attention to itself because of its remoteness and isolation, and received scant consideration from those who wrote the history of beaver skins and mountain men. Even Chittenden, who, among the host of students of the Western fur trade, towers like Saul head and shoulders above his brethren, dismissed one of the most important trapping regions of the whole Southwest with little more than a disparaging paragraph.

"The Colorado river proper below the confluence of the Green and Grand," he wrote, has but little connection with the history of the fur trade. The physical character of the country precluded access to the river for the greater part of its length until it emerged from the Grand Cañon near the mouth of the Virgin river. By that time it was in a latitude where the trapping business was no longer profitable. Most of its tributaries, likewise, along this stretch of the river, were shut in between the walls of deep cañons and, like the main stream, were inaccessible. However interesting and attractive this region may now be to lovers of natural scenery, it was not so to the people of the fur trade, and was but little frequented by them. . . .[3]

Chittenden, in this rare instance, was grossly ignorant of the facts. Draw a huge arc from the lower reaches of the Columbia River to the valley of the Salt Lake. Extend that arc to the old Spanish settlement of Santa Fe. Project the line south and west to the head of the Gulf of California and the delta of the Colorado. Carry it on to the missions and pueblos of California. Swing it back to the Columbia, through the San Joaquin and Sacramento valleys. Such an imaginary line will enclose about a fourth of the territory now included in the United States and roughly define the geographic limits of this present study. The region thus delineated, as truly as the more famous lands "across the wide Missouri," was the dominion of the mountain man. There he set his traps, meandered his streams, fought his unrecorded battles, and left his bleaching and forgotten bones. Across that trackless waste he extended the trails to the West begun by Daniel Boone and the backwoodsmen

---

[3] Op. cit., Vol. II, pp. 782–3. Chittenden added that the Gila River, in reality one of the most important beaver streams of the West, "was too far south to be of any importance in the fur trade."

from the valley of the Yadkin. He was the vanguard of the American advance that blazed a new Wilderness Trace to the Pacific and established the sovereignty of the United States over the empire commonly spoken of today as the "Great Southwest."

CHAPTER 1

Beaver and Mountain Men

THE BEAVER, whose peltry constituted the basis of the Western American fur trade, flourished in North America from the Arctic Circle to the gulfs of Mexico and California. After the close of the eighteenth century, three great river systems west of the Misssissippi — the Missouri, Columbia, and Colorado — constituted the principal hunting-grounds for American trappers; but beaver were also found in large numbers on the Rio Grande, Arkansas, Humboldt, Sacramento, San Joaquin, and a hundred other independent streams.

Contrary to common opinion, many of the desert or semi-desert rivers of the Southwest were major trapping fields. For the beaver was — and still is — at home alike in the deep chasms of the San Juan and Colorado rivers, where the summer heat becomes almost unbearable for human beings; in the warm, sluggish waters of the lower Gila; and along the winding channels of the Colorado delta. The fur of the desert river beaver, though somewhat lighter in color and practically worthless from early spring to late fall, is only slightly inferior to that of the northern beaver during the remainder of the year.

As a preface to this study. it is also necessary to point

out that the Spanish province of Alta California once had a large beaver population. California beaver were of three types or races: the Shasta beaver in the interior, the large golden beaver in the central delta area of San Francisco Bay, and the Sonora beaver on the Colorado. The rivers of southern California apparently had too little water to maintain beaver colonies; but the animal flourished in large numbers in the northern drainage basins of the state, especially on the Sacramento and San Joaquin rivers and their tributaries, and in the low, marshy regions tributary to San Francisco Bay.

A few beaver were found in the streams that flowed out of the northern Coast Range Mountains into the Pacific; but though the animal thrived at high altitudes in other mountain systems, it had not established itself above the thousand-foot level in the Sierra Nevada by the time the trappers reached California, and the fur-hunters' narratives make no mention of beaver in the Owens, Walker, Carson, Truckee, and other rivers that flow eastward out of the central and southern Sierra.[1] No satisfactory explanation has been found for this curious restriction of the animal's habitat.

A beaver of average size weighs between thirty and forty pounds, but fifty- or sixty-pound adults are not uncommon,

[1] For confirmation of these statements and the beaver's present distribution in California, see Grinnell, Dixon, and Linsdale: *Fur Bearing Mammals of California* (Berkeley, 1937), Vol. II, pp. 635–6. I am also indebted to Seth B. Benson of the Museum of Vertebrate Zoology of the University of California at Berkeley, for further information on the subject.

Silt from mining operations apparently drove the beaver out of many northern California streams after 1850.

and a few authentic specimens running over a hundred pounds have been reported. The animal's hind feet are webbed, his scaly tail possibly furnished the pattern for the first Indian canoe paddles. The beaver finds it an instrument of many uses — a rudder when he swims, a balancing device when he runs or gallops, a prop when he sits down or squats on his haunches, and a convenient artifice for slapping or plopping the surface of the water when he wishes to warn other beaver of approaching danger.

The bark and leaves of the aspen, cottonwood, willow, and similar trees furnish the animal's chief supply of food. His teeth and jaws are powerful enough to cut through the hardest oak, but the old belief that a beaver felled a tree in a predetermined direction has been discarded. In quiet water the beaver builds a house of branches, twigs, and mud. He is then called a lodge beaver. In swift-running streams the same beaver tunnels into the bank and makes his nest above the water level. He is then spoken of as a bank beaver.

In his monumental work on the American fur trade Chittenden thus described the methods commonly used in trapping this traditionally sagacious animal:

The universal mode of taking the beaver was with the steel trap, in the use of which long experience had taught the hunters great skill. The trap is a strong one of about five pounds' weight, and was valued in the fur trade period at twelve to sixteen dollars. The chain attached to the trap is about five feet long, with a swivel near the end to keep it from kinking. The trapper, in setting the trap, wades into the

stream, so that his tracks may not be apparent; plants his
trap in three or four inches of water a little way from the
bank, and fastens the chain to a strong stick, which he drives
into the bed of the stream at the full chain length from the
trap. Immediately over the trap a little twig is set so that
one end shall be about four inches above the surface of the
water. On this is put a peculiar bait, supplied by the animal
itself, castor, castorum, or musk, the odor of which has a
great attraction for the beaver. To reach the bait he raises
his mouth toward it and in this act brings his feet directly
under it. He thus treads upon the trap, springs it and is
caught. In his fright he seeks concealment by his usual
method of diving into deep water, but finds himself held by
the chain which he cannot gnaw in two, and after an inef-
fectual struggle, he sinks to the bottom and is drowned. Not
infrequently he wrests the chain from the stake, drags the
trap to deeper water before he succumbs, or, taking it to the
shore, becomes entangled in the undergrowth.[2]

In addition to the castoreum, "a granular, sticky, yellow
substance of a rather pleasant odor," to which Chittenden
refers, both male and female beaver secrete a thick, pun-
gent, yellow oil from two small glands behind the castors.
During the mating season beaver of both sexes deposit oil
and castoreum on spots regularly visited by other beaver
and add mud, sand, dead leaves, and other material to
form so-called "scent-mounds." These hillocks, the largest

---

[2] *History of the American Fur Trade,* Vol. II, p. 820. In the summer of
1947 Charlie Young, of Ovando, Montana, a trapper of seventy-seven
years' experience, told me that a cottonwood wand planted beside a trap
would serve as well for bait as the twig dipped in castoreum. While attempting to strip the bark from the wand, the beaver stepped on the
trigger, sprung the trap, and was caught as Chittenden described.

of which are about a foot high, served the trappers as markers for the trails or runways of the beaver. Some trappers believed that the beaver also rubbed castoreum on his fur to make it waterproof.[3]

Beaver-skinning, like trapping, was an art. After being slit along the animal's belly and on the inside of the four legs, the hide was carefully removed, dried on a willow hoop, and later scraped or grained to rid it of all adhering particles of flesh. A trapper smoked the hides of other animals on a framework of sticks planted around the edge of a hole containing a fire of rotten wood or punk. The process required ten or twelve hours. The Indians followed a somewhat different technique.

"Their mode of dressing the skins is very simple," said an early American writer on the West.

When they wish to preserve the hair, they first extend the skins in the shade, and spread a thin covering of the recent ordure of the buffalo mixed with clay, on the fleshy sides, which for two or three days, are kept constantly moistened with water. In the next place, they are thoroughly cleansed, and subsequently rubbed in the brain of some animal, till they become dry, soft, and pliant.

They are then washed in water thickened with corn bran, dried, and finally scraped with bones, sharp stones, or knives, or sometimes they are worked soft, by drawing them backwards and forwards over the rounded end of a piece of timber, fixed permanently in the ground. When sufficiently dressed, in the manner above described, they are hung up to

---

[3] The castors, sexual organs of both male and female beaver, ran about six pair to the pound. Castoreum itself was worth approximately three dollars a pound in the mountains.

be smoked, either in the smoke aperture of the lodges, or in places constructed exclusively for the purpose.[4]

Beaver skins were folded with the fur inside and packed in bundles by means of a crude press. The bundles were then tied with green buckskin thongs, which contracted while drying and finally became almost as hard and inelastic as iron bands. More elaborate and efficient "wedge presses" were used at the fur-trading posts to bale much larger packs.[5] According to Chittenden, the standard pack contained "ten buffalo robes, fourteen bear, sixty otter, eighty beaver, eighty raccoon, one hundred and twenty foxes, or six hundred muskrat skins." [6]

Upon reaching a promising beaver country, a trapping expedition usually established a base camp from which small parties or single trappers radiated out for many miles to carry on their operations. In the northern and central Rocky Mountain region the trapping season was limited to the spring and fall; but in some parts of the Southwest, where there was little snow or ice, trapping was continued through the winter.

The American trapper borrowed the word *cache* from his French associate and used it as both noun and verb. A cache was a hiding-place, usually a hole or pit — square, circular, or bottle-shaped — in which food, supplies, or furs were stored for safekeeping or to await more convenient means of transportation. A cache was designed to

[4] John D. Hunter: *Manners and Customs of the Western Indians* (Philadelphia, 1823), p. 295.

[5] Carl P. Russell: *Picture Books of the Fur Trade History*, reprint from the *Missouri Historical Society Bulletin*, April 1948.

[6] Chittenden, op. cit., Vol. I, p. 40 n.

keep its contents dry, safe from destruction by wild animals, and secure from discovery by Indians. All the skill and ingenuity of the trappers were used in the construction of such a hiding-place, but frequently the cache was ruined by flood or seeping water, or found and plundered by keen-eyed Indian thieves. The expectant trapper then returned to the site only to face the loss of goods, fortune, or even life itself.

By 1820, after more than a decade of experimental development, the Rocky Mountain fur trade had assumed a fairly clear-cut, standardized pattern. It was carried on by independent or "free" trappers and by powerful, well-organized partnerships or companies. The free trapper — or freeman, as he was called in the usage of the Hudson's Bay Company — operated entirely on his own. He furnished his own equipment, trapped where he pleased, sold his furs to the highest bidder, and recognized no overlord. His status was distinctly higher than that of a regular company trapper or *engagé*. If a free trapper served temporarily with a company brigade, he received his outfit from the company and sold his skins to his employer.

Instead of joining a company expedition, however, the typical free trapper usually chose either to unite with a large number of other freemen like himself, to set out with only one or two companions for "tother side of the great mountains" or across the continent, or to trap entirely alone.

A band of free trappers, though much looser in organization than a company expedition, customarily elected a leader, drafted a set of regulations governing the conduct of the expedition, and provided stringent penalties for the violation of these self-imposed rules. In actual practice, however, such punishments were seldom imposed. Each man's equipment in such a party usually included a gun with two locks, a hundred flints, twenty-five pounds of powder, a hundred pounds of lead, a good powder horn, a double shot bag, a butcher or skinning knife, a tomahawk or shingling hatchet, and from four to six traps.

The partnership or company represented "big business" in the fur trade. It had the advantage of capital, organization, continuity, and large-scale operations. It sought to monopolize both trade and trapping wherever large-scale operations were profitable, and often employed drastic methods to discourage competition. The trappers regularly in its employ were outfitted by the company, trapped under orders of one of its captains, turned their furs over to their leader, and lived under semimilitary discipline.

With the exception of John Jacob Astor's American Fur Company, an enterprise comparable in its field to the Standard Oil Company in the early petroleum industry of the United States, most American organizations, such as the Rocky Mountain and the Missouri fur companies, originated in St. Louis and had their headquarters in that gateway to the continent.[7] Almost always the partners in such companies were themselves successful and experienced mountain men. Many of them were capable executives, as imaginative, adventurous, and persistent in their business undertakings as they were bold, resourceful, and resolute

[7] For Chittenden's criticism of the monopolistic tendencies and ruthless practices of the American Fur Company, see op. cit., Vol. I, pp. 378, 380.

in their leadership of an actual trapping party in the field.

A full-scale trapping expedition sometimes numbered as many as fifty or a hundred men. Its personnel included trappers, hunters, packers, cooks, and miscellaneous camp attendants, hired on a year-to-year basis. In the wilderness the leader, captain, or partisan (to use a term borrowed from the Hudson's Bay Company's terminology) had almost as much authority over the personnel of the company as the captain of a ship exercises over the passengers and members of the crew; and disobedience of his orders was punishable by fine, flogging, or even death. The equipment of a trapping party, though fairly well standardized, depended in part upon the size of the company, the nature of the country, and the length of time the expedition proposed to be away.

Before the members of a trapping party separated into small bands to trap the surrounding country, the leader selected a conspicuous and easily identified spot at which the trappers could rejoin their companions. In 1825 one of Ashley's companies made an extensive reconnaissance of the Seedskedee or Green River Valley, and for several months the leader, William L. Sublette, kept an illuminating diary of the expedition. The following extract indicates the care with which he marked the site of the rendezvous and briefed his lieutenants in recognizing it:

Sunday 19th [April 1825]
We left the creek which turned south traveled west 6 miles over a broken sandy country & came to the Shetkedee which runs SE by Se & NW — is one hundred yards wide 4 to five

feet deep with a rapped current — mountains W.N. — & westerly about 15 or 20 miles — and a range of mountains at a great distance say 40 or 50 miles southwardly — pleasant weather — game scarce some fresh sign of beaver on this river and much old sign — timbered with long leaf cotton wood & small yellow —

. . . .

Tuesday 21st

The 5 men sent to procure skins arrived early this morning with six with which we proceeded to make a boat. They also brought meat. The day is fine and our work advances rapidly —

Wednesday 22nd

Our boat 16 by 7 feet was finished this morning at 9 ock AM, arrangements made for starting to make our hunt. The following are the directions given to Wm. Ham & Clyman who conduct each a party, one of six; The other of five men — [8]

That I will transport the goods and extra baggage down the river to some conspicuous point . . . [and] make choice of the entrance of some river that may enter on the West side of the Shetskedee for a deposite should there be any such river. Should the mountains through which the river first passes be a less distance than we imagine, the deposite will be made on or near the river a short distance above the mountain at some suitable place — The place of deposite as aforesaid, will be the place of randavoze for all our parties on or before the 10th July next & that the place may be known — Trees will be pealed standing the most conspicuous near the junction of the rivers, or above the mountain as the case may be — should such point be without timber I will raise a mound of earth five feet high or set up rocks the tops

[8] William Ham, for whom a branch of the Green River is named, and James Clyman, whose name appears frequently in later pages of this book.

of which will be made red with Vermillion. Thirty feet distant from the same — and one foot below the surface of the earth northwest direction will be deposited a letter communicating to the party any thing that I may deem necessary — Mrss C. & H. will each at a proper time apoint each a man of their party to take charge of their business should anything occur to make it necessary — the men so appointed will be informed of my arrangements will with their parties proceed accordingly in the most carefull & alert manner for my interest — copies of the foregoing directions were delivered to Mrss Ham, Cly. & Fitzpatrick, our boat launched and at 3 ock P.M. the parties started. Clyman with six men to the sources of the Shetskedee Ham westerly to a mountanous country that lay in that direction Fitzpatrick with 6 men southwardly — & myself with 7 men embarked on board the boat with all my goods and extra baggage of the men, we decended the river a short distance and encamped — [9]

The trapper's costume, which nearly every writer who visited the mountains took pains to describe in considerable detail, was more distinctive than that of any other American frontiersman. "His dress and appearance are equally singular," wrote Rufus Sage, a merchant trapper of unusual descriptive ability.

His skin, from constant exposure, assumes a hue almost as dark as that of the Aborigine, and his features and physical structure attain a rough and hardy cast. His hair, through inattention, becomes long, coarse, and bushy, and loosely dangles upon his shoulders. His head is surmounted by a low crowned wool-hat, or a rude substitute of his own manufacture. His clothes are of buckskin, gaily fringed at the seams with strings of the same material, cut and made in a fashion

[9] Missouri Historical Society Collection, Sublette Papers (microfilm).

peculiar to himself and associates. The deer and buffalo furnish him the required covering for his feet which he fabricates at the impulse of want. His waist is encircled with a belt of leather, holding encased his butcher-knife and pistols — while from his neck is suspended a bullet-pouch securely fastened to the belt in front, and beneath the right arm hangs a powder-horn traversely from his shoulder, behind which, upon the strap attached to it, are affixed his bullet-mould, ball-screw, wiper, awl, &c. With a gun-stick made of some hard wood, and a good rifle placed in his hands, carrying from thirty-five balls to the pound, the reader will have before him a correct likeness of a genuine mountaineer when fully equipped.

This costume prevails not only in the mountains proper, but also in the less settled portions of Oregon and California. The mountaineer is his own manufacturer, tailor, shoemaker, and butcher — and, fully accoutred and supplied with ammunition in good game country, he can always feed and clothe himself and enjoy all the comforts his situation affords.[10]

In dangerous country, trappers sometimes wore a deerskin overshirt that reached from chin to thighs. Soaked in water and wrung out, the dried shirt became a veritable buckskin coat of mail that only the hardest-driven Indian arrow would penetrate.

The American fur trade, as distinct from the French or British, made use of three separate institutions — the factory, the fortified trading post, and the rendezvous. The factory was in effect a government monopoly designed to safeguard the welfare of the Indians and prevent their ex-

---

[10] Rufus Sage: *Scenes in the Rocky Mountains* (Philadelphia, 1846), p. 18.

ploitation by aggressive and unscrupulous whites. Though ineffective in some particulars, the system on the whole served a useful and beneficent purpose. It was never a feature of the trade of the Southwest, and went out of existence elsewhere at the beginning of the most important decade of the fur trade, partly because of changed conditions and partly because of the constant pressure of private interests.[11]

Following the policy used so successfully by the British companies in Canada and the Northwest, most of the large American fur companies and a few independent trappers built fortified trading posts at strategic locations in the beaver country.[12] Such establishments, like the presidio, pueblo, and mission of the Spaniard, were distinctive, highly effective frontier institutions. They were civilization's outposts in the wilderness and served not only as important trading centers but also as military forts, supply depots, and havens of refuge for trappers, immigrants, and other wilderness refugees.

The director of one of these great trading posts was a man of unusual and varied talents. He had to be. His authority extended over a region larger than many a European kingdom, and his decisions involved the fate of the post, the welfare of Indians as well as trappers, and the grave issue of peace or war.

He was required to organize the post's numerous trap-

---

[11] For a detailed description see Edgar B. Wesley: "The Government Factory System among the Indians, 1795–1822," *Journal of Economic and Business History,* Vol. IV, pp. 509–10.

[12] A detailed description of one of these posts will be found in Chapter 4.

ping expeditions, to instruct the parties where and how to operate, to exercise control over the most independent and undisciplined product of the Western frontier, and to maintain the peace of the border, despite the presence of many hundreds or even thousands of warlike savages, hostile to the whites by nature and often the implacable foes of other tribes. The men who successfully met such tests were indeed well qualified "to command armies, manage great railroads, or fill any high calling to which the fortunes of life might have led them."

In 1825 General William H. Ashley, most famous of the fur-trading entrepreneurs of St. Louis, revolutionized the Rocky Mountain fur business by introducing the rendezvous as a substitute for the fortified trading post. Unlike the trading post, the rendezvous was not confined to a fixed or permanent location, but followed the movement of the trappers from one region to another and thus created much more accessible trading centers for Indians and mountain men alike.

In contrast again to the company fort, where the Indians and trappers might trade the year round, the rendezvous was held only once a year, usually at the close of the spring hunt. The site for the grand event, an accessible, well-known valley, abounding in game, grass, and water, was usually selected one or two years in advance so that word could be widely circulated through the mountains of the time and place of the gathering. As the opening of a rendezvous drew near, trappers and Indians hundreds of miles away began to move toward the site to participate in the combined festival and fair.

The trappers' rendezvous, in some of its features the wilderness version of the medieval fair, was distinctly an American institution. It was held only in the Rocky Mountains. It was picturesque, spectacular, riotous, magnificently barbaric. To it the company brought its goods, gewgaws, and merchandise — blankets from England (because both wool and workmanship were notably superior to the products of the American mills); powder from the Du Ponts of Delaware; lead from the mines of Missouri; rifles from the Bolton Gun Works of New York and other factories and establishments of St. Louis or the East; shortbarreled guns known as fusils or fusees from American or English gun works; traps, light and strong, from England, Montreal, ironworking plants on the Atlantic seaboard, and smithies in Pennsylvania and St. Louis; gaudy-colored shawls and calicoes from the mills of New England; little bells and mirrors from Cologne, beads from Italy, merinos and calicoes from France; coffee, sugar, and tea from importers of New York, Philadelphia, and New Orleans; and liquor — raw, crude, and poisonous — from Turley's distillery in New Mexico and the devil knew where else besides.

Beaver fur, like the cowhide on the Spanish-American cattle frontier, was the standard medium of exchange. A prime skin weighed at least a pound and a half, and during the heyday of the industry the price ranged from four to six dollars a pound in the mountains. Trade goods sold at the rendezvous at prices that neither the risk of loss nor the high cost of transportation could properly justify; but the trappers and Indians must either buy or go without. Even as late as the mid-forties, tobacco brought from one to three dollars a pound, blankets from twelve to sixteen dollars each, coats as high as forty dollars, sixpenny calicoes fifty cents a yard, and beads a dollar a bunch.[13] Russell estimated the gross profits of such transactions, before deducting necessary costs, at two thousand per cent.[14]

As already suggested, the rendezvous, like the medieval fair, was an extraordinary mixed and colorful affair. It was a place of buying, selling, haggling, cheating, gambling, fighting, drinking, palavering, racing, shooting, and carousing. Here a majority of the trappers traded the furs that had cost them months of incredible danger and hardship for a year's supply of powder, lead, knives, traps, tea, coffee, and blankets that would enable them to return to the lonely reaches of the Green, Yellowstone, Snake, Gila, or Sacramento.

An additional part of the catch went for trinkets and gewgaws for their Indian wives and concubines, as well as for their own adornment. The remainder was then too often squandered in roaring, riotous debauch, devoted in about equal measure to lethal whisky, reckless gambling, usually at euchre, poker, or seven-up, and an orgy of sexual abandon with the complacent Indian girls and squaws.

In soberer moments there were horse races, shooting matches, athletic contests, and long hours of feasting, smoking, and talk around the campfires. Thus the rendezvous furnished a market for the trapper's furs, provided him with a relatively convenient source of supplies, and af-

---

13 Sage, op. cit., p. 29.
14 Osborne Russell: *Journal of a Trapper* (Boise, Idaho, 1921), p. 63.

forded almost his only opportunity for social intercourse and contact with civilization's ragged fringe.

In the regions drained by the Missouri and its larger tributaries, canoes, bullboats, and keelboats were common means of transportation. A keelboat was a heavy, flat-bottomed affair with a raised cargo box running down the middle, a battery of six oars on a side, and a sail for auxiliary use. The boat, usually from fifty to seventy-five feet long, was commonly towed upstream by means of a long rope or cordelle, manned by a tough, hard crew of twenty or thirty men who "scrambled along shore, through water, over rocks, sometimes swimming, sometimes wading, sometimes on solid, dry ground." Such a boat was used only on the largest rivers when heavy cargoes of furs or other freight required transportation.

The bullboat, in striking contrast to the slow, cumbersome keelboat, could be manned by a single trapper. In his account of the activities of Jedediah Smith, Stanley Vestal vividly described the making of one of these awkward-appearing but serviceable craft:

Smith had made bullboats before. He knew how to cut limber willow shoots nearly as thick as his wrist, how to set the butts in the ground in a four-foot circle — as big as the round coracle was to be, how to bend them over and lash them into a rounded framework, how to weave and lash smaller branches across this sturdy frame into a basket.

That done, he skinned several buffalo, and . . . sewed the skins tightly together, making a sheet of hide large enough to cover his willow framework. Then he stretched this skin, flesh-side out, over the basket, and fastened it securely to the gun-wale all around. He next built a small fire under the raw-hide tub, to make the hides shrink and harden, all the time smearing melted buffalo tallow over the seams and surface of the hides. The smoking and soaking in warm grease made the boat waterproof.

Finally, Smith had a leather tub big enough to float him and his packs, light enough to be carried on his back, and small enough to be easily concealed in any thicket or patch of tall grass near which he might drift on his lonely way down the muddy Missouri. . . .[15]

With rare exceptions, the streams of that vast region of uncertain extent and indefinite boundaries called the Southwest were too small and erratic or too swift and tumultuous to permit the use of boats of any type. In its lower reaches the Colorado was navigable by canoes and even larger craft, but from Green River, Utah, to the Mojave villages the river was not a highway but a menace. The trappers were a rash and reckless breed, but even they had no stomach for the rapids, whirlpools, and gray, jagged rocks of that stretch of the Colorado, or for its almost equally treacherous tributary, the San Juan.

This lack of navigable rivers compelled the fur traders of the Southwest to rely almost entirely upon the caravan or pack train for transportation. For such overland travel each trapper had one or more riding-animals equipped with saddles usually of the Mexican type, and two pack mules or horses. The pack animals were equipped and packed after the Mexican fashion and usually carried a load of from two hundred to two hundred and fifty pounds. The stock foraged for itself the year round, and when grass

[15] Stanley Vestal: *Mountain Men* (Boston, 1937), pp. 168–9. Reprinted by permission of the publishers, Houghton Mifflin Company.

and bushes failed, the inner bark of the quaking aspen or sweet cottonwood furnished a satisfactory substitute. Warren A. Ferris, an educated and experienced trapper, noted that the trappers bled their horses every spring "to make them thrive, and render them healthy," and that stock thus treated invariably became fatter, stronger, hardier, and more active than the others.[16]

Each trapper carried his personal articles — pipe, flints, bullet-mold, and the like — in a buckskin bag known as a "possible sack." Traps were carried in a similar but larger bag called a trapsack. Except for running buffalo, a form of sport for which some hunters preferred the fusil or short-barreled shotgun especially designed for the Indian trade, the mountain men employed a forty- to sixty-caliber "plains rifle," the barrel of which ranged in length from thirty to thirty-six inches. Such a gun fired a long, heavy lead bullet and used two to four times as much powder as the famous Kentucky squirrel rifle of Daniel Boone's day. The latter was a little larger in bore than the modern thirty-two-caliber rifle and had a barrel at least four feet long. The plains rifle was a powerful gun, designed under the stress of necessity to deal successfully with buffalo, elk, mounted Indians, and grizzly bears. Its effective range was well over two hundred yards.[17]

[16] Warren A. Ferris: *Life in the Rocky Mountains* (Denver, 1940), pp. 264–5. I have found no other references to this custom, though Texas ranchers, according to J. Frank Dobie, the authority on the Western mustang, used to bleed their horses for certain kinds of sickness. In bleeding, a vein was opened above one of the horse's hoofs.

[17] Chauncey Thomas: "Frontier Firearms," *Colorado Magazine,* Vol. VII, No. 3, p. 103. See also Ferris: *Life in the Rocky Mountains,* p. 241; John G. W. Dillin: *The Kentucky Rifle* (New York, 1946), *passim.*

The most celebrated of the plains and trappers' rifles was made in the gun works of two brothers, Jacob and Samuel Hawken, of St. Louis. Both brothers were born in Hagerstown, Maryland. Jacob moved to Missouri before 1820, and Samuel followed in 1822. The rifle was handmade and had a thirty-six inch barrel of soft iron instead of steel.[18]

The trapper used a peculiar technique in buffalo-running which the following contemporary account very adequately describes:

When running buffaloes the hunters do not use rifle-patches but take along several balls in their mouths; the projectile thus moistened sticks to the powder when put into the gun. In the first place, on buffalo hunts, they do not carry rifles, for the reason that they think the care required in loading them takes too much time unnecessarily when shooting at close range and, furthermore, they find rifle balls too small. The hunter chases buffaloes at full gallop, discharges his gun, and reloads without slackening speed. To accomplish this he holds the weapon close within the bend of his left arm and, taking the powder horn in his right hand, draws out with his teeth the stopper, which is fastened to the horn to prevent its being lost, shakes the requisite amount of powder into his left palm, and again closes the powder horn. Then he grasps the gun with his right hand, holding it in a vertical position, pours the powder down the barrel, and gives the gun a sidelong thrust with the left hand, in order to shake the powder well through the priming hole into the touchpan (hunters at this place discard percussion caps as not practical).

---

[18] A Hawken rifle is on exhibit in Pioneer Hall, Society of California Pioneers, San Francisco. The above data was taken from the exhibition cards.

Now he takes a bullet from his mouth and with his left hand puts it into the barrel, where, having been moistened by spittle, it adheres to the powder. . . . Hunters approach the buffaloes so closely that they do not take aim but, lifting the gun lightly with both hands, point in the direction of the animal's heart and fire.[19]

As tracker, scout, plainsman, or woodsman the mountain man was at least the equal of the Indian. He had to be if he intended to survive. "A turned leaf," wrote George Frederick Ruxton, one of the best-informed observers in the Rocky Mountains, "a blade of grass pressed down, the uneasiness of the wild animals, the flight of birds, are all paragraphs to him written in Nature's legible hand and plainest language." [20]

With the exception of scant supplies of salt, flour, tea, and coffee, the trapper, like the Indian, lived wholly off the country. His favorite meat, day in and day out, was the buffalo, and trappers who had once formed a liking for buffalo humps, ribs, marrow, and steaks were never content with other kinds of meat for any length of time. The craving, in fact, was so pronounced that one wonders if there was not a definite physiological reason for it.

When a hunter killed a buffalo, he often cut the animal's throat and drank the thick, red blood, a draught that reportedly had the taste of warm milk.[21] The heavy layer of fat that ran from the buffalo's shoulder along the backbone

---

[19] Bureau of American Ethnology: *Journal of Rudolph Friederich Kurz* (Bulletin 115. Washington, 1937), pp. 194–5.

[20] *Adventures in Mexico and the Rocky Mountains,* p. 235

[21] Thomas James: *Three Years among the Indians and Mexicans* (St. Louis, 1916), p. 116.

was stripped off, dipped in hot grease, and then smoked. It was eaten with lean or dried meat.[22]

Deer, elk, antelope, and bear were also favorite food animals with the mountain men. Beaver tail was a great delicacy, but the rest of the beaver was eaten only when other meat was scarce. According to many reports, a true mountain man preferred lynx meat to any other delicacy.[23] French dumplings, a very special treat, were made of minced meat rolled in balls of dough and fried in buffalo marrow.[24]

Thomas Jefferson Farnham, whose writings on the West attained wide popularity in the early forties, made his reader hunger-conscious with the following vivid account of a trapper's feast on buffalo:

The marrow bones were undergoing a severe flagellation; the blows of the old hunter's hatchet were cracking them in pieces, and laying bare the rolls of "trapper's butter" within them. A pound of marrow was thus extracted, and put into a gallon of water heated nearly to the boiling point. The blood which he had dipped from the cavity of the buffalo was then stirred in till the mass became of the consistency of rice soup. A little salt and black pepper finished the preparation. It was a fine dish; too rich, perhaps, for some of my esteemed acquaintances, whose digestive organs partake of the general laziness of their habits; but to us who had so long desired a healthful portion of bodily exercise in that quarter, it was the very marrow and life-blood . . . of

[22] Alpheus H. Favour: *Old Bill Williams* (Chapel Hill, N. C., 1936), pp. 200–1; William Thomas Hamilton: *My Sixty Years on the Plains* (New York, 1905), p. 33.

[23] Ferris: *Life in the Rocky Mountains,* p. 248.

[24] Ibid., p. 240.

whatsoever is good and wholesome for famished carniverous animals like ourselves. It was excellent, most excellent. It was better than our father's foaming ale. For a while it loosed our tongues and warmed our hearts toward one another, it had the additional effect of Aaron's oil: it made our faces to shine with grease and gladness. But the remembrance of the palate pleasures of the next course, will not allow me to dwell longer upon this. The crowning delight was yet in store for us. While enjoying the said soup, we believed the bumper of our pleasures to be sparkling to the brim; and if our excellent old trapper had not been there, we never should have desired more. But how true is that philosophy which teaches, that to be capable of happiness, we must be conscious of wants! Our friend Kelly was in this a practical as well as theoretical Epicurean. "No giving up the beaver so," said he; "another bait and we will sleep." Saying this, he seized the intestines of the buffalo, which had been properly cleaned for the purpose, turned them inside out, and as he proceeded stuffed them with strips of well salted and peppered tenderloin. Our *"boudies"* thus made, were stuck upon sticks before the fire, and roasted till they were thoroughly cooked and browned. The sticks were then taken from their roasting position and stuck in position for eating. That is to say, each of us with as fine an appetite as ever blessed a New-England boy at his grandsire's Thanksgiving Dinner, seized a stick spit, stuck it in the earth near our couches, and sitting upon our haunches ate our last course — the dessert of our mountain host's entertainment. These wilderness sausages would have gratified the appetite of those who had been deprived of meat a less time than we had been. The envelopes preserve the juices of the meat with which while cooking the adhering fat, turned within, mingles and forms a gravy of the finest flavor. Such is a feast in the mountains.[25]

[25] *Travels in the Great Western Prairies* (Poughkeepsie, 1841), pp. 85–6.

On the prairies the trapper usually built his fire of buffalo chips — not a bad substitute for wood when the chips were old and dry, but poor fuel indeed when wet by rain or snow. Pitch-pine was the most inflammable of all mountain wood; dry aspen burned without smoke and made a brilliant light; juniper gave out a hot, steady flame and lasted as long as oak. Buffalo fat made excellent candles.

In choosing a site for its winter camp, a trapping party selected a hidden, well-watered valley, sheltered as far as possible from wind and snow, remote enough to escape the notice of small bands of roving Indians, and sufficiently wooded to afford shelter for the company's horses and mules and provide an adequate supply of sweet cottonwood, willow, or aspen bark to supplement the supply of grass. Here the trappers erected skin lodges or rough log cabins and "holed up" for the winter.

"The winter-camp of a hunter of the Rocky Mountains would doubtless prove an object of interest to the unsophisticated," wrote Sage.

It is usually located in some spot sheltered by hills or rocks, for the double purpose of securing the full warmth of the sun's rays, and screening it from the notice of strolling Indians that may happen in its vicinity. Within a convenient proximity to it stands some grove, from which an abundance of dry fuel is procurable when needed; and equally close the ripplings of a watercourse salute the ear with their music.

His shantee faces a huge fire, and is formed of skins carefully extended over an arched frame-work of slender poles, which are bent in the form of a semicircle and kept to their places by inserting their extremities in the ground. Near this is his "graining block," planted aslope, for the ease of the operative in preparing his skins for the finishing process in the art of dressing; and not far removed is a stout frame, contrived from four pieces of timber, so tied together as to leave a square of sufficient dimensions for the required purpose, in which, perchance, a skin is stretched to its fullest extension, and the hardy mountaineer is busily engaged in rubbing it with a rough stone or "scraper," to fit it for the manufacture of clothing.[26]

The dirt floors of the skin lodges, such as Sage describes, were covered with reeds, dried grass, or small evergreen boughs, and on these the trappers spread their fur robes and heavy woolen blankets. The larger pieces of baggage were then placed inside the lodge, close against the walls, to help exclude the wind and cold.

Of all frontier callings, that of the trapper was the most hazardous and rash. Indians, grizzly bears, quarrels, hunger, thirst, flood, storm, accident, and disease — perils of nature, man, and beast — took unremitting toll even of the most seasoned of the mountain men. Chittenden estimated that at least a hundred men lost their lives in the service of the American Fur Company. In 1856 Antoine Robidoux declared that he could account for only three survivors out of a force of three hundred hunters and trappers who were in the Rocky Mountains thirty years before. James Ohio Pattie thought that only sixteen men out of a total of a hundred and sixteen survived their first year's trapping experience in the Southwest.

The Indian was the trapper's greatest menace. Responsibility for the traditional blood feud between the mountain

---

[26] Rufus Sage, op. cit., p. 288.

man and certain Indian tribes is hard to apportion. Perhaps both were equally at fault. Encounters between the two were grim, savage, merciless; and if the savage practiced nameless cruelties on wounded or captured whites after a victorious engagement, the trappers not infrequently killed the wounded enemy and on occasion burned Indian villages and shot the fleeing inmates, men, women, and children, without discrimination.

Following the Indian practice, the trapper customarily scalped his victim. "Scalp-taking is a solemn rite," wrote an English traveler about the middle of the last century. "When the Indian sees his enemy fall he draws his scalp-knife . . . and twisting the scalp-lock — round his left hand, makes with his right two semicircular incisions, with and against the sun, about the part to be removed. The skin is next loosened with the knife point. . . . The operator then sits on the ground, places his feet against the subject's shoulders by way of leverage, and holding the scalp-lock with both hands he applies a strain which soon brings off the spoils with a sound which, I am told, is not unlike 'flop.' " [27] According to Ferris, the Flatheads "raised the scalp" of a dead Indian "by cutting around the edge of the hair and pulling off the entire skin of the head from the ears up." [28]

In justice to the mountain men, however, it may be said that they inherited the practice of scalping Indians from an earlier generation of frontier whites. In 1791, for example, "an association of the most civilized, humane, and

---

[27] Richard F. Burton: *The City of the Saints* (London, 1861), p. 138.
[28] *Life in the Rocky Mountains,* p. 129.

pious inhabitants of Pittsburg" offered a reward of a hundred dollars "for every hostile Indian's Scalp, with both ears to it." [29]

In general, however, the more responsible, far-sighted leaders of the mountain men, and the more humane trappers among the rank and file, endeavored to remain on friendly terms with the Indians and deal fairly with them. Liquor was one of the major sources of difficulty between Indians and whites and the most demoralizing of all factors in the Western trade. The better class of traders deplored its use; but when a company's representative brought it into a locality, other traders were forced to follow suit or lose the trade of Indians and trappers alike to their unscrupulous competitor. American companies damned the Hudson's Bay Company for thus debauching and ruining the Indians; the Hudson's Bay Company laid the blame on the Americans. The independent companies charged the American Fur Company with responsibility for the practice; the American Fur Company accused the independents.

Meanwhile, despite well-intentioned but unenforced federal laws to the contrary, poisonous and adulterated liquor poured into the rendezvous and trapping-grounds, and Indians and trappers alike paid the Devil's price. From the accounts of contemporary observers, who, almost without exception, emphasized the ruinous influence of the traffic, Chittenden drew the following composite picture:

In retailing the poisonous stuff (a pure article never found its way to the Indian) the degree of deception and cheating

---

[29] See *Magazine of American History*, Vol. II, Part I, p. 58.

could not have been carried further. A baneful and noxious substance to begin with, it was retailed with the most systematic fraud, often amounting to a sheer exchange of nothing for the goods of the Indian. It was the policy of the shrewd trader first to get his victim so intoxicated that he could no longer drive a good bargain. The Indian, becoming more and more greedy for liquor, would yield up all he possessed for an additional cup or two. The voracious trader, not satisfied with selling his alcohol at a profit of many thousand per cent, would now begin to cheat in quantity. As he filled the little cup which was the standard of measure, he would thrust in his big thumb and diminish its capacity by one-third. Sometimes he would substitute another cup with the bottom thickened up by running tallow in until it was a third full. He would also dilute the liquor until, as the Indian's senses became more and more befogged, he would treat him to water pure and simple. . . . the duplicity and crime for which this unhallowed traffic is responsible in our relations with the Indians have been equalled but seldom in even the most corrupt of nations.[30]

Nearly all mountain men had Indian wives or concubines; some of the trappers were adopted into Indian tribes; a few, such as Jim Beckwourth, Old Bill Williams, and Edward Rose became influential chiefs. The mountain man who smoked the peace pipe with an Indian chief, "one puff to the skies, one to the earth, two to the winds and waters on the right and left," [31] was assured of a measure of temporary security; but even when the two races were ostensibly at peace, some act of treachery, skulduggery, or open hostility might end the hair-trigger truce and start

---

[30] *The American Fur Trade of the Far West,* Vol. I, pp. 23–4.
[31] James: *Three Years among the Indians,* p. 205.

a conflict that knew no mercy on either side. The trapper's typical attitude found expression in the saying that the rifle was the only pen with which a treaty could be written that the Indians would not forget.[32]

But before too harshly condemning the perfidy and treachery of the savages, it would be well if the uninformed American acquainted himself, at least in some slight measure, with the other side of the picture. Somewhere in the archives in Washington there is a dust-covered file of treaties running into the score, if not the hundred, that the government of the white interloper who trespassed on the savage's homelands and hunting-grounds negotiated with the Indian and then deliberately violated, grossly neglected, or carelessly forgot.

Yet wherever the fault lay, the Indian menace was a constant, inescapable factor in the trapper's life. It dogged the trail of the solitary mountain man as he explored the streams for beaver signs, set and visited his string of traps, hunted or loafed, ate or slept, sat by his campfire, or rode his wild and lonely trails. Even the largest trapping expeditions were subject to raids, ambush, and attack. The battles of Pierre's Hole, of Fort Mackenzie, and of Ashley's men with the Arikaras were typical examples of such large-scale engagements.

It is true that many tribes — the Cheyennes, Snakes, Gros Ventres, Utes, even the Apaches — at times made common cause with the trappers against their traditional Indian foes; but only one tribe, the Flatheads or Salish, kept their relations with the whites permanently inviolate.

---

[32] Osborne Russell: *Journal of a Trapper*, p. 63.

They alone were never guilty of theft or violence against trapper, settler, or passing emigrant. The small tribe lived in western Montana. Its members spoke a language "remarkable for its sweetness and simplicity," and were noted, as Ferris wrote, for their "humanity, candour, forbearance, integrity, truthfulness, piety, and honesty." To this he added:

They were the only tribe in the Rocky Mountains that can with truth boast of the fact that they have never killed or robbed a white man, nor stolen a single horse, how great soever the necessity and the temptation. I have . . . been often employed in trading and travelling with them, and have never known one to steal so much as an awl-blade. Every other tribe in the Rocky Mountains hold theft rather in the light of a virtue than a fault, and many even pride themselves on their dexterity and address in the art of appropriation, like the Greeks deeming it no dishonor to steal, but a disgrace to be detected.[33]

Ferris might have explained the Flathead character by adding that the Indians had learned some of the great truths of Christianity from early missionaries or Christian traders and very naïvely determined to put these truths into daily operation.

The danger of ambush, the horrors of Indian torture, and the stark necessity either of outwitting his savage enemies or losing his own scalp, made the Anglo-American frontiersman, whether Kentucky long-rifleman or Far Western mountain man, a superb master of woodcraft, self-de-

---

[33] *Life in the Rocky Mountains,* p. 88. Notwithstanding many writers to the contrary, Flathead mothers did not deform the heads of their children. The name was a misnomer.

fense, and border warfare. The trapper's skill with the rifle has become an authentic American tradition. He could throw a tomahawk or scalping knife (probably the most dangerous of all border weapons at close range) more ac- curately than an Indian, and developed a resourcefulness in combat that matched the savage's uncanny skill. In an account of one of his many skirmishes Russell gave the following excellent example of the trapper's ingenuity: "When I first stationed myself at the tree, I placed a hat on some twigs which grew at the foot of it and would put it in motion by kicking the twigs with my foot in order that they might shoot at the hat and give me a better chance at their heads." [34]

As previously suggested, the Indians with whom the trappers traded or fought, as occasion demanded, were proverbially warlike, crafty, treacherous, and cruel. Their principal native weapons were the bow, scalping knife, tomahawk, and war club. The Indian bow, which differed both in effectiveness and craftsmanship from tribe to tribe, was distinctly inferior as a weapon either to the English longbow of Crécy and Agincourt or to the bows of modern manufacture. But an Apache bowman could send an arrow clear through the body of his enemy at a hundred yards, and Kit Carson found the Klamath Indians of northern California and southern Oregon able to drive an iron- pointed arrow four inches deep into the trunk of a pine tree.

Arrowheads and even rifle balls were poisoned in a variety of ways. The Snake and Mojave Indians, both of

[34] *Journal of a Trapper*, p. 22.

Shoshonean stock, dipped their arrows in a mixture of antelope or deer liver and rattlesnake venom. To secure the venom, the Indians placed the snakes in a small enclosure and tormented them with sticks until they struck the pieces of liver and injected the contents of their poison sacs into the spongy flesh. The liver was then placed in the sun and allowed to putrefy. A wound made by an arrow smeared with this repulsive poison was nearly always fatal, for if the victim survived the rattlesnake venom, he still faced death from blood poisoning or tetanus. Some trappers asserted that the Shoshones added the blood of a woman to the deadly mess to increase its potency.

The literature of the fur trade is full of the drama of Indian warfare. The story runs the whole gamut of border conflict, from single-handed combat to pitched battle, from incredible escape to wholesale massacre and torture. A few concrete examples, chosen almost at random, will confirm this general statement.

"From the time we parted from Maj. Riley, at the western terminus of the Arkansas sandhills, until we were met by Ewing Young and his ninety-five hunters," wrote William Waldo, "we seldom obtained more than three or four hours sleep out of the twenty-four. Men became so worn down with toil by day and watching by night, that they would go to sleep and fall from their mules, as they rode along. For forty or fifty days, we were not permitted to take off our clothes or boots at night, and all slept with their pistols belted around them and their guns in their arms. In several instances, men seized their knives in their sleep and stove them into the ground, and the men became afraid to sleep together, for fear of killing each other in their sleep." [35]

While searching for two lost members of a company of trappers on one of the tributaries of the Colorado, the Kentucky adventurer James Ohio Pattie came upon a party of Indians engaged in cooking the dismembered bodies of his companions over a campfire in much the same way that the trappers roasted the flesh of a buffalo or beaver.

Pursued by Indians, four members of a trapping party became separated from their companions and attempted to cross the Snake River. Forcing their horses to swim to the other side, the trappers stripped themselves naked, placed their belongings on a raft, and attempted to push the awkward craft across the current. Now, the Snake River is not to be trusted, as too many tragedies even among present-day trout fishermen attest. The raft capsized, and everything — clothes, shoes, guns, food, and saddles — disappeared. Naked as the day they were born, the wretched trappers suffered an experience as cruel and painful as it was novel and grimly ludicrous. Ferris gave this vivid picture of their predicament:

The burning heat of the sun parched their skins, and they had nothing to shield them from his powerful rays; the freezing air of the night chilled and benumbed their unprotected bodies, and they had no covering to keep off the cold; the chill storms of rain and hail pelted mercilessly on them, and they could not escape the torture; the friction produced by riding without a saddle or anything for a substitute, chaffed

---

[35] Recollections of a Septuagenarian," *Missouri Historical Society Quarterly,* Vol. V, Nos. 4–6, pp. 77–8.

off the skin, and even flesh, and without any means of remedying the misfortune, or alleviating the pain, for they were prevented from walking by the stones and sharp thorns of the prickly pair [pear], which lacerated their feet. They were compelled though the agony occasioned by it was intense, to continue their equestrian march, till amidst this accumulation of ills, they reached our camp; where by kind treatment, and emollient applications, their spirits were restored and their sufferings relieved. Add to the complication of woes above enumerated, the knawing pangs of hunger which the reader will infer, that they must have experienced in no slight degree, from the fact that they did not taste a morsel of food during those four ages of agony, and we have an aggregate of suffering hardly equalled in the history of human woe." [36]

Next to the Indian, the grizzly bear was the trapper's greatest menace. "An enormous animal, a hideous brute, a savage looking beast," the grizzly, gray, or white bear, as the trapper indiscriminately called him, was one of the most formidable creatures modern man has ever had to face. He was enormously powerful, fearless, truculent, and crafty and as tenacious of life as a rogue elephant. Few trapping expeditions returned from the mountains without having lost some of their members to the savage fury of this great gray monarch of the wilderness.

In places the grizzly was found in numbers that now seem as incredible to us, the children of an overcrowded, over-

---

[36] Reprinted by permission from *Life in the Rocky Mountains; a Diary of Wanderings on the Sources of the Rivers Missouri, Columbia, and Colorado from February, 1830, to November, 1835,* by Warren A. Ferris; edited by Dr. Paul C. Phillips; published by The Old West Publishing Company (Denver, 1940), p. 208.

civilized land, as the stories our grandsires told of the passenger pigeon and the buffalo. Pattie saw two hundred and twenty in a single day. "They were everywhere — upon the plains, in the valleys and on the mountains," said George C. Yount, "so that I have often killed as many as five or six in one day, and it is not unusual to see fifty or sixty within the twenty-four hours." [37]

If he escaped the Indian and the grizzly, the luckless fur trader too frequently died — or suffered even greater agony than death — from cold, hunger, thirst, prairie fires, cloudbursts, snowslides, and disease. Snow-blindness made his eyes feel "as if they were filled with coarse sand." Hunger sometimes led him to bleed his horses and cook and eat the blood. Mosquitoes, especially of the snow and swamp varieties, tormented him almost beyond endurance. Wounds became infected and produced blood poisoning and tetanus. Poisoned liquor and venereal disease brought paralysis, madness, and lingering death.

Except in rare instances, the services of a physician or surgeon were unavailable, and the victim of wounds, accident, or disease was compelled to rely on the crude ministrations of his fellow trappers. Novel remedies, the efficacy of some of which might even warrant investigation by modern medical science, were used for many ills. Rattlesnake bites were cauterized by burning small quantities of gunpowder on the open wound. A salve for wounds and lacerations was made from sugar and soap or from beaver's oil

[37] Mrs. F. H. Day: "Sketches of the Early Settlers of California," the *Hesperian,* March 1859, p. 1.

and castoreum.[38] Liver pills of calomel and tar drops for colds and sore throats were common remedies.

"I here became for the first time acquainted with a kind of beverage very common among the mountaineers," wrote Sage.

The article alluded to may with much propriety be termed "bitters," as the reader will readily acknowledge on learning the nature of its principal ingredient.

It is prepared by the following simple process, viz: with one pint of water mix one-fourth gill of buffalo-gall, and you will then have before you a wholesome exhilarating drink.

As a sanative, it tends to make sound an irritated and ulcerated stomach, reclaiming it to a healthful and lively tone, and thus striking an effective blow at that most prolific source of so large a majority of the diseases common to civilized life.

From what I have seen of its results, I consider it one of the most innocent and useful medicines in cases of dyspepsy. . . .[39]

In reply to a request for medicine, Captain William Becknell sent some rhubarb and camphor to Bartolomé Baca, Governor of New Mexico. Becknell was not an educated man, in the narrow sense of that term, and his directions for the use of the two remedies involved certain liberties both with syntax and spelling. His letter read:

The Rubarbe you can take at ny time what will Ly on the pinte of apocket Knif sum shuger and a spunful of cold warter you may Eaeght or drinke any thing Hot or Cold.

---

[38] Sage, op. cit., p. 295; Maurice S. Sullivan: *The Travels of Jedediah Smith* (Santa Ana, California, 1934), p. 78.

[39] Sage, op. cit., pp. 132–3.

The Best time to take it is of aneight [a night] When you go
to Bed it is not apecke [ipecac?] agental purge and wil
creteefy [gratify?] the stomak when in Bad order The
Campor you can desolve in whiskey put a few drops in a dram
of whiskey in the morning will Help the stomake very much.
I send you A few of the qusawit Barks [Jesuits' bark or cam-
phor] put them in to abotel of whisky 1 quart in and . . .
stand in the sun for one or 2 days and then drinke them. . . .[40]

The trappers, though inclined to let Nature work her
own cures, sometimes resorted to crude surgery to save a
man's life or limb. When Dr. Marcus Whitman visited
Fort Hall on his way to Oregon, he removed a three-inch
Blackfoot iron arrowhead that had been embedded in Jim
Bridger's back for several years. "It was a difficult operation," wrote the Reverend Samuel Parker, "in consequence
of the arrow being hooked at the point by striking a large
bone, and a cartilaginous substance had grown around it.
The doctor pursued the operation with great self-possession
and perseverance; and Captain Bridger manifested equal
firmness." [41]

Ferris was once wounded so severely in the shoulder by
a rifle ball that the blood ran out of his mouth and nose
and covered his body. A friend, "who had some knowledge
of practical surgery," probed the wound with a ramrod and
"dressed it with a salve of his own preparation." [42]

[40] The letter was sent from Santa Cruz, New Mexico, October 29, 1824.
It is number 80 of the Ritch Collection (hereafter indicated as RI) of
the Huntington Library Manuscripts.
[41] *Journal of an Exploring Tour beyond the Rocky Mountains* (Ithaca,
New York, 1840), p. 76. Dr. Whitman also removed an arrowhead which
had lain under the shoulder of another hunter for two and a half years.
[42] *Life in the Rocky Mountains*, p. 178.

In his historic account of the Santa Fe trade Josiah Gregg vividly described a rough-and-ready operation performed on a member of the caravan whose arm was shattered by an accidental gunshot wound. Gangrene had set in and the man's death seemed inevitable. In response to the sufferer's desperate plea, however, three or four of his companions undertook to amputate the infected arm.

Their only case of instruments [wrote Gregg] consisted of a handsaw, a butcher's knife, and a large iron bolt. The teeth of the saw being considered too coarse, they went to work and soon had a set of fine teeth filed on the back. The knife having been whetted keen and the iron bolt laid upon the fire, they commenced the operation, and in less time than it takes to tell it the arm was opened round to the bone, which was almost in an instant sawed off; and with the whizzing hot iron the whole stump was so effectually seared as to close the arteries completely. Bandages were now applied and the company proceeded on their journey as though nothing had occurred. The arm commenced healing rapidly and in a few weeks the patient was sound and well, and is perhaps still living to bear witness to the superiority of the hot iron over ligatures, in taking up arteries.[43]

In the literature of a popular or semipopular character that has grown up around the fur trade, the mountain man is portrayed, almost without exception, as illiterate, drunken, licentious, brutal. The picture is exaggerated and too one-sided. Though a majority of the trappers perhaps belonged in this familiar category and gave themselves free

---

[43] Josiah Gregg: *The Commerce of the Prairies* (New York, 1844), Vol. I, pp. 59–60.

license whenever they had the opportunity, they did not constitute the dominant, stabilizing element in the fur trade.

That element, to which many of the leaders and responsible trappers belonged, was sober, literate, and often deeply religious. Peter Skene Ogden, one of the most illustrious of the explorers of the Far West, gathered his men together daily for public prayers when they were on the march.[44] Louis Vasquez requested his brother to send him some novels and to tell Emilie, his sister, "not to worry about my health; tell her that the God of men who are above reproach is with me and besides I have nothing to fear."[45]

Jedediah Smith, perhaps the greatest of all the American mountain men, was as devout a Christian as a Scotch Covenanter and as faithful in his prayers and daily reading of the Bible. Harrison G. Rogers, who served as clerk of Smith's historic expedition to California in 1826, was equally sincere in his religious experiences and conviction. On New Year's Day, 1827, he delivered an address "to the Reverend Father of San Gabriel Mission" on the early history and missionary activities of the Christian Church that for diction, range of knowledge, and Scriptural allusion would have put to shame most ministers or priests.[46]

[44] Constance L. Skinner: *Adventurers of Oregon* (New Haven, 1920), Vol. XXII, p. 243.

[45] LeRoy R. Hafen: "Mountain Men," *Colorado Magazine*, January 1933, p. 17.

[46] There are many baffling aspects of this address. I cannot explain its style and phraseology, which differ radically from the rest of Rogers's diary, or account for Rogers's amazing knowledge of the subject. The subsequent history of the diary makes it virtually impossible that the address was added by a later writer.

Months later, in the midst of the trackless wilderness, perhaps with the premonition of death before him, Rogers wrote in his revealing diary, "Oh! God, may it please thee, in thy divine providence, to still guide and protect us through this wilderness of doubt and fear, as thou hast done heretofore, and be with us in the hour of danger and difficulty, as all praise is due to thee and not to man, oh! do not forsake us Lord, but be with us and direct us through." [47]

By direct reference or casual allusion many another fur trader's diary shows clearly enough that the writer enjoyed a superior educational and cultural background. Describing his camp in the Yellowstone, Osborne Russell wrote that during the long winter evenings the men collected in the larger buffalo-skin lodges and entered into debates and arguments in what they called the "Rocky Mountain College." [48] Elsewhere Russell added: "There were four of us in the mess. One was from Missouri, one from Massachusetts, one from Vermont, and myself from Maine. We passed an agreeable winter. We had nothing to do but to eat, attend to the horses and procure firewood. We had some few books to read, such as Byron, Shakespeare and Scott's works, the Bible and Clark's Commentary on it, and other small works on geology, chemistry and philosophy. . . ." [49]

---

[47] Reprinted by permission of the publishers, The Arthur H. Clark Company, from *The Ashley-Smith Explorations and the Discovery of a Central Route to the Pacific, 1822–1829,* by Harrison C. Dale (Glendale, California, 1941), pp. 210–12, 249–50.

[48] *Journal of a Trapper,* p. 55.

[49] Ibid., p. 109.

"I found the Scotchman and Kentuckian well educated men," wrote another trapper. "The latter presented me with a copy of Shakespeare and an ancient and modern history which he had in his pack. We had an abundance of reading matter with us; old mountain men were all great readers. It was always amusing to me to hear people from the East speak of old mountaineers as semi-barbarians, when as a general rule they were the peers of the Easterners in general knowledge." [50]

Thomas Jefferson Farnham, traveler, propagandist, and popular writer, spoke of a trapper from New Hampshire, whom he encountered in the heart of the Rocky Mountains, as one of the most remarkable men of his acquaintance. The trapper was a graduate of Dartmouth College, a gentleman in manners and bearing, "a finished scholar, a critic on English and Roman literature . . . an Indian." [51]

"The trapper in his solitude seldom wasted his time," said Frederic E. Voelker, of St. Louis.

Time left over from physical activity necessary to his business and his subsistance was mostly devoted to reading and thought. Many of them carried on their solitary travels newspapers, magazines, and books — chiefly the Bible and Shakespeare. Their tastes ran, also, to history, biography, science and (hold your hat!) — poetry. They read little or no fiction. Being men of thought, it is not surprising that many of their favorites in their chosen fields of literature were or have become classics. Their reading matter was passed from hand to hand until it became so worn and filthy

---

[50] W. T. Hamilton: *My Sixty Years on the Plains* (New York, 1905), p. 68.
[51] *Travels in the Great Western Prairies*, p. 38.

it fell apart. Many a good book was carried through storm, flood, fire and blood bath.[52]

But whether religious or pagan, cultured or illiterate, the fur trader had certain fundamental traits that were the common heritage of all who wore the badge and livery of his calling. "To me," wrote Timothy Flint, who aspired to be the Richard Hakluyt of the fur traders, "there is a kind of moral sublimity in the contemplation of the adventures and daring of such men. They read a lesson to shrinking and effeminate spirits, the men of soft hands and fashionable life, whose frames the winds of heaven are not allowed to visit too roughly. They tend to re-inspire something of that simplicity of manners, manly hardihood, and Spartan energy and force of character which formed so conspicuous a part of the nature of the settlers of the western wilderness." [53]

Even the rudest and most boisterous of the mountain men were fundamentally honest, just, and kind. They dealt fairly and generously with each other, never "lifted" another's cache unless the mountain code recognized the act as necessary, rarely violated their word or suffered from an associate's dishonesty, protected their own rights, and enforced a few simple, self-made laws.

The nature of his life and calling left its stamp, deep, permanent, and unmistakable, upon the trapper's face, movements, reactions, and entire personality. "He was or-

---

[52] "The Mountain Men and Their Part in the Opening of the West," *Bulletin of the Missouri Historical Society,* Vol. III, No. 4, p. 158.
[53] *The Personal Narrative of James Ohio Pattie of Kentucky* (Cincinnati, 1831), p. v.

dinarily gaunt and spare," wrote Chittenden, "browned with exposure, his hair long and unkempt, while his general makeup, with the queer dress which he wore, made it often difficult to distinguish him from an Indian. The constant peril of his life and the necessity of unremitting vigilance gave him a kind of piercing look, his head slightly bent forward and his deep eyes peering from under a slouch hat, or whatever head-gear he might possess,.as if studying the face of the stranger to learn whether friend or foe." [54] His life was indeed one of "enigmas, contrasts, and contradictions." According to his scale of values, freedom of life and action was the greatest of the virtues. He was at ease only in the "atmosphere of elevated, unembarrassed regions."

Farnham observed that the typical mountain man had the same manners as the Indians, the same "wild, unsettled, watchful expression in the eyes; the same unnatural gesticulation in conversation, the same unwillingness to use words when a sign, a contortion of the face or body or movement of the hand," would serve. He stood, walked, rode, dressed, and wore his hair after the same pattern, and Washington Irving even went so far as to say: "You can not pay a free trapper a greater compliment than to persuade him that you have mistaken him for an Indian."

In his tribute to James Clyman, companion of Smith, Bridger, Sublette, and other great figures of the trapping era, Charles L. Camp wrote an appropriate epitaph not only for his particular hero but for all the notable company of mountain men:

[54] *The American Fur Trade of the Far West,* Vol. I, pp. 59–60.

The moving force in his career was an intense love of the freedom of the wilderness. He, and probably his father before him, typified that class of borderers who were never satisfied with a patch of land if there was a chance of finding something better a thousand or three thousand miles farther on. He wandered restlessly for forty-one years over the breadth of the continent and into the farthest recesses of the mountains, carrying with him an intimate knowledge of the geography of the regions he explored. . . . He outlived his times completely. Scarcely one of his mountain comrades survived him. Trails that he found across the mountains were now traversed by highways and steel rails. Cities had grown up on his camp grounds, farms had invaded the old cattle ranges of the California valleys, and the beaver and the buffalo had gone from the land that knew them, forever.[55]

Such was the American beaver-hunter or mountain man, the reckless, daring, hawk-eyed wanderer who roamed through half a continent and vanished from the earth a long, long century ago. He was the product of the wilderness, its deserts, mountains, forests, winds, and streams. He was the first to take seizin of the vast and lonely spaces of the West, to explore its mysteries, discover its hidden trails, and "march with the sun to the last frontiers."

---

[55] *James Clyman, American Frontiersman,* ed. by Charles L. Camp (San Francisco, 1928), p. 10.

CHAPTER 2

Jedediah Strong Smith:

From the Big Lake to the Sea

B Y 1825 American fur traders had extended their operations far west of the Continental Divide and equally far south of the Mexican border. The line of exploration at that time ran in a great jagged arc from the Mexican settlements of the upper Rio Grande, through the valley of the Green River and the basin of the Great Salt Lake, to the Snake and Columbia rivers. During the next ten years a series of further explorations extended the radius of this arc till it reached the coast of California, the Gila and lower Colorado rivers, and the Mexican states of Chihuahua and Sonora.

Most of the expeditions that invaded the wilderness lying beyond the strategic outposts of 1825 were Anglo-American in their origin and leadership, but a few set out from the forts and trading posts of the Hudson's Bay Company on the Columbia. The "Great Company" was especially active in the exploration of the northern and western part of the Great Basin and in trapping the beaver streams of California. On occasion it even sent its motley brigades as far south as the Gulf of California.[1]

The story of these expeditions, American and British

---

[1] Chapter 9 contains an account of these activities.

alike, is "a tale which holdeth children from play and old men from the chimney corner." It is also a chapter in the destiny of nations, a part of the unfolding drama of the westward course of British and American empire.

The first of the historic expeditions to reach the Pacific Ocean from the central Rocky Mountain trapping-grounds started from the recently discovered Salt Lake basin in the summer of 1826. Its leader was Jedediah Strong Smith, a pathfinder beyond the Rocky Mountains who deserves a place in national tradition equal in every respect to that accorded Meriwether Lewis, William Clark, Daniel Boone, Kit Carson, or any other American explorer.

Born in Bainbridge, New York, of pioneer New England stock, Smith acquired a fair education from a small-town doctor who took time to teach reading, writing, Latin, and English to the serious-minded boy. Smith gratefully remembered this service down to the close of his life and in later years made financial provision for his benefactor.

At the age of thirteen Smith obtained a minor clerical position on a freight boat on the Great Lakes. There he came in contact with fur traders from Canada and the upper Missouri wilderness and apparently developed a consuming interest in the life and opportunities of the West. In 1822 he found his way to St. Louis, already the recognized center of the rapidly developing Western fur trade.

Smith's arrival in St. Louis was well timed. The trapping industry was just coming into its own, and before it lay a crowded decade of rapid expansion and mounting profits. The historic trade between the Missouri frontier and the

northern Mexican provinces, usually spoken of as the Santa
Fe trade, was already well under way; and General William Ashley, the John Jacob Astor of St. Louis, was about
to embark on his most ambitious undertaking, a venture as
profitable in the end as it was hazardous and unpromising
at the start.

The following advertisement, which appeared in the
Missouri Republican of March 22, 1822, announced the
inauguration of Ashley's enterprise and marked the beginning of Smith's heroic and singularly great career:

TO ENTERPRISING YOUNG MEN. The subscriber
wishes to engage one hundred young men to ascend the Missouri River to its source, there to be employed for one, two,
or three years. For particulars inquire of Major Andrew
Henry, near the lead mines in the county of Washington, who
will ascend with, and command, the party; or of the subscriber near St. Louis.

(Signed) William H. Ashley

Major Andrew Henry, Ashley's partner in the venture,
was one of the pioneer fur traders of the upper Missouri
territory. He had been an associate of Manuel Lisa and
Pierre Chouteau in the organization of the St. Louis Missouri Fur Company in 1809 and served as the leader of
the first American trapping party to winter west of the
Rocky Mountains.[2] In the undertaking that Ashley and he
now jointly sponsored, Henry proposed to ascend the Missouri River as far as the junction of the Madison, Gallatin,

---

[2] The party spent the winter of 1810–11 on a branch of the Snake or
Lewis River, now known as Henry's Fork. The St. Louis Missouri Fur
Company soon came to be known as the Missouri Fur Company.

and Jefferson, the historic "Three Forks" in southwestern Montana, and trap a region reputed to contain a "wealth of furs not surpassed by the mines of Peru." The expedition intended to spend three years in the mountains and perhaps go as far west as the mouth of the Columbia.

Between eighty and one hundred men joined Henry's first expedition to the mountains. The party left St. Louis on April 3, 1823, reached the mouth of the Yellowstone sometime the next fall, and began the erection of a fortified trading post. During the course of the next six months Ashley brought at least two other companies up the river until there were close to two hundred men in the Ashley-Henry command.

According to James Clyman, a young man employed by Ashley to recruit members for the expedition, many of the applicants came from the grogshops and other sinks of iniquity in the rough frontier river town of St. Louis; but the roster of Ashley's motley bands, more disreputable in appearance than Falstaff's tatterdemalion battalion, contained the names of a minority who were destined to live for generations in the history and heroic tradition of the race — Jim Bridger, Thomas Fitzpatrick, Andrew Henry, James Clyman, Milton and William Sublette, Hugh Glass, Etienne Provost, Jedediah Strong Smith, David E. Jackson, Daniel T. Potts, and perhaps half as many more — a company that constituted "the most significant group of continental explorers ever brought together." [3]

Jedediah Smith, though a stranger to the mountains and the trapper's calling when he started for the Rockies as one

[3] Dale: *The Ashley-Smith Explorations,* p. 84.

of Ashley's men, was destined to immortality. He was in his twenty-fourth year — strong, observant, dependable, modest, courageous, self-reliant, a man who commanded the confidence of others and kept truth with himself. As emergencies arose and misfortune overtook the Ashley company, Smith revealed unusual qualities of leadership. A bloody melee with the Arikara Indians made his courage, initiative, and resourcefulness even more conspicuous and ended his apprenticeship as a trapper. Thereafter he became one of Ashley's chief lieutenants.

During the next three years Smith perfected himself in the many accomplishments required of a leader of the mountain men. He studied the art of Indian diplomacy and the grimmer art of Indian warfare; he mastered the techniques of trapping and mountain woodcraft; he absorbed all the information that those who crossed unknown frontiers brought back to the rendezvous and camp.

Danger and hardship became part of the normal routine of his daily life. He escaped death at the hands of the Indians and eluded other perils of the wilderness by the narrowest of margins. Once a grizzly bear catapulted from a thicket, sent him sprawling from the saddle, and horribly mutilated his head and scalp. Clyman's account of the affair is almost as brutally direct, graphic, and curious in its syntax and spelling as a passage from *Beowulf*:

. . . late in the afternoon while passing through a Brushy bottom a large Grssely came down the vally we being in single file men on foot leding pack horses he struck us about the center then turning ran paralel to our line Capt. Smith being in the advanc he ran to the open ground and as he im-

merged from the thicket he and the bear met face to face
Grissly did not hesitate a moment but sprung on the capt
taking him by the head first pitc[h] sprawling on the earth
he gave him a grab by the middle fortunately cat[c]hing by
the ball pouch and Butcher K[n]ife which he broke but
breaking several of his ribs and cutting his head badly none
of us having any sugical Knowledge what was to be done
one Said come take hold and he wuld say why not you so it
went around I asked the Capt what was best he said one or
2 [go] for water and if you have a needle and thread git it
out and sew up my wounds around my head which was bleeding freely I got a pair of scissors and cut off his hair and
then began my first Job of d[r]essing wounds upon examination I [found] the bear had taken nearly all his head in his
capcious mouth close to his left eye on one side and clos to his
right ear on the other and laid the skull bare to near the
crown of the head leaving a white streak whare his teeth
passed one of his ears was torn from his head out to the
outer rim after stitching all the other wounds in the best way
I was capabl and according to the captains directions the
ear being the last I told him I could do nothing for his Eare
O you must try to stitch up some way or other said he then
I put in my needle stiching it through and through and over
and over laying the lacerated parts together as nice as I
could with my hands water was found in about one mille
when we all moved down and encamped the captain being able
to mount his horse and ride to campt whare we pitched a tent
the onley one we had and made him as comfortable as circumstances would permit this gave us a lisson the character of
the grissly Baare which we did not forget. . . .[4]

Though young in years when he set out on the historic
expedition of 1826, Jedediah Smith was thus old in ex-

[4] "James Clyman, His Diaries and Reminiscences," ed. by Charles L.
Camp, *California Historical Society Quarterly* (1925), Vol. IV, pp. 122–3.

perience, adventure, and responsibility. Moreover, even then he was one of the foremost of his contemporaries in the field of exploration. He began that phase of his career almost as soon as he became a trapper. With Thomas Fitzpatrick he crossed the South Pass, historic gateway of the continent, in the spring of 1824.[5]

"South Pass," wrote Donald McKay Frost,

does not fulfill the ordinary conception of a mountain pass. It is no mountain cleft, but a treeless, bleak plateau about fifteen miles broad. Easy grades of only twelve miles divide the upper waters of the Sweetwater River from Pacific Spring, the headwaters of a tributary of the Green River. From the Canadian border to the abrupt termination of the Wind River Range at the South Pass plateau, the Continental Divide follows a series of mountain ridges. Its course to the south for the next hundred miles is across plains. First it meanders across the South Pass plateau where its exact location can be determined only by instrumental survey, then crosses the Antelope Hills at right angles to the line of the ridge and follows a subsidiary spur down to the Great Divide Basin where it is lost; for as the waters drain from all sides into this desert bowl and sink into the sands, no true divide exists. From this descent it rises again to the high peaks of the mountains of Colorado. South Pass is therefore the northern and most elevated portion of a hundred mile break in the chain of the Rocky Mountains. No railway or through motor road crosses it today, only an unsurfaced byway across the desert floor.[6]

---

[5] The discovery of the South Pass is variously credited to Andrew Henry's men in 1810 and to Robert Stuart, one of the returning Astorians in 1812. In either case its extensive use began with the Fitzpatrick-Smith expedition just mentioned.

[6] "Notes on General Ashley, the Overland Trail, and South Pass," *Pro-*

Smith was also one of the first to trap the virgin streams of the Green River Valley — the upper tributaries of the turbid Colorado — and to look out across the strange, dead waters of the Great Salt Lake.[7]

On the western slope of the Rockies, Ashley's men encountered a brigade of rival trappers under Peter Skene Ogden, a partisan of the Hudson's Bay Company, and became involved in a rivalry that almost led to open conflict. Some of the results of the incident, which is treated more at length in a later chapter, were even more significant than beaver skins.

In 1824–5 Ashley made a memorable expedition in person to the new trapping-grounds west of the Rockies. Beyond the Continental Divide, in what is now the state of Wyoming, his small party of six men embarked on the Green River — the Seedskedee or Prairie Hen of the Indians — and made the first recorded exploration by boat of that important tributary of the Colorado. The voyage ended in one of the treacherous rapids at Desolation Cañon, fifty miles below the mouth of the Duchesne. Later explorers found Ashley's name and the date 1825 inscribed "on a high rock" on the west bank of the Green.[8] Abandoning the

ceedings of the American Antiquarian Society, October 1944 (Worcester, Massachusetts, 1945), pp. 213–14.

[7] In 1818 Donald Mackenzie crossed from the Snake to the Green River Basin, where he found "a rich field of beaver, besides deer, otters, foxes, martens, black foxes, mountain sheep, goats and wild horses." W. A. Ferris: *Life in the Rocky Mountains*, p. lxxv.

[8] T. D. Bonner's *Life and Adventures of James P. Beckwourth* (New York and London, 1856), pp. 71–2; reprinted, New York, 1931, pp. 44–6) contains a detailed and probably fanciful account of Ashley's voyage through the Green River Cañon and a notorious stretch of the river filled with rapids and whirlpools called the "Suck."

useless boat, Ashley and his men apparently returned and ascended the Duchesne, crossed the Uinta Mountains, and met the rest of his trappers at a rendezvous on Henry's Fork.

Ashley returned to St. Louis on October 4, 1825, with the most valuable collection of furs ever brought to that city.[9] St. Louis newspapers reported that he had reached the headwaters of the "Rio Colorado of the West," sailed down the river some four hundred miles, and then crossed overland to the sources of the famous Buenaventura River, a mythical stream, almost as elusive as the Spaniard's long-sought Strait of Anian, which supposedly carried the waters of the Salt Lake into the Pacific Ocean.

The wealth derived from the new beaver country discovered by Smith, Fitzpatrick, and Sublette enabled Ashley to leave the mountains and enter upon a successful political career. "The correspondence of the traders at this time shows how completely Ashley had fired the minds of every one with visions of wealth no less real than if he had discovered mines of gold," wrote Chittenden.

And there was much reason for it. He had brought down in 1824 one hundred packs, in 1826 one hundred and twenty-three packs, in 1827 one hundred and thirty packs. If we add reasonable returns for the years 1823 and 1824, he must have brought in something like five hundred packs of beaver, worth in St. Louis over a quarter of a million dollars. After deducting the cost of the expedition, and all losses, there still remained what at that period was an ample fortune for those engaged in the enterprise. Ashley had acquired a reputation

---

[9] *Missouri Advocate and St. Louis Enquirer* of October 29, 1825.

as an authority on the Western fur trade that never afterward deserted him and in his subsequent career in Congress he was looked to as much as was Senator Benton for information upon all measures relating to the West.[10]

Ashley made his last journey to the Rockies in the spring of 1826 and at a notable rendezvous, presumably in Cache Valley, on Bear River, sold his interests in the fur trade to three of his associates — Jedediah S. Smith, William L. Sublette, and David E. Jackson. As a condition of the contract, Ashley undertook to furnish his successors with necessary trade goods and supplies, and they agreed in turn to trade exclusively with him. After Ashley's return to St. Louis he invited Pratte & Company and Pierre Chouteau to participate with him in this trade. His letter to Pratte & Company contains so many important items relating to the agreement and the Rocky Mountain trade in general that it is published here in *extenso*.

St. Louis, Oct. 14, 1826

Gentlm.

I contemplate sending an expedition across the R mountains the ensuing Spring for the purpose of trading for and trapping Beaver, and with a conversation had with Genl. B. Pratte a few days since, I am induced to propose to you an equal participation in the adventure. That you may better understand the situation of my business in the mountains and future prospects of success, I will observe that when I left that country I placed under the direction of three young men, Messrs. Smith, Jackson and Sublett my remaining stock

10 *The American Fur Trade of the Far West,* Vol. I, p. 281. Ashley's returns for the year 1827, to which Chittenden referred, consisted of skins he received for supplies furnished to Smith, Jackson, and Sublette as well as of those given in payment on account.

of merchandize amounting altogether to about sixteen thousand dollars which (after deducting therefrom five thousand dollars I paid Mr. Smith on dissolution of Partnership with him) they promise to pay me in beaver fur delivered in that country at three dollars per pound or I am to receive the fur, transport the same to St. Louis and have it disposed of on their account, deductions from the amount of sale one dollar twelve and half cents per pound for transportation, and place the net proceeds to their credit in discharge of the debt aforesaid. I have also transfered to the s^d Smith, Jackson and Sublett the services of a number of men employed by me as hunters whose terms of service will expire in July next. I have also promised to furnish Messrs. Smith, Jackson and Sublett with any amount of merchandize etc. etc. not less than eight, nor exceeding fifteen thousand dollars when they may think proper to order, provided that they give me timely notice by an express which they propose sending to this place in the course of the winter. They bound themselves to deliver me all the beaver furs they may collect from the time I left them, until the first of July next, (when the merchandize last mentioned is to be delivered) on the terms above mentioned, any amount which may appear from the proceeds of the fur after paying for the goods already delivered and any balance which may be due the men transferred as aforesaid, is to be appropriated towards the payment of the goods to be delivered in July next, and any ballance of that debt which may remain after that appropriation is to be paid on or before the first of July 1828.

It is also understood between the said Smith, Jackson and Sublett and myself that provided they [h]and in the goods as last mentioned, that I will not furnish any other company in that Country with merchandize, except such as I may employ on my own acct. The following are the prices at which some of the articles of merchandize are to be furnished.

To wit

Gunpowder	$1.50	per pound
Lead	1.00	″ ″
Shot	1.25	″ ″
3 pt. Blankets	9.00	each
Scarlett Cloth	6.00	per yard
Blue (common)	5.00	″ ″
Flannel (common)	1.50	″ ″
Callico	1.00	″ ″
Butcher knives	.74	each
A. W. Fusils	24.00	each
Beavertraps	9.00	″
sugar	1.00	per pound
coffee	1.25	″ ″
Flour	1.50	″ ″
alspice	1.50	″ ″
Beads (assorted)	2.50	″ ″
Vermillion	3.00	″ ″
Rum	13.50	per gallon

The expedition which I propose sending in the spring will consist of about forty men, one hundred and twenty mules and horses. The merchandize necessary to supply them for twelve months, and that to be furnished Messrs. Smith, Jackson & Sublett all of which must be purchased for cash on the best terms.

If you are disposed to join me in the adventure, you will please signify the same by letter previous to my departure for the East — [11]

In the formal agreement between the three partners and General Ashley, entered into "near the grand lake West of

[11] Missouri Historical Society Collection, Ashley MSS. See also Ashley's letters of February 27, April 4, and April 27, 1827, and Ashley's statement dated October 1, 1827, in the Sublette Papers of the same collection.

the Rocky Mountains," Ashley undertook to deliver not less
than seven thousand nor more than fifteen thousand dollars'
worth of goods "at or near the west end of the little lake
of Bear river a watter of the pacific ocean on or before the
first day of July 1827 without some unavoidable occurrence should prevent." [12]

The members of the Smith, Jackson, Sublette partnership were young, bold, imaginative. As Ashley's men, they
had crossed the known frontiers to pre-empt the trapping
rights of a new land and make a fortune for their patron.
Now, as their own men, they were determined to find a
virgin beaver empire for themselves, to prospect a region
wholly unknown to the trapping fraternity, possibly to discover a usable waterway from the Salt Lake Valley to the
Gulf of California, and to develop a place of deposit on the
Pacific for the furs that might be taken west of the Rocky
Mountains. The dream of Ledyard, Jefferson, and Astor
died hard.[13]

We know little of the start of Smith's expedition into the
unexplored region extending south of the valley of the Salt
Lake to the Gulf of California and west to the gray Pacific,
for the surviving records of the undertaking are as frugal
of detail as a Bible narrative. We only know that the company of eighteen adventurers left the rendezvous on Bear
River, an inviting, well-wooded tributary of Salt Lake, on

[12] Ibid., the Sublette Papers, Article of Agreement, July 18, 1826.

[13] As late as 1856 Moses Carson, Kit Carson's older brother and a nota-
ble mountain man in his own right, proposed to Abel Stearns to make
Los Angeles the place of deposit for this Oriental outlet. See Cleland:
The Cattle on a Thousand Hills (San Marino, California, 1941), p. 260 n.

August 26, 1826, and literally went out into a new country not knowing whither they went.

California, one of the company's principal objectives, was vaguely known to the American people through the reports of New England sea-otter hunters, whalers, and hide and tallow traders. Most of these reports were colorful and alluring. They pictured the region as a western Eden, a land of perennial sunshine and infinite natural resources, a province sparsely inhabited by a backward, indolent population and ruled by a government both ineffective and despotic.

To what extent this picture led Smith and his partners to initiate the California expedition, or how far it played upon the curiosity and imagination of the trappers who composed the company, must be left to speculation. In any event the outcome was the same whether the men in buckskin dreamed some vague dream of national expansion or went in quest of virgin beaver streams or sought an opportunity to visit the half-legendary land of California. Destiny used them to complete the crossing of the continent, to breach the hitherto impenetrable wall that guarded California from invasion on the east, to blaze a new Wilderness Trace over which the feet of a nation would eventually travel to the western sea.

In addition to traps, provisions, and ammunition, Smith's party carried with it a considerable quantity of trade goods to barter with the Indians — lead, mirrors, rings, awls, ribbons, butcher knives, arrow points, combs, hawk bells, tobacco, and the like. The route from the rendezvous on

Bear River lay east of the Salt Lake, approximately through the sites of the present-day cities of Brigham, Ogden, Salt Lake City, Provo, Spanish Fork, Payson, and Nephi. Striking the modern Sevier River, which Smith named the Ashley in honor of his friend and former patron, the trappers followed up the course of that stream till they came to the range of high, rough mountains that separates the Great Basin proper from the tributaries of the lower Colorado.

Crossing the divide near the source of the Sevier, the expedition struck the headwaters of the present-day Virgin River, which Smith called the Adams "in compliment to our president," and kept along that stream till the men were forced to detour south of the formidable gorge now known as Parunweap Cañon. Returning to the Virgin west of Zion National Monument, the trappers continued down the river till the mountains again forced them to leave the cañon and strike out across the barren region west of the present city of St. George.[14]

Here Smith's route lay through a country almost devoid of game and water, a region of waste and savage desolation, and the trappers not only suffered severely from thirst but, in the leader's restrained language, "learned what it was to do without food." In desperation they finally ate the dry, tasteless, leather-like meat of their dying horses.

---

[14] En route the expedition crossed the modern Beaver River, or "Lost River," as Smith called it, the Santa Clara, or "Corn Creek," and Beaver Dam Wash, or "Pautch Creek," Smith's route after he reached the upper Sevier River is a matter of controversy and conjecture. I have followed the conclusions of A. M. Woodbury: "The Route of Jedediah S. Smith . . ." *Utah Historical Quarterly,* Vol. IV, pp. 262, 35–42.

Pautch Creek, or Beaver Dam Wash, offered the company a passable route to the lower reaches of the Virgin River, and that desolate stream, in turn, brought the trappers to the Colorado.[15] Smith crossed the silt-laden Colorado and continued down the east bank till he reached the inviting gardens and green melon patches of the Ammuchaba or Mojave Indians. The tribe was one of the most unpredictable and warlike of the Colorado basin, but the trappers rested fifteen days in the villages, trading for horses, food, and miscellaneous articles with apparently no unfriendly incident on either side.

At the end of that pleasant interlude the expedition left the river and set out with two native guides for the coast. The trail was older than the white man's knowledge of America. Over it, even in pre-Columbian days, the Indians of the Colorado basin had visited the coast and brought back the iridescent sea shells that figured in intertribal trade perhaps as far east as the Mississippi and as far south as the kingdom of the Aztecs.[16]

Two waterless days brought Smith and his men to the Mojave River, a stream that flowed at times along the surface between green banks of willow trees and cottonwoods and again disappeared for long stretches in the thirsty sands. With a nice choice of words, Smith named the river the "Inconstant." Making their way along the course of this intermittent stream to the base of the San Bernardino Mountains, the trappers continued over the old Indian path

---

[15] Smith applied the Indian name of the Green River — Seedskedee, or Prairie Hen — to the Colorado.

[16] From the Mojave villages the trail ran to Paiute Springs, Cedar Pass, Marl Springs, Soda Lake, and the Mojave.

that cut diagonally across the Sierra east of the Cajon Pass and emerged from the mountains above what is now the little settlement of Etiwanda.

In contrast to the dry, desolate wastes that Smith and his men had traversed for nearly seven hundred miles, the new land was a semi-paradise. Before them, bounded on the north by a range of bold, rough mountains and on the south by a line of low, rolling hills, a gentle sloping plain stretched away to the west as far as the eye could reach. Occasional watercourses, bordered with willow, sycamore, and elder, cut through the plain on their way from the mountains to the sea. Live oaks dotted the landscape, the first winter grass made the earth a velvet green, and fields of wild flowers added their flaming color to the hills. Herds of long-horned, long-legged cattle stared curiously at the intruders, and the keen, appraising eyes of the trappers noted hundreds of unprotected horses grazing on the open plain.

On Monday afternoon, November 27, 1826, the company made an early halt in a forest of noble live oaks near the Franciscan mission of San Gabriel. Here, as nearly as can be determined from the diarist's somewhat confused account, two friars, preceded by a Spanish-speaking mayor-domo, visited the camp, invited Smith to return with them to the mission to spend the night, and left the trail-worn, half-starved wanderers feasting to their hearts' content on good corn meal and the tender meat of a fat young cow.

The day following, the company broke camp and moved to the settlement about the mission. The Franciscan missions of California were then almost at the height of their temporal prosperity. The herds of cattle, horses, swine, and sheep of the Mission San Gabriel alone numbered into the tens of thousands. Its grazing lands ran from the mountains to the sea and extended from the Arroyo Seco and the boundaries of the near-by pueblo of Los Angeles on the west to the barren sands of the Colorado Desert, nearly a hundred miles distant, on the east. A handful of brown-robed friars exercised paternal but absolute authority over some twenty-five hundred Indian wards who lived in the shadow of the mission church or in small villages, called rancherias, on its distant grazing lands.

The trappers' arrival at the flourishing but isolated mission represented the first encounter of the rough, ragged, westward-moving vanguard of the Anglo-American frontier with what had once been the outposts of Spanish empire at the end of the continent. The empire itself had fallen to pieces, and the remnants in California were soon to pass into the hands of an alien race, but the historical implications of Smith's arrival were far too big for trapper, priest, or Indian neophyte to grasp. None recognized that Smith's appearance in California marked the completion of the Anglo-American's long march across the continent, the fulfillment of his age-old search for a highway to the western sea, the extension of the Wilderness Trace to the "extreme end of the great West."

It was part, too, of a tradition of conflict as old as the age of Philip and Elizabeth. For the rivalry for empire that began before the Armada unconsciously entered upon a new phase when Boone and his backwoods companions crossed the Alleghenies, and came to an end at Manila and

Santiago Bay. The characters in the opening scene of this drama in California were few and inconspicuous — a band of uncouth mountain men, a handful of devoted friars, a few ragged troops attached to a mission that stood on the rim of Spain's farthest American frontier, and some hundreds of wondering, half-wild Indian neophytes.

The coming of the Americans presumably created some stir in the placid affairs of California and the uneventful life of the isolated mission. The educated padres were hungry for news and companionship; the Indians displayed the consuming curiosity and interest of children in the bearded, long-haired strangers. The trappers, in turn, found the life of the mission full of novelty and fascination. With the trained eye of a mountain man, Harrison G. Rogers, clerk and second in command of the expedition, noted both the prosaic and the colorful details of the life around him and preserved in his journal a description of California mission life invaluable today for its realism and variety.

To his over-all picture of the mission, with its church and secular buildings, its orchards, vineyards, irrigated fields and pasture lands, herds of cattle, horses, sheep, and swine, soap works, watermill, weaving and sewing rooms, pleasant setting of high, timbered mountains on the north and low, grass-covered hills on the south, Rogers added an illuminating account of customs, ceremonials, and incidents that filled the day's routine.

Though a devout Protestant, taught to regard the Roman Catholic ritual as near-idolatry, Rogers repeatedly paid his tribute to the kindness, tolerance, hospitality, and good-fellowship of the San Gabriel friars. "Old Father Sanchus

[Sánchez]," he gratefully wrote on the eve of his departure from the jurisdiction of the mission, "has been the greatest friend that I ever met with in all my travels, he is worthy of being called a christian, as he possesses charity in the highest degree, and a friend to the poor and distressed. I ever shall hold him as a man of God, taking us when in distress, feeding, and clothing us, and may God prosper him and all such men. . . ." [17]

According to the diarist, the Indian women at the mission were a brazen lot, in both manner and speech, and one who came to his room to beg him to get her a white pickaninny was so shameless in her words and behavior that the disgusted trapper refused her request and sent her away unsatisfied. Rogers also noted that petty theft, a vice common to all California Indians, was so ineffectually exorcised by the conversion of the Gabrielaño neophytes to Christianity that he "was asked by the priest to let the company blacksmiths make a large trap to set in his orange garden, to catch the Indians in when they came up at night to rob his orchard." The friars also disciplined the Indians by imprisonment, branding, and flogging. Flogging, however, was a common punishment in many circles in that day, and one learns from Rogers's own journal that Smith flogged an obstreperous trapper in much the same way that the priests whipped the Indians.

Soon after the company's arrival at San Gabriel, Smith went to San Diego to make his peace with the Provincial Governor, José María Echeandía. Smith's men had neither proper passports nor trapping licenses and were techni-

---

[17] Dale: *The Ashley-Smith Explorations*, p. 222.

cally liable to imprisonment under Mexican law as soon as they entered California. Mexico had the traditional Spanish fear of Anglo-American designs, the trappers were not strong enough to defend themselves against an attempt at arrest in force, and the fate of the expedition lay in Echeandía's hands.

From the Governor's standpoint, the situation was full of unpleasant possibilities. If he assumed a friendly attitude toward the interlopers, his enemies would certainly report such action to the Mexican government, accuse him of betraying the interests of the province, and jeopardize his political future. On the other hand, if he dealt too harshly with the Americans, the Washington government would protest, diplomatic relations, already delicate enough, might be broken off, and the Mexican authorities could be expected to make Echeandía the scapegoat.

So the harassed Governor, who at this time apparently cherished no personal ill will against the Americans, found himself between the upper and the nether millstones. To arrest the eighteen heavily armed, self-reliant trappers would probably prove a dangerous and bloody business and almost certainly lead to Echeandia's recall from California. To permit the intruders to remain indefinitely in the province or travel extensively through the poorly defended settlements would increase the ever present danger of American infiltration into California and jeopardize the Governor's own political fortunes.

To avoid this dilemma, Echeandía resorted to a convenient compromise. Without attempting to arrest the trappers, he refused Smith's request for permission to travel northward along the coast to Oregon and ordered the Americans to retrace their steps across the desert to Salt Lake. This relatively lenient action was probably due in part to a testimonial to Smith's character and intentions that six American hide and tallow traders presented to the governor. The document read as follows:

WE, THE UNDERSIGNED, having been requested by Capt. Jedediah S. Smith to state our opinions regarding his entering the Province of California, do not hesitate to say that we have no doubt but that he was compelled to, for want of provisions and water, having entered so far into the barren country that lies between the latitudes of forty-two and forty-three west that he found it impossible to return by the route he came, as his horses had most of them perished for want of food and water; he was therefore under the necessity of pushing forward to California — it being the nearest place where he could procure supplies to enable him to return.

We further state as our opinions, that the account given by him is circumstantially correct, and that his sole object was the hunting and trapping of beaver, and other furs.

We have also examined the passports produced by him from the Superintendent of Indian affairs for the Government of the United States of America, and do not hesitate to say we believe them perfectly correct.

We also state that, in our opinion, his motives for wishing to pass, by a different route to the Columbia River, on his return is solely because he feels convinced that he and his companions run great risk of perishing if they return by the route they came.

IN TESTIMONY WHEREOF we have hereunto set our hands and seals, this 20th day of December, 1826.

William G. Dana, Captain of schooner Waverly.
William H. Cunningham, Captain of ship Courier.
William Henderson, Captain of brig Olive Branch.
James Scott.
Thomas M. Robbins, Mate of schooner Waverly.
Thomas Shaw, Supercargo of ship Courier.[18]

During Smith's prolonged absence at San Diego, the trappers made the most of their leisurely stay at San Gabriel, familiarized themselves with the life and customs of the mission, busied themselves in some of the activities of the establishment, and obtained a fairly accurate idea of the topography of California — in so far, at least, as that was known to the mission authorities themselves.

For the most part there was little friction between the visitors and the people of the mission. Rogers found himself embarrassed when he sat down at mealtime in his dirty, uncouth trapper's garb "amongst the dandys with their ruffles, silks, and broadcloths"; but the padres liked Rogers and he liked them, so differences in dress, language, and religion were courteously ignored. An occasional experience, however, gave Rogers cause for some anxiety. One such incident he recorded under date of January 6, 1827:

This being what is called Epiphany or Old Christmas day, it is kept to celebrate the manifestation of Christ to the gentiles, or particularly the Magi or wise men from the East. Church held early as usual, men, women, and children attend; after church the ceremonies as on sundays. Wine issued abundantly to both Spanyards and Inds., musick played by the Ind. band. After the issue of the morning, our men, in com-

---

[18] Titus F. Cronise: *The Natural Wealth of California* (San Francisco, 1868), p. 43.

pany with some Spanyards, went and fired a salute, and the old padre give them wine, bread, and meat as a treat. Some of the men got drunk and two of them, James Reed and Daniel Ferguson, commensed fighting, and some of the Spanyards interfered and struck one of our men by the name of Black, which come very near terminating with bad consequence. So soon as I heard of the disturbance, I went among them, and passified our men by telling what trouble they were bringing upon themselves in case they did not desist, and the most of them, being men of reason, adheared to my advice.

Our black smith, James Reed, come very abruptly into the priests dining room while at dinner, and asked for argadent; the priest ordered a plate of victuals to be handed to him; he eat a few mouthfuls, and set the plate on the table, and then took up the decanter of wine, and drank without invitation, and come very near braking the glass when he set it down; the padre, seeing he was in a state of inebriety, refrained from saying anything.[19]

After completing his unsatisfactory negotiations with the Governor, Smith returned to San Gabriel and began to collect fresh horses and supplies for a resumption of the journey. The Americans had no intention, however, of obeying Echeandía's orders to leave California. It was one thing, indeed, for the Governor to close the way along the coast and keep the trappers out of the settled portions of the province; it was a very different thing to control their movements in the no man's land of the interior. Orders and decrees did not run beyond the mountains. For all practical purposes Echeandía's authority stopped where the wilderness began.

The great interior valleys of the province, known only

---

[19] Dale, op. cit., pp. 215–16.

vaguely to the Californians and as yet unvisited by British, French, or American trappers, appealed alike to Smith the explorer and Smith the beaver-hunter. His partners had sent him to California to find new trapping-grounds and virgin beaver streams. Well and good. Before he returned to Salt Lake, he proposed to trap whatever streams the savage hinterland possessed; but he also proposed to gratify his never satisfied curiosity and see what lay beyond the long, frowning range that paralleled the sea and confined the Californians to their narrow coastal plain.

Some forty miles east of San Gabriel, near what is now the city of Redlands in the heart of the navel-orange belt of southern California, the Franciscans had established an *asistencia*, or outpost of the parent mission. Here Smith and his company established camp and spent a week or more in breaking horses, drying meat, and getting their gear and packs in order for a resumption of the march.

Leaving the *asistencia* about the 1st of February, the party crossed the rough San Bernardino Mountains through the Cajon Pass, skirted the edge of the Mojave Desert north of the San Gabriel Range, traversed the weird Joshua-tree forests of Antelope Valley, ascended the Tehachapi Mountains, presumably by way of Oak Creek Cañon, and dropped down into the great San Joaquin Valley on the other side.

In spite of the early explorations of Fages, Garcés, Moraga, and a few other Spanish priests and soldiers, the region through which Smith's route now lay was still a primeval wilderness, untouched by ax or plow, with neither trail nor settlement. The blue line of the Coast Range Mountains defined the limits of the valley on the west; on the east the trappers saw the huge uplift of the Sierra Nevada — a giant, unscaled wall that ran in majesty and silence from the white glory of Mount Lassen on the north to the gray wastes of the Mojave Desert in the south.

The physical characteristics of the region were full of arresting contradictions. Alkali plains, white, dry, and desolate, covered part of the valley's floor. Other areas held lakes and sloughs and miles of rank, almost impenetrable tule marshes. Leagues of bare, rolling hills gave place to broad, tree-lined rivers, and fertile plains dotted with stands of oak and sycamore. During the long dry summers much of the valley lay withered and dead in the shimmering heat, but the touch of rain clothed all the dusty earth with beauty and transformed the landscape into a garden filled with the riotous and glowing colors of lupine, poppy, godetia, Indian paintbrush, and kindred flowers, each growing only with those of its own kind.

The valley was also a hunter's paradise. Deer, wild horses, and antelope roamed across it by the thousand. Bear, both brown and grizzly, multiplied in it unmolested. Bands of elk were almost as numerous as the cattle on the California ranges.[20] Wild fowl darkened the sun and literally hid from sight the surface of lakes and ponds. Beaver flourished in the rivers that flowed along the floor of the valley, in the lower reaches of the streams that came down

---

[20] Twenty years later the wild elk of the San Joaquin and Sacramento valleys were profitably hunted for their hides and tallow.

from the Sierra Nevada Mountains, and in the sloughs and estuaries near the coast.[21]

Our knowledge of Smith's activities in the San Joaquin and lower Sacramento valleys is disappointingly meager and comes chiefly from a letter that he wrote the following summer to General William Clark, Superintendent of Indian Affairs, in St. Louis.[22] After leaving the Spanish settlements, according to this document, Smith traveled three hundred miles through a well-populated country of almost naked Indians who knew nothing of firearms and lived principally on fish, acorns, roots, and grapes. The company established a base camp on a branch of the San Joaquin River, presumably the Stanislaus, which Smith called the Wimilchi, after a tribe of Indians living along its banks.

After trapping as far north as the stream known thereafter as the American River, Smith attempted to lead his company across the Sierra and return to the appointed rendezvous with his partners, Jackson and Sublette, in Bear River Valley. But the deep mountain snows defeated his efforts and forced the party to return to the lower levels of the valley.[23]

---

[21] Apparently Smith's party was the first to trap these inland waters, though the Russians hunted beaver earlier in San Francisco Bay.

[22] The letter, written after Smith returned to the rendezvous with his partners in the valley of the Salt Lake, is now in possession of the Kansas Historical Society. A copy appeared in the *Missouri Republican* of October 25, 1827, and this, or the original, has been reprinted in whole or in part by a number of later writers.

[23] According to Cronise: *The Natural Wealth of California,* p. 42, a company of American trappers, which included Caleb Greenwood, reached the American River before Smith. See also Charles Kelly: *Old*

On May 20, 1827, after the party had made a number of other unsuccessful attempts to scale the mountain barrier, Smith and two companions, Robert Evans and Silas Gobel, undertook again to cross the wide Sierra, dazzling white "from crest to crest." The snow was still from four to eight feet deep on the upper ridges, and the men were alone with the winds and the rocks and the singing trees. Eight days after entering the mountains the adventurers stood on the edge of the desolate Nevada plains. In crossing the Sierra the three had done what no one, so far as there is any record, had ever done before. Of the seven horses and two mules with which the trappers began the journey, only five horses and one mule survived. Smith's laconic account contains no further details. The reader's imagination must complete the tale.

The location of Smith's base camp in the San Joaquin Valley and the route by which he crossed the mountains are still, and possibly always will be, matters of dispute. Because of the proximity of the Mission San José to his headquarters in the San Joaquin, or possibly out of gratitude to old Father José Sanchez of San Gabriel (whom the trappers customarily referred to as Father Joseph), Smith called the whole chain of the Sierra Nevada Mountains Mt. Joseph or Mt. St. Joseph.

This peculiar nomenclature confused later writers, who applied the name to some specific mountain (instead of to the entire range) and fixed Smith's route by reference to that erroneous landmark. The trappers' already obscure

Greenwood (Salt Lake, 1926), p. 64. There seems to be little evidence, documentary or circumstantial, to support the statement.

itinerary thus became still more uncertain and perplexing. The best available (though inconclusive) evidence indicates that Smith followed the course of the Stanislaus River into the mountains north of the Yosemite Valley, and descended the eastern side of the range by way of Sonora or Carson Pass.

The privations and difficulties that Smith and his two companions suffered in the crossing of the mountains, whatever their severity, were soon forgotten in the greater hardships of the Nevada plains.

Smith kept a desultory record of the entire journey, but the first part of his journal has not yet come to light. The extant entries, however, are poignant and brief. They began when the trappers, having taken a direct course toward Salt Lake after leaving the mountains (thus missing the comparatively easy, well-watered Humboldt River route a little farther north), were fast approaching the limit of human endurance, though some of the worst ordeals of the journey still lay ahead.

Fighting a deathlike weariness of body and spirit, sometimes burying themselves in the earth to find shelter from the fierce midday heat, eating the dry, black flesh of one of the remaining horses, which died along the way, driven to the verge of madness by the searing heat of sand and sun — without water, without hope, without prospect of escape — the three men staggered on.

Evans, the weakest of the three, at last gave out and lay down, like the prophet of old, in the thin shade of a juniper tree to die. Smith and Gobel, half-dead and semi-delirious themselves, stumbled a few miles farther on. Then, on the

actual verge of collapse, they reached the base of a mountain and found a flowing spring.

Maddened by thirst, Gobel threw himself into a small
pool and drank down the water in frenzied gulps, a dangerous, often fatal thing for one in such an extremity to do.
More cautious and self-disciplined than his companion,
Smith momentarily held back; but such thirst is stronger
than human will. Presently he also threw discretion to the
winds, lay down bodily in the stream, and drank and drank
till his swollen stomach could hold no more.

Smith then filled a kettle with water, added to it a piece
of meat, and hurried back to rescue the victim whom the
desert was about to claim. Completely prostrated and
scarcely able to speak, Evans put the kettle to his mouth
and kept it there "until he had drunk all the water, of which
there was at least 4 or 5 quarts." With the kettle dry and
the madness of thirst still on him, he querulously complained because Smith had brought so little water.[24]

According to Charles Kelly, foremost authority on the
Salt Desert trails, Smith's probable route ran some twenty
miles from Goshute Springs (on the western edge of Utah's
great salt plain) to Granite Mountain; thirty miles farther
on to the southern end of Skull Valley; and then an additional twenty miles to the spring that saved the trappers'
lives.

Quoting from Isaac K. Russell, author of *Hidden Heroes
of the Rockies,* Kelly adds: "For years after Smith's journey, the Piute Indians of Skull Valley, Utah, repeated the

---

[24] Maurice Sullivan: *The Travels of Jedediah Smith* (Santa Ana, California, 1934), p. 22.

tradition that the first white men they ever saw were three who staggered, almost naked in from the western desert, and were half-crazed from breathing alkali dust."

Kelly's eloquent and vivid tribute deserves a place in any account of Smith's heroic exploration:

The feat of crossing this great unknown country between the Sierras and the Salt Lake, with only two companions, has never been fully appreciated by historians, partly because Smith himself makes such brief mention of it, but principally because of the historians' lack of knowledge concerning that section of the west. Few persons today — few even in Utah — have ever seen the Great Salt Desert or the country which lies to the west of it. The desert between the Sierras and the Sink of the Humboldt is desolate enough, dangerous enough, even for the hardiest explorer. But the Great Salt Desert, stretching for 75 miles without water and without any vegetation whatever, reflecting from its salt-encrusted surface all the heat of the summer sun, confusing the traveller with its beautiful mirages and choking him with its salt-laden winds; enmeshing his feet in its bottomless mire and sapping his energy with its shifting sand dunes, presents the most desolate and dangerous stretch of desert in America, with the exception of Death Valley itself.

Jedediah S. Smith, crossing this desert for the first time, with no knowledge of what lay before him, achieved one of the greatest single exploits in the whole history of western exploration.[25]

The worst of the refugees' hardships ended with the discovery of the life-saving spring. On June 27 Smith caught sight of the shining expanse of the Big Salt Lake, already

[25] *Utah Historical Quarterly*, Vol. III, No. 1, p. 27. Reprinted by permission of the Utah State Historical Society, Salt Lake City, Utah.

84

a familiar and cherished landmark to the wanderer, a home and refuge in the wilderness, despite its loneliness and isolation. Six days later the three refugees, by that time little more than skeletons, reached the rendezvous in Bear Valley where Jackson and Sublette were camped.

Smith's account of the reunion with his partners, after so many months of separation, peril, hardship, and epoch-making exploration, was typical of the man's habitual restraint and understatement. "My arrival caused a considerable bustle in camp," he wrote, " for myself and party had been given up as lost. A small cannon, brought up from St. Louis, was loaded and fired for a salute." [26]

[26] Sullivan, op. cit., p. 26. Ashley had brought the cannon to the rendezvous the year before.

CHAPTER 3

Jedediah Strong Smith:

The End of the Long Trail

B EAR LAKE, the site of the Smith-Jackson-Sublette
rendezvous, has been described as "one of the most beautiful lakes in the West, and therefore in the world." "From
the east shore," wrote Harrison Dale, "bare hills of burnt
sienna rise sheer from the water's edge, culminating in the
gentle domes of the Bear River divide, while to the west,
beyond a narrow hem of gently sloping arable land, rise
sparsely covered hills of hock and quaking aspen, topped
by the dark timber of the main Wasatch ridge." [1]

The contrast between the streams and trees and grass of
Bear Valley and the abomination of desolation of the Ne-
vada-Utah plains might well have symbolized to the three
victims of the desert's torment the contrast between paradise and hell. But Smith lingered in this valley of Avilion
only long enough to recuperate his exhausted strength, review the affairs of the partnership with Jackson and Sublette, and organize a second company for California — a
matter of ten short days.

The expedition consisted of the leader and eighteen men,

---

[1] Dale: *The Ashley-Smith Explorations*, p. 226.

including the hard-bitten blacksmith, Silas Gobel, and left Bear Lake on July 13, 1827. "My object," wrote Smith, "was to relieve my party on the Appelamminy (or Stanislaus) and then proceed further in examination of the country beyond Mt. St. Joseph and along the sea coast. I of course expected to find Beaver, which with us hunters is a primary object, but I was also led on by the love of novelty common to all, which is much increased by the pursuit of its gratification." [2]

The expedition followed, in the main, Smith's first route into California, though his journal notes an occasional deviation. Instead of pursuing the rough course of the Santa Clara River through the mountains of southern Utah below St. George, for example, the company proceeded up the stream some twenty-five miles, then turned southwest and entered the lower Colorado basin by a comparatively easy trail across the divide. The dry bed of Beaver Dam Wash brought the trappers to the Adams or Virgin River, and the latter led them to the Colorado. Crossing to the east bank as he had done before, Smith abandoned his trail of the preceding year in favor of an easier route to the Mojave villages.

Up to this point the journey had been relatively uneventful except for one arresting incident. North of the Sevier River the Indians, friendly enough on Smith's former visit, now kept themselves so well hidden that the keen-eyed mountain men caught sight of only a single native, and he "kept as close to Rock as a Mountain Sheep." The change in attitude was explained when a little later Smith found

[2] Sullivan: *The Travels of Jedediah Smith*, p. 26

the well-preserved tracks of horses and mules along the river and learned from the Indians at Utah Lake that a party of men, "nearly starved to death," had come up from the south the preceding spring and passed through their country on the way to Taos. These inhabitants of the lake region, curiously enough, assumed an entirely different attitude toward the strangers from that of their neighbors to the north, so that Smith wrote: "the indians who were so wild when I passed the year before came to me by dozens. Every little party told me by signs and words . . . of the party of White Men that had passed the year before, having left a knife and other articles at the encampment when the Indians had ran away."

From the Mojaves, Smith learned more of the mysterious party that had visited the region since his previous expedition. An Indian interpreter named Francisco told him that a mixed party of Americans and Spaniards (that is, Mexicans or New Mexicans) had followed the Gila to the Colorado and traveled up the latter river to the Mojave villages. There, after trading briefly with the Indians, the strangers had quarreled among themselves and divided into two companies. One of these continued up the Colorado to leave the traces that Smith found along the Virgin and Sevier rivers; but the Mojaves apparently did not have any knowledge of the other's whereabouts.

Smith remained some time at the Mojave villages, camping in a rich, grassy bottom to prepare his horses and mules for the long desert crossing to California, while his men traded with the Indians for horses, beans, and corn. Outwardly the Mojaves, friendly and hospitable on Smith's

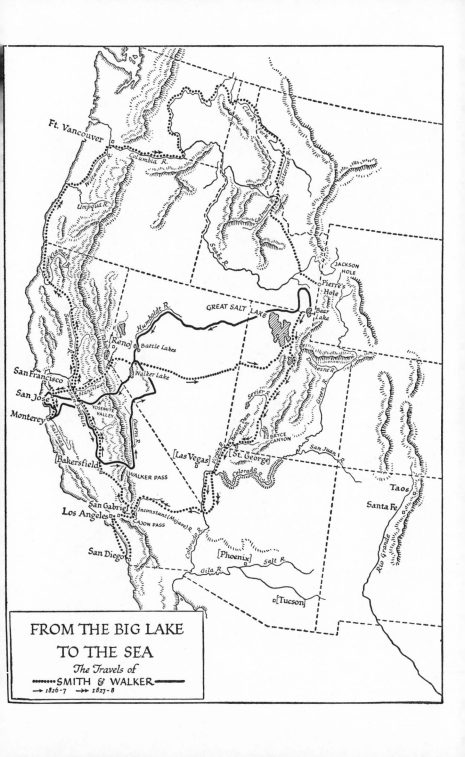

Ft. Vancouver

Columbia R.
Willamette

Umpqua R.

Snake R.

Clark Fork

Bitterroot R.

JACKSON
HOLE

Pierre's
Hole

Klamath

Sacramento R.

GREAT SALT LAKE

Humboldt R.

Bear Lake

[Reno]
Battle Lakes

Walker Lake

San Francisco

San Jose

Stanislaus

YOSEMITE VALLEY

San Joaquin R.

Owens R.

Sevier R.

Duchesne R.

Green R.

San Juan R.

Monterey

Salinas R.

Bakersfield

WALKER PASS

[Las Vegas]

Virgin R.

San Gabriel
Los Angeles

CAJON PASS

Inconstant (Mojave) R.

San Diego

Colorado R.

[Phoenix]

Gila R.

Salt R.

[Tucson]

Beaver Dam Wash

BRYCE CANYON

St. George

Colorado R.

Taos

Santa Fe

Rio Grande

FROM THE BIG LAKE
TO THE SEA
The Travels of
●●●●●●SMITH & WALKER━━━
→ 1826-7 ⇒ 1827-8

Josiah Gregg: Customs House Permit, Chihuahua

previous visit, appeared equally so on this. But their friendship was only make-believe. Behind the scenes, unrevealed by sign or word, the warriors poisoned their arrowheads, made ready their war clubs, and rehearsed the plans for a massacre.

The Indians struck when the trappers, swimming their horses and ferrying their food, equipment, and furs on makeshift tule rafts across the Colorado, were totally unprepared. In a few tragic minutes arrows, lances, and war clubs had taken their bloody toll. Ten members of the surprised, divided, and almost defenseless company were killed at the first onslaught. Thomas Virgin, one of the oldest and most seasoned of the men, lay helpless from wounds about the head. Two Indian squaws, wives or companions of the trappers, were taken captive. Almost all the baggage and supplies fell into the hands of the Mojaves.[3]

Few men ever faced a more desperate plight than the nine survivors, one nearer dead than alive, of this grim massacre. It was impossible for them to recross the Colorado and return to Salt Lake. A hundred and fifty miles of desert, rendered furnace-hot by the midsummer sun, separated them from the California settlements. An inventory of the articles salvaged from the massacre offered only the bitter mockery of hope: horses, none; guns, five; ammunition, a few rounds; food, fifteen pounds of dried

---

[3] Among the victims were David Cunningham, Francis Deramme, William Campbell, Boatswain Brown, Gregory Ortega, John B. Ratelle, Pale, Polita, Robiseau, and Smith's companion of the Sierra and Nevada desert crossing, Silas Gobel. Missouri Historical Society Collection, Sublette Papers (microfilm).

meat. Hundreds of blood-crazed Indians, whose war clubs were known and feared "from the pueblos east of the Zuñi to the western Ocean, and from the big Salt Lake in the north to the river of the Yaquis in the south," were preparing to enact the final scene in the tragedy.

Telling his men to help themselves to the scant supply of equipment that had escaped the hands of the Mojaves, Smith threw some of the remainder of the goods into the river and strewed the rest on a sand bar to serve as bait to divert the Indians, even briefly, from their pursuit. He then ordered his men to take refuge in a clump of small cottonwoods and make breastworks out of the trunks and limbs of the young trees. Giving the rifles to his best marksmen, he directed the latter to fire "only when the shot would be certain of killing," and never to discharge more than three of the five guns at one time. Meanwhile the trappers hurriedly lashed butcher knives to the ends of cottonwood poles to provide makeshift lances as additional weapons of defense.

It was indeed "a fearful time," as Smith wrote in his journal. Some of the men asked their intrepid leader if he thought they could hold off the Indians. "I told them I thought we would," he replied; then dryly added: "but that was not my opinion."

Taking advantage of rocks, brush, and other cover, the Mojaves crept closer and closer to the trappers' flimsy barricade. But when some of the more reckless savages ventured out into the open, Smith ordered two of his men to fire. The range was long, but the shots went home. Two Indians fell dead; a third lay badly wounded. This deadly reception cooled the blood lust of the mercurial Mojaves so effectively that they abandoned the attack and ran away, like so many frightened sheep, to a safer distance. Scarcely able to believe their miraculous escape, the surprised trappers left the river and began their desperate retreat toward California.

The massacre was one of the major tragedies of the Western fur trade. What lay behind it? Did the attack spring out of the notorious fickleness of the Mojave temperament? Was it due to some unrecorded friction or hostility between the Indians and the whites? Did the California officials, as Smith later believed, or emissaries from New Mexico, secretly instruct the Indians to turn back or destroy any further American companies that sought to cross the Colorado?

Any one of these motives offers a possible explanation of the massacre. But a more logical answer lies in another quarter. Smith's visit to the Colorado in 1826 apparently marked the first contact of the Mojave Indians with Americans. The relations of the two peoples were then altogether friendly. Between that visit and the arrival of Smith's second expedition, the trapping company from New Mexico, which Smith frequently mentioned in his journal, traveled up the Colorado River from the Gila and visited the Mojave villages. One might hazard the guess that this party offended or perhaps attacked the Mojaves and that a few months later the Indians massacred Smith's men by way of retaliation.[4]

---

[4] There is even a faint possibility that the trappers from the Gila belonged to the Young-Pattie expedition described in Chapter 5.

But whatever the cause of the massacre, the plight of the nine men reprieved by the Indians' panicky withdrawal offered little hope. The fleeing whites looked for the enemy to renew the attack in overwhelming force at any moment, and even if the fugitives escaped torture and death at the hands of the Mojaves, the desert waited to destroy them by hunger, heat, and thirst.

The survivors of the massacre followed substantially the same route between the Colorado River and the Cajon Pass that Smith's former expedition had traversed. Midsummer temperatures reached fantastic heights; watering-places were far apart; the sandy waste was like the anteroom of hell.

Burdened with the care of their wounded companion, lying by at some brackish spring or water-hole through the day, traveling at night to escape the cruel sun, chewing pieces of cactus to ease their intolerable thirst, sometimes wandering from the course, occasionally retracing their steps to succor a weaker member of the party, the handful of trappers struggled for nine days to complete the crossing of the desert.

Some miles from the sink of the Mojave River, near the present town of Baker, Smith found a friendly Indian village from whose inhabitants he obtained a few horses in exchange for some of the beads, cloth, butcher knives, and vermilion that his men had salvaged from the massacre. Farther up the river he found a second village and made a similar exchange. There the company left the old Indian trail along the Mojave and cut directly across the desert to the "Gap of the Mountain," as Smith called the Cajon Pass, gateway between the desert and the coastal plain. Ragged as scarecrows, gaunt as sun-dried mummies, the trappers descended the cañon, now used daily by thousands of automobiles and endless freight and passenger trains of the Santa Fe and Union Pacific railroads, and again found themselves within the jurisdiction of the friendly Father Sánchez.

Near the foot of the Cajon Pass the ravenous company came to the fringe of the vast cattle herds of the San Gabriel Mission, and Smith ordered his men to kill enough steers to satisfy their immediate hunger and supply sufficient dried meat for the completion of their journey into the San Joaquin Valley. The necessity for this action he later explained in a letter to Father Sánchez.

Worn out by his experiences on the Colorado and the crossing of the desert, and anxious if possible to avoid a second meeting with Governor Echeandía, Smith made no attempt to reach San Gabriel, but camped at the *asistencia*. There he bartered the remainder of the trade goods that his men had brought on their backs from the Colorado and obtained a horse and saddle for each unmounted trapper from the mayordomo.

At the end of five days he set out over his former trail through the Cajon Pass for the lower San Joaquin. By this time the party had been reduced to only six men. Ten of the original company had been killed on the Colorado. Thomas Virgin, still suffering from his bad head wound, remained at the *asistencia* with instructions to make his way to San Francisco as soon as he recovered. Daniel Ferguson, one of the survivors of the massacre, deserted. Isaac Galbraith, another survivor, obtained Smith's formal release from the company and remained in southern California.[5]

Galbraith was a man of gigantic stature. According to an unsupported story by William Waldo, though out of ammunition and wounded in the forehead by a rifle ball on the Colorado, he "performed such prodigies of strength and valor with his gun barrel" that the Indians ran away and allowed him to escape. He then wandered across the desert without gun or blankets and lived on snakes and frogs until he reached California.[6]

Unfortunately we have no record of Smith's journey from the *asistencia* to the trappers' headquarters on the Stanislaus. He reached their camp on September 18, 1827, only two days before the deadline fixed the preceding spring for his return, and found that the trappers were becoming concerned over his absence. His unannounced appearance roused great enthusiasm for the moment; but when the exiles learned of the massacre of their companions on the Colorado and the loss of the long-awaited goods and supplies, their rejoicing came to a quick and gloomy end.

During Smith's absence the California camp had been under command of Harrison G. Rogers, clerk of the expedition, and the trappers had spent a pleasant if uneventful summer. Game had been plentiful and the Indians friendly. "A gentle Northwestern Breeze that rose and sank with the

---

[5] Ferguson was paid a hundred dollars before he left the company. Smith later discharged a trapper named John Wilson at "Chintache Lake," better known as Lake Tulare, in the lower San Joaquin Valley.
[6] William Waldo: "Recollections of a Septuagenarian," Missouri Historical Society, *Glimpses of the Past,* Vol. V, Nos. 4–6, p. 84.

rising and setting of the sun" had kept the temperature of the valley within bounds, and a detachment of California troops that visited the camp gave every evidence of friendship and raised no objection to the presence of the Americans so far from the settlements along the coast.

Smith remained only two or three days on the Stanislaus. Then, with two of his men and as many Indian guides, he crossed the Coast Range Mountains and presented himself before the authorities at the Mission San José. There he expected to find a welcome similar in kind if not in degree to the friendly reception he had received at San Gabriel the year before. But in this he was rudely disappointed; for neither Father Narciso Durán of the Mission San José nor Father José Viader of the near-by Mission Santa Clara followed the example of the friars of San Gabriel. Instead of offering kindness and hospitality, these two more realistic fathers treated the trappers as spies and interlopers, refused to give them supplies, and placed them under informal arrest; and as Smith, with one of his rare expressions of humor, dryly remarked, apparently expected them "to live on faith instead of food."

Some days later Lieutenant Ignacio Martínez, whom Smith had met at San Gabriel the year before, came down from the presidio of San Francisco to take official cognizance of the arrival of the Americans at San José. Martínez, who proved more friendly than the friars, told Smith that he and his men were to be tried for illegal entry into the province — an offense of which they were at least technically guilty — and for claiming the region drained by the River San Joaquin for the United States — a charge, obviously preposterous, which originated with a talebearing Indian neophyte.

Worn out as much by the backing and filling of the padres and local officials as by ill treatment, Smith finally appealed unto Cæsar, in the person of Governor Echeandía, at Monterey, and left San José under armed escort for the seaport.

From Echeandía's standpoint, Smith was neither a welcome nor an honored guest. Through the good offices of William E. Hartnell, an English trader of more than transient reputation, the American explained that he had returned to California only to rescue the men whom he had left in the San Joaquin Valley the year before and had suffered cruel disaster at the hands of the Mojaves on the Colorado. But Echeandía refused to be placated or convinced. Why, he querulously asked, had Smith returned to California over his first long trail, by way of the Colorado, instead of using the more direct route that he had opened across the Sierra Nevada and the Utah-Nevada plains? Again, why had he failed, in violation of Mexican law, to notify the Governor of his arrival at San Gabriel after his escape from the Mojave massacre?

To the first of these charges Smith replied that he followed the Salt Lake-Colorado trail only because the expedition's horses and mules could not survive the heat, rocks, and waterless stretches of the shorter Utah-Nevada route. In reply to the second he explained that he had notified Father Sánchez of his arrival at the mission *asistencia* and took it for granted that the padre would forward the message to Echeandía.

Under normal conditions Smith's replies would probably have satisfied Echeandía, but the Governor was so exasperated and embarrassed by the American's reappearance in California that he brushed aside his explanations and charged him with willful violation of Mexican law.

As on Smith's first visit, Echeandía was once more caught on the horns of a difficult dilemma. If he permitted the Americans to remain in the province, he jeopardized his standing with the unpredictable authorities in Mexico; his case was no better if he left the trappers at large and again allowed them to leave California without arrest. On the other hand, seizure and imprisonment of the Americans might well involve the Mexican government in unwelcome international complications and render Echeandía extremely unpopular in the capital. The possibility that Smith's detention might bring the formidable body of American trappers posthaste to Monterey to effect their leader's release was an even stronger and more realistic argument for caution.

Unable to reach a decision in the face of these difficult alternatives, Echeandía played with the idea of getting rid of Smith by sending him to Mexico for trial. But the Governor had no funds to pay the trapper's passage, and Smith bluntly refused either to travel as a prisoner at his own expense or to wait indefinitely for a government transport to carry him away. So, falling back upon a useful, time-old Spanish custom of meeting a difficult or disconcerting situation, Echeandía resorted to evasion, inaction, and ambiguous pronouncements.

Meanwhile time was running on. Smith's enforced stay at Monterey threatened to keep the company from taking advantage of the fall trapping season, his supply of money was almost gone, and the trappers, most of whom had been in California the better part of a year, were impatient to begin the return journey to Salt Lake.

In this crisis Smith sought the assistance of some of the well-known foreigners at Monterey, including Captain John Rogers Cooper, a Boston trader of good reputation on the coast, and William Hartnell, the versatile agent for the English firm of John Begg & Company. One of the traders, Captain John Bradshaw, of the New England ship *Franklin*, agreed to supply Smith with badly needed funds by purchasing from him sixteen hundred pounds of beaver fur at $2.50 a pound. The price was much lower than the rate then prevailing in the mountains, but the difference was less real than apparent. The transaction was in cash instead of goods, and the sale relieved Smith of the further risk and burden of transportation.

Smith's difficulties with Echeandía were finally resolved on November 12, 1827, when four Americans gave bond to assure the trapper's peaceful withdrawal from California and his proper future conduct.[7] The text of the bond was as follows:

[7] The four were Captain Joseph Steele and Thomas B. Park of the *Harbinger*; Henry Pease and Benjamin Clark of the *Hesper*. John Cooper acted as representative of the bondsmen. On June 26, 1828, J. Lenox Kennedy, the United States Vice-Consul at Mazatlán, wrote "Juan Bautista R. Cooper" as follows:

"I have been favoured with your letter of the 26 March last, enclosing me one from our countryman Mr. Smith, with a document you had been generous enough to give to enable Mr. Smith to direct his

Therefore, in the name of the Government of the United States, I provisionally guarantee the good conduct and behavior of Captain Smith in whatever concerns his return to the settlement called "the deposit," and for the furnishing of such equipment as shall be necessary, I hereby bind myself and all property in my possession or to be received, to be responsible to the Republics of Mexico and of the United States, and to anyone who may be concerned, for each and every one of the following articles:

1. That Captain Smith and his men are citizens of the United States, honest and faithful to our Government, and as such they should be considered friends and bound by the same agreement as exists between the two nations.

2. That for this reason such help as shall be absolutely necessary for their return, such as arms, ammunition, horses, provisions, etc., shall be furnished them at their just prices, the same being for the purpose of protecting them and their property until their safe return to the settlement called the Salt Lake deposit, following the road from Mission San José by way of Carquinex Straits and Bodega.

3. That under no condition will he delay on the way a longer time than is necessary, and that having reached his destination, he will make no hostile excursion, and will make no trip toward the coast or in the region of his establishment south of the 42nd parallel not authorized by his Government in accord with the latest treaties, unless he has a legal passport expressly [permitting it] from one or the other of the aforesaid Governments.

---

route towards his hunting deposit within the territories of the United States.

"All these papers I shall forward on to Mr. Poinsett, our Minister at Mexico, and I shall transmit you his answer as soon I receive it, and can meet with an opportunity of sending it with safety to you." Mariano Guadalupe Vallejo: *Documentos para la Historia de California,* Bancroft Library MSS.

4. Four copies of this direct guarantee to the Governor of California shall be drawn — one to be filed with the Governor, one to be retained by Captain Smith, one to be sent to Mexico, and the other to be kept in my possession. In witness whereof, we have set our hands in Monterey, November 12, 1827.

I acknowledge this Bond.

Jedediah S. Smith.[8]

The text of Smith's acknowledgment ran as follows:

I Jed^h S. Smith of Greentownship of the State of Ohio do hereby bind myself, my heirs, executors and principals in the penal sum of thirty thousand dollars for the faithful performance of a certain Bond given to the Mexican Govt.

Monterey 15 Nov. 1827

Jedediah S. Smith

Witness
Rufus Perkins.[9]

In compliance with the provisions of the bond Echeandía formally granted Smith and his men free passage to the trappers' depot in the Salt Lake Valley and made them a baggage allotment of 75 pounds of powder, 125 pounds of lead, five pack-loads of clothing and other goods, six of provisions, one of tobacco, six of merchandise for trade with the Indians, a gun for each man, and the remnants of the equipment that Smith had originally brought into California.[10]

---

[8] Vallejo: *Documentos,* Bancroft Library MSS. Quoted in Sullivan, op. cit., p. 172.

[9] From a copy in the papers of John C. Parish, Library of the University of California at Los Angeles. The original document is in the Sublette Collection of the Missouri Historical Society.

[10] Apparently the customs officials at San Francisco appraised these goods at $1,178.12, levied a 15 per cent duty on them, and refused Smith

Unfortunately the truce with Echeandía did not bring Smith's troubles to an end. Devious activities on the part of certain California officials, inadequate supplies, runaway stock, horses stolen or "appropriated" by the Californians, torrential rains, and impassable streams delayed the start of the expedition for another month.[11]

By January 1, 1828, however, the trappers were again back in the San Joaquin Valley, over the edge of the wilderness, beyond the reach of Echeandía's vacillating authority. Four days later Smith feelingly wrote: "Having been so long absent from the business of trapping and so much perplexed and harassed by the folly of men in power, I returned again to the woods, the river, the prairie, the Camp & the Game with a feeling somewhat like that of a prisoner escaped from his dungeon and his chains." [12]

For more than two weeks the homeward bound Americans floundered through the swollen estuaries, tule marshes, and miry bottoms of the San Joaquin and Sacramento delta region. Beaver were plentiful, but the company had few traps and the flooded lowlands forced the men to use canoes

---

a passport until he had made arrangements to pay the charge of $176.69. Raymundo Estrado to General Commander, March 30, 1829. Papers of John Parish, loc. cit. See also David E. Jackson in Account with William L. Sublette, January 31, 1832. Missouri Historical Society Collection, Sublette Papers (microfilm).

[11] Meanwhile Rogers had brought the company out of the San Joaquin Valley to the straggling village of San Francisco. There Henry Virmond, a German merchant with important political connections in both Mexico and California, supplied the trappers with food and other necessities.

[12] Maurice Sullivan: *The Travels of Jedediah Smith* (Santa Ana, California, 1934), p. 54. Reprinted by permission of the publishers, The Fine Arts Press, Santa Ana, California.

of green elk skin to carry on their trapping operations. Thus engaged, the Americans reached the vicinity of the present towns of Stockton and Lodi, passing en route through a country as green "as a flourishing wheat field." Smith then swung northwest till he came to the Sacramento, or Buenaventura, River.

Keeping on the east bank of the Sacramento, meanwhile looking in vain for a pass across the Sierra, the company moved slowly north till it came to the flood-swollen American River,[13] and Smith recalled the rushing streams, thick falling snow, and bitter cold of the cloud-wrapped Sierra Nevada Mountains that he and his two half-frozen companions had crossed the previous spring. With a tragic foretelling of his own fate, the trapper wrote: "It seems that in times like those men return to reason and make the true estimate of things. . . . But a few days of rest makes the sailor forget the storm and embark on the perilous Ocean and I suppose that like him I would soon become weary of rest." [14]

From the American River northward Smith found the country one vast quagmire; and though beaver were plentiful, floods, mud, and the scarcity of traps, already mentioned, greatly handicapped the hunters.[15] The company reached the Feather River early in March. The surround-

---

[13] On this occasion Smith named the stream Wild River, because the Indians were so frightened and hard to make friends with. "To this river," he wrote, "I had before that time applied a different name." Ibid., p. 66.

[14] Ibid., p. 63.

[15] Louis Pombert and James Read (whom Smith had flogged at San Gabriel) deserted the company early in January and carried off eleven of the company's traps.

ing region was full of bear, and Harrison Rogers was almost killed by one of the wounded animals. Smith's account of the incident, vivid though tantalizingly laconic, ran as follows:

> On this river I found a plenty of Beaver sign. 13 were caught the first setting. Mr. Rodgers killed a Brown Bear and wounded another. . . . Early in the Morning Mr. Rodgers went after the wounded Bear in company with John Hanna. In a short time Hanna came running in and said that they had found the Bear in a verry bad thicket. That he suddenly rose from his bed and rushed on them. Mr. Rodgers fired a moment before the Bear caught him. After biting him in several places he went off, but Hanna shot him again, when he returned, caught Mr. Rodgers and gave him several additional wounds. I went out with a horse to bring him in and found him verry badly wounded being severely cut in . . . 10 or 12 places. I washed his wounds and dressed them with plasters of soap and sugar.[16]

Rogers' hurts, which Smith continued to treat at frequent intervals "with cold water and salve of Sugar and Soap," forced the company to lie by for nearly a week, and even then the wounded man could travel only a short distance every second or third day. The men spent the time to good advantage trapping and hunting. Beaver were so plentiful that the trappers caught twenty in one night, a feat that led Smith to break through his habitual reserve and write in his journal: "as I had but 28 traps I considered it great trapping."

In addition to beaver, the hunters found the country

---

[16] Sullivan, op. cit., p. 68.

well stocked with elk, black-tailed deer, antelope, coyotes, wolves, otter, coons, and bear. There were also large numbers of swan, geese, brant, and wild ducks. The Indians were numerous but inoffensive. They went naked, or nearly so, lived like animals, and appeared to Smith, whose acquaintance with Indian tribes was probably as extensive as that of any American of the time, "to be the lowest intermediate link between man and the Brute creation."

In hunting wild fowl, however, the skill of the Sacramento Indians aroused the admiration of the mountain men. The natives wove nets, not unlike those with which the frontier American settlers caught wild pigeons, and made such lifelike imitations of ducks and geese that the decoys deceived the keenest eye and led even Smith's experienced hunters to fire at them.

By the last week in March, Rogers was again able to take active part in camp affairs, and the company resumed its full-scale march up the Sacramento. Trapping was good, though sloughs, mud, and lack of traps continued to hamper the operations. South of the present city of Red Bluff the company entered a bear-infested region that put even the most experienced hunters constantly on guard.

Smith himself was attacked twice in a single day. The first incident occurred while he and some of his men were following a wounded bear in heavy brush. Suddenly they came face to face with a second bear. Smith fired. The bear fell with a bullet in his head. As Smith walked over to the animal, one of his companions shouted: "He's alive!" But with the bear stretched out before him, Smith paid no attention to the warning. An instant later a third bear sprang up from behind the body of the dead animal and rushed the hunters.

As Smith mildly remarked, the charging bear made "no pleasant noise"; and since his gun was empty, Jed dived headlong into a stream that ran beside the thicket. The bear knocked the next man down and rushed on to attack a hunter named La Point, who had a bayonet fixed to his rifle. La Point used his novel weapon so effectively that the bear ran off, badly wounded, and took refuge in a near-by clump of brush. By that time Smith had climbed out of the pool and rejoined his companions. Before long the hunters found and killed the bear that La Point had stabbed, and wounded still another of the dangerous beasts.

While looking for this last bear, Smith had his second hair-raising adventure of the day, which he briefly described as follows:

I rode up close to the thicket in which I supposed him to be and rode round it several times halloeing but without making any discovery. I rode up for a last look when the Bear sprang for the horse. He was so close that the horse could not be got underway before he caught him by the tail. The Horse being strong and much frightened exerted himself so powerfully that he gave the Bear no opportunity to close uppon him and actually drew him 40 or 50 yards before he relinquished his hold.

The Bear did not continue the pursuit but went off and [I] was quite glad to get rid of his company on any terms and returned to camp to feast on the spoils and talk of the incidents of our eventful hunt. 16 Beaver taken.

A little beyond the scene of these adventures, the outlook to the east and north became so discouraging that Smith gave up his original plan to cross the Sierra Nevada Mountains and strike directly eastward to Salt Lake. Instead he forded the swollen Sacramento and turned toward the coast. Veering to the northwest, he found the new route through present-day Trinity, Siskiyou, and Del Norte counties even worse than the one he had just abandoned, and the trappers were soon caught in a tangled wilderness of massive boulders, sheer precipices, foaming streams, dense fogs, and almost impenetrable forests. Hunger, cold, fatigue, discouragement, and danger became the traveling companions of the men by day and their blanket mates by night.

Starting at dawn and floundering along till darkness blotted out all semblance of the way, the exhausted company was thankful to make a mile or two a day. Many of the horses were killed or maimed by the rough going, and the men wore themselves to the bone breaking a makeshift trail for each day's slow advance. The Indians, much more warlike and dangerous than the backward natives of the Sacramento Valley, added greatly to the company's trials and tribulations. Moving in small bands, the savages killed or crippled the trappers' unguarded horses, wounded some of the men, and kept the expedition in a constant state of tension and alarm. And still the trail grew worse. In places travel was "awful," again it was "amazing bad." Some of the pack mules fell over precipices; twenty-three horses drowned in three days; often an injured or exhausted animal had to be abandoned by the trail.

In addition to the severe physical hardships, shared on equal terms with his men, Smith carried the heavy responsibilities that leadership entailed. The welfare of the company, the profit of the expedition, the lives of the men depended on his actions and decisions. But through all these days of utter weariness, uncertainty, and discouragement Smith's diary holds no word of complaint or despair and seldom mentions his own personal trials, misfortunes, or painful physical injuries.

The company crossed the Klamath River on May 25 and reached the sea on June 8. Keeping close to the beach, the trappers came to the present California-Oregon line on the 23rd and forded the Rogue River on rafts four days later. On July 9 they were at Coos Bay and two days later reached the mouth of the Umpqua River. The following day the trappers forded the river and followed its course to the northeast for about three miles. On July 13, a Sunday, they traveled four miles, pitched camp near a small tributary (later called Defeat River) and spent the rest of the day trading with the Indians for beaver skins, eels, and elk meat. For all but four of the company, this was the end of the long trail.[17]

Early the next morning Captain Smith, John Turner, Richard Leland (an Englishman who had joined Smith's party in California), and an Indian guide set out in a canoe to look over the country and map out the day's route, according to the customary procedure. Contrary to Smith's explicit orders, Harrison Rogers, his deputy commander, permitted the Umpqua Indians to come into camp and

---

[17] For the identification of the camp, see Lancaster Pollard: "Site of the Smith Massacre of July 14, 1828," *Oregon Historical Quarterly*, Vol. XLV, pp. 133–7. Pollard used the field notebook kept by Harry Gordon on a survey of the Klamath River region in 1857–8 for the United States Land Office.

mingle freely with the men. Whether due to the trappers' eagerness to trade with the Indians or their lust for the Indian women, this breach of discipline opened the flood-gates of disaster. Awaiting a favorable opportunity, the Umpquas fell upon their unsuspecting victims and shot and stabbed and clubbed almost all of them to death. In the bedlam and confusion one man managed to escape. Arthur Black, a trapper of unusual size and strength, broke away from his assailants, fled to the brush, and made his way alone through the heavy forests toward the Hudson's Bay post at Fort Vancouver. Smith, Turner, and Leland, absent on the day's reconnaissance when the Indians fell upon the camp, also escaped the massacre and fled north toward the Columbia.[18] By a singular coincidence the three reached Vancouver within a day of Black's arrival.

Many hearsay accounts of the Umpqua massacre subsequently found their way into print; but the report that Black made in person to Dr. John McLoughlin, most famous of the Hudson's Bay factors of the old Northwest, is the best that has so far come to light. McLoughlin transmitted Black's report in the following letter:

Fort Vancouver 10*th August 1828*
To the Governor Deputy Govt. & Committee
Honble. Hudsons Bay Coy.
HONBLE. SIRS,
On the 8th Inst. at 10 P.M. an American of the name of Black reached this place, in his opinion at the time, the only survivor of a Party of Nineteen (19) Americans, the remain-

---

[18] There is also presumptive evidence that the Indians spared the lives of four other trappers at the time of the massacre, only to put them to death later on.

der having been massacred by the Natives of the Umpqua River. Black says that he and seventeen others were engaged to Mr. Smith (this is the same that came to the Flat Heads 1824–5 and also whom Capt. Simpson saw last Jany. at St. Francisco) & they left St. Francisco January last with about three hundred Horses bound for their Depot at Salt Lake.

Leaving St. Francisco they ascended the North Branch of Bonaventura trapping Beaver as they went along till the 14th May, when finding it impossible to cross the Mountains with their Horses in an Eastern direction they turned West & fell on a River which took them to the Coast, & proceeded along it to the Umpqua where they were defeated. At the moment of attack Mr. Smith was off with two men in a Canoe to ascend & examine Bridge River, a stream that flows into the Umpqua, to see if he could find a road to take his Horses — a short time after Mr. Smiths departure, their being about a hundred Indians in the Camp & the Americans busy arranging their arms which got wet the day previous, the Indians suddenly rushed on them, two got hold of his (Blacks) Gun to take it from him, in contending with them he was wounded on the hands by their Knives & another came with an axe to strike him on the head, which he avoided by Springing on one side & received the blow on the back. He then let go his Gun & rushed to the woods, as he was coming away he saw two Indians on one Virgil, another, Davis was in the water & Indians were pursuing him in a Canoe, a third was on the ground & a band of Indians were butchering him with axes — after wandering in the woods during four days he fell on the Ocean about (by his description of the place) two miles North of the Umpqua & knowing this Establishment to be here followed the Coast to the Killemau Village; the first Indian he saw wanted to pillage him of his knife but this he resisted. A little after he fell in with seven who stripped him of all his cloathing except his Trousers, another party joined

109

these & a quarrel took place between the two Parties as he thinks about himself: during the fray he found an opportunity of reaching the Woods & saw no Indians till he got to the Killimaux Village, here he got some to take him across Land to the Willamette to one of our Freemen who forwarded him to this place — on the 10 Inst. (yesterday) at midday Mr. Smith arrived with the two men who were with him in the Canoe, he was as I already stated gone with them to examine the Banks of the River; after proceeding a few miles he returned & when within sight of his Camp seeing none of his people at the place, it struck him with surprise & while looking about to see where his people could be, an Indian from the shore spoke to an Indian with him, the latter immediately turned round, seized Mr. Smiths Rifle & dived in the River, & at the same time natives that were hid in the Bushes fired on Mr. Smith & his two men, who escaped by paddling to the opposite bank; he ascended a Hill from whence he saw his Camp distinctly, but seeing none of his people & from none of them coming forward when he was fired on though within reach, he naturally concluded they were all cutt off, shaped his course for the ocean & fell on it at Alique River & followed the Coast to the Killamau Village where he got Indians to take him to the Williemette & accompany him to this place. When he was attacked he had two hundred & twenty eight Horses & Mules, about Seven Hundred & eighty Beaver, fifty or Sixty large Otters & two or three Sea do. two hundred wt. of Beads & one hundred wt. of Goods & Tobacco, the Indians who brought Mr. Smith say their were fifteen killed, which with four that got here accounts for the whole party. Immediately on hearing this melancholy intelligence Indian Messingers were dispatched towards the Umpqua with directions to the Natives if they found any of the survivors to shew them every kindness & to convey them to this place & that we would reward them handsomely for their trouble. On hearing Blacks narrative I enquired of him if they had any quarrel with the Natives, he says the only difference they had was about an Axe which the Natives stole ten days before they attacked the Party, to recover which Mr. Smith secured an Indian & tied him, but on the latter promising to bring it back he was liberated & he brought it back & that previous to reaching the Umpqua, they had two skirmishes with the natives in which they killed two of them. Mr. Smith gives the same account. The Indians who accompanied Mr. Smith to this place also report that the quarrel originated about an axe & the Natives conceiving them to be a different people from us had acted in this treacherous manner towards them; this unfortunate affair is extremely injurious to us as the success & facility with which the Natives have accomplished their object lowers Europeans in their estimation & consequently very much diminishes our security. As for us every means in our power will be exerted to assist Mr. Smith in recovering his property.

I am Honble. Sirs Your Obt. Humble Sert.

JNO. McLOUGHLIN [19]

Though a dangerous and aggressive competitor, with whom the Hudson's Bay Company had a heavy account to settle, Smith was a man after McLoughlin's own courageous, hospitable, and deeply religious heart. So, in spite of the company's past grudges and growing British-American friction in the Northwest, the "White-Headed Eagle" offered both his friendship and resources to his destitute

---

[19] *The Letters of John McLoughlin from Fort Vancouver to the Governor and Committee, First Series, 1825–38,* ed. by E. E. Rich (Toronto: The Champlain Society; 1941), pp. 68–70. Reprinted by permission of the publishers, The Champlain Society, University of Toronto Library, Canada.

rival and with characteristic vehemence went at once into action. One who witnessed the scene declared that after taking off his spectacles and throwing them on the table, McLoughlin

grabbed his cane and bareheaded out he goes upon the porch before the house, and called out at the top of his voice, "Mr. McCay, Thomas McCay, Tom, where in the d—l is Mc-Cay?" Out comes old Tom from the store. As loud as usual the Doctor cries out, "This American has been robbed, all his men massacred; take fifty men, have the horses drove in. Where is Laframboise, Michel, Babtiste, Jacque, where are all the men? Take twenty pack horses; those who have no saddles ride on blankets, two blankets to each man. Go light; take some salmon, peas, grease, potatoes; now be off, cross the river tonight, and if one of you is here at sunset I will tie you to that (pointing to a twelve pound cannon, just below where he was speaking) and you'll get a dozen." Mr. Smith says he never before saw men so anxious to leave a place, as those men going and coming, all on a trot, the Doctor going out occasionally and hurrying up the men. McCay gets ready and comes for orders. "Take this paper," said the Doctor, "and be off; read it on the way; you'll observe that the place is beyond the Umpqua. Good-bye Thomas, God bless you. Be off." And off he goes.[20]

---

[20] For other accounts, see Francis Ermatinger to Edward Ermatinger, March 14, 1829, "Letters of Francis Ermatinger, 1823–1853," Typescript No. 127007, Huntington Library MSS.; Smith, Jackson, and Sublette to John Eaton, Secretary of War, St. Louis, October 29, 1830, Ex. Docs. 21st Congress, 2d sess., Vol. I, No. 39, p. 23; Dale: *Ashley-Smith Explorations,* p. 280 n.

Among the men killed on the Umpqua were Harrison Rogers, Thomas Virgin, Joseph Lapoint, Peter Rannee, John Hanna, Emmanuel Lazarus, Thomas Daw, Charles Swift, Toussaint Maréchal, J. Scott, J. O'Harra, Martin McCoy, John Gaither, Bell, Logan, Marion, and three others.

McKay and Laframboise proceeded as rapidly as possible to the Umpqua. Alexander McLeod, though prepared to start on a long fall hunt to the south and impatient of the delay, followed hard at their heels with a much larger company. Smith and the other survivors of the massacre accompanied the McLeod party. The expedition traveled up the Willamette, reached the Umpqua early in October, and succeeded in recovering some of the furs, horses, and other stolen articles from different Indian villages in the vicinity. On the 28th the party arrived at the site of the massacre. The scene was one that even the hard-bitten trappers could not look upon unmoved. Eleven skeletons, "a Sad Spectacle of Indian barbarity," lay whitening in the sun. Four bodies were unaccounted for.[21]

After holding a simple burial service over the bleaching bones, McLeod's men continued along the river to the coast. Using both threats and diplomacy, the party obtained additional furs, horses, and miscellaneous booty from the Indians in the neighborhood and then turned back to Fort Vancouver, arriving there on or about the 10th of December. Thanks to McLoughlin's efforts, Smith thus regained some 700 beaver skins, 39 horses, and a miscellaneous assortment of other goods from the plunder taken by the Indians.

According to Sir George Simpson, Governor General of the Hudson's Bay Company, who was then at Fort Vancouver on a tour of the Western posts, the recovery of Smith's property cost his company a thousand pounds in

---

[21] This supports the report that the Indians temporarily spared four of the trappers, only to put them to torture and death later on.

actual outlay and probably a much larger sum in the aban-
donment of McLeod's contemplated fall trapping expedition to California. Simpson declined all compensation from
Smith, however, generously saying that "the satisfaction
we have derived from these good offices will repay the
honble Hudsons Bay compy amply for any loss or inconvenience in rendering them." [22]

Smith eventually sold the recovered furs and horses to
the Hudson's Bay Company for about $3,200 and spent
the winter with Dr. McLoughlin, the feudal lord of the
great Northwest. Turner, on his part, served as guide for
McLeod's postponed trapping expedition to the southern
beaver streams.[23] Almost a decade later he became an associate of the renowned American trapper Ewing Young in a
cattle drive from California to the Willamette. In 1847 his
name appears as a member of the second relief expedition
that left Sutter's Fort to rescue the survivors of the ill-fated
Donner party from the Sierra Nevada snows.

Unlike Turner, who thus elected to remain in the Oregon country, Smith and Black took the first opportunity
to return to the territory in the Rocky Mountains in which
Jackson and Sublette proposed to hold the summer rendezvous. The region between Fort Vancouver and the eastern
Rockies was so full of known and unknown dangers that
employees of the Hudson's Bay Company would not attempt the journey with parties of less than forty or fifty

[22] Dale: *The Ashley-Smith Exploration,* p. 284. Simpson, McLoughlin,
and other Hudson's Bay Company leaders recognized that the plunder
had to be regained or the Indians would be encouraged to think that
they could attack any trapping party of white men with impunity.
[23] See Chapter 9.

men. Sir George Simpson warned Smith of the desperate nature of the undertaking and advised him that one who rashly embarked on it was "sporting with Life or courting danger to madness."

But Smith and Black, without benefit of guides, companions, or knowledge of the country, somehow got through. Their objective was Jackson's Lake, near the source of the Snake River, on the northern border of Jackson's Hole, where the rendezvous of the three partners, Smith, Jackson, and Sublette, had been agreed upon two years before. The route of the two men lay up the Columbia, beyond the site of the present Grand Coulee Dam, to the Hudson's Bay posts of Fort Colville and Kettle Falls, near the northeastern corner of what later became the state of Washington, down Clark's Fork to the present city of Missoula, up the Bitter Root Valley, and across the divide to the Salmon.

Somewhere in the wild Kootenais territory of northwestern Montana the lone travelers fell in with a combined trapping and searching party under David E. Jackson. So far as we have any record, the reunion of the two partners, after so many momentous and tragic happenings, was outwardly as commonplace and undemonstrative as the meeting of Livingstone and Stanley in the heart of Africa.

Augmented by Smith and Black, Jackson's party turned southeast to the Snake River basin and met Sublette on the important tributary known as Henry's Fork. Later the three partners — Smith, Jackson, and Sublette — moved their combined force to Pierre's Hole, west of the Tetons, for the summer rendezvous.

Smith's expeditions to California and the Columbia had

far-reaching effects. They aroused the interest of the mountain men and the United States government in the Far Western territories, particularly California and the Oregon wilderness, which Smith had traversed. They also led the Hudson's Bay Company to send out reconnaissance expeditions as far south as the Gulf of California and ushered in more than a decade of profitable trapping on the watersheds of California for Dr. McLoughlin and his associates.

Smith expressed his gratitude to his benefactors at Fort Vancouver in three very practical ways: he placed his hard-won knowledge of the routes, Indians, and fur resources of the Southwest at their disposal; from that time on he endeavored to counteract the criticisms so freely levied against the Hudson's Bay Company by other American trappers; and he and his associates were careful not to trespass again upon the long-established trapping-grounds of McLoughlin's men.

After his return from the disastrous second California expedition Smith's activities seldom touched even the fringe of the Southwest. In July 1830 the Wind River Valley of Wyoming witnessed the last rendezvous of the historic partnership of which he was a member. To that rendezvous Sublette brought a train of ten wagons heavily loaded with trade goods from St. Louis, and when the festivities and bartering were over, the firm of Smith, Jackson, & Sublette sold its interests to a group of equally famous mountain men — Thomas Fitzpatrick, Milton A. Sublette, James Bridger, Henry Fraeb, and Jean Baptiste Gervais. Out of that transaction came the Rocky Mountain Fur Company, an enterprise that ran its course in a few brief, dramatic, history-making years.[24]

The *Missouri Intelligencer* of October 9, 1830 thus described the triumphant return of the three famous partners from their last mountain rendezvous:

On Tuesday last a large company of trappers and traders from the Rocky Mountains passed through this place [Franklin], with Furs and Mules valued at one hundred and fifty thousand dollars. The cavalcade extended a considerable distance. The gentlemen who fitted out this expedition are Messrs. Smith, Jackson and Sublette, and we are much gratified that they are likely to be so well rewarded for their hazardous enterprise. A considerable number of large and substantial waggons, laden with the fruits of their toils, accompanied them, exclusive of the pack horses and mules, of which there were a great number.[25] We should judge about fifty individuals. These hardy and sun-burnt *Mountaineers*,

---

[24] The following memorandum shows the "amount of property lost by the firm of Smith, Jackson & Sublette from depredations of different tribes of Indians from July 1826 to July 1830":

480 head of horses, at the lowest mountain price $60. per head	$28,000
Gross amount of goods lost	10,000
Traps and Camp Equipage lost	1,000
Beaver furs taken from us by Indians	4,500
	$43,500

. . . .

"Among our parties in the mountains, sickness and natural deaths are almost unknown.

[signed]   Smith-Jackson & Sublette."

[25] This was the first wagon train taken to the Rocky Mountains. The wagons, of which there were ten, carried about 1,800 pounds of freight apiece, and each was drawn by five mules. The caravan traveled between fifteen and twenty miles a day.

who had been so long excluded from the pleasures of civilized society, exhibited great demonstrations of satisfaction, at their near approach to their families and homes.[26]

With a modest fortune at last in his possession, Smith proposed to quit the fur trade and settle down to a quiet and safely ordered life. But he was no longer his own master. He had given himself forever to the deserts and mountains, the forests, winds, and streams. Civilization walled him in; like the air of a fetid dungeon, the ease and comforts and petty conventions of society stifled his restless spirit. He yearned for the wilderness as a land-marooned sailor yearns for the danger and freedom of the sea.

So, in spite of his announced determination to leave the mountains, Smith soon found himself at the head of a caravan of twenty-three wagons and eighty-five men en route to the Mexican pueblo of Santa Fe. The company included two of Smith's brothers, his former associates in the fur trade, David E. Jackson, William and Thomas Sublette, and Thomas Fitzpatrick, the "Broken Hand" of the Indians and a prominent figure among the mountain men.

The expedition followed the usual route of the Santa Fe traders to the Arkansas and reached that river, near the present site of Dodge City, without special incident or trouble. Here, instead of taking the longer but safer route along the Arkansas, the leaders of the caravan decided to ford the river and strike directly across country to the Cimarron.

[26] Donald McKay Frost: *Notes on General Ashley, the Overland Trail, and South Pass* (Worcester, Massachusetts, 1945), pp. 310–11.

A waterless plain, almost as dangerous and desolate as the trackless deserts that Smith had crossed on his California expeditions, separated the two streams. Two days of hard travel failed to bring the expedition to the Cimarron. On the third day the animals were near collapse and some of the men had begun to grow delirious. All sense of organization disappeared, and small groups wandered off, some in this direction, some in that, to look for water. For a time Smith and Fitzpatrick rode together along the sand-choked trail. Then Fitzpatrick's horse gave out and Smith went on ahead. Long after his last companion had dropped from sight behind an intervening ridge, Smith reached the sandy course of the Cimarron entirely alone. The bed of the stream was dry, but moist places here and there gave evidence of water. One of these betrayed him.

Robbed by thirst of his habitual sense of caution, Smith knelt down and dug a shallow hole in the damp depression. The basin slowly filled with water; and there Death laid a final ambush for this chief of mountain men. As he drank, a band of Comanche Indians closed in, swiftly and silently, upon the unsuspecting man. No one knows the details of the tragedy that followed. According to one account, Smith tried to persuade the Indians to return to the wagon train for trade and presents. They answered by frightening his horse with waving blankets and flashing mirrors. Then, while he sought to control the frantic animal, one of the Comanches threw his lance and wounded the trapper in the back. Smith killed two of his assailants with a pistol ball. The rest of the Indians joined the attack and the curtain fell. In the words of Maurice Sullivan, "on the twenty-seventh of May, in the year 1831, Jedediah Smith came to the end of his last trail." [27]

That trail, begun on the memorable day nine years before when Smith left St. Louis for the Rocky Mountains as one of Ashley's men, had carried him farther across the continent, taken him to more unknown places, and broken down more barriers of geographic isolation than that of any other American. "In the brief space of six years," wrote Dale, Smith "had crossed and recrossed . . . the American west from the upper Missouri southward to the Platte and from the Columbia to the Colorado and westward to the Pacific. His geographic knowledge excelled that of all his contemporaries. He travelled, too, with wide-open eyes. Everywhere observant and greedy for information, he returned from each expedition with something more than a superficial acquaintance with the business resources of the regions he had traversed." [28]

Smith's worth as an explorer, his resourcefulness as a leader, and his skill as a mountain man were only surpassed by his integrity and faith. Men spoke of him as a Christian gentleman. Those who knew him best said that he made religion "an active principle from the duties of which nothing could seduce him." Like the young men of Oliver Cromwell's never defeated army, he had the fear of God before him and made some conscience of what he did. He was a man of good and honest and courageous heart.

[27] In July 1831 the Rocky Mountain Fur Company bought goods at Santa Fe to the value of $2,800 from Smith's estate. Missouri Historical Society Collection, Sublette Papers (microfilm).
[28] Dale, op. cit., p. 312.

CHAPTER 4

To Santa Fe and Beyond

THOUGH a distinct enterprise in itself, the historic overland trade between St. Louis and Santa Fe, which Josiah Gregg appropriately styled the "Commerce of the Prairies," was inseparably interwoven with the fur trade of the Southwest. Soon after the Louisiana Purchase, American settlers in Missouri made tentative efforts to establish commercial relations with the Spanish settlements of New Mexico. As early as 1804 William Morrison, a well-known merchant of the Missouri Fur Company, entrusted Baptiste Le Land, a French creole, with a consignment of merchandise to be sold in Santa Fe. Le Land disposed of the goods, pocketed the money, and remained in New Mexico.[1]

In 1805, after hunting three years in the country of the Osage Indians, a Kentuckian named James Purcell (or Pursley) reached Santa Fe. The next year Manuel Lisa, the distinguished merchant trapper of St. Louis, also outfitted a trading venture to the Mexican settlements. Zebulon R. Pike, government agent and explorer, however, was by far the most important of these early American adven-

[1] On May 6, 1812 James and Jessee Morrison gave Robert McKnight a letter of introduction to Baptiste Le Land. The letter spoke of Le Land as "a good young man" and urged him to return to the United States with McKnight. Missouri Historical Society MSS. (Santa Fe Envelope).

turers to enter Spanish territory. After wittingly or unwittingly crossing the vaguely defined boundary between the recently annexed Louisiana Territory and the domains of His Catholic Majesty, Pike built a fort of cottonwood logs on the Conejos branch of the Rio Del Norte. There he was visited by a body of Spanish troops who escorted him first to Santa Fe and later to the much larger and more important commercial center of Chihuahua.[2]

This enforced but welcome tour of Mexican territory enabled Pike to bring back to the United States, especially to the ambitious merchants of St. Louis, a first-hand account of the political and economic conditions of the southern provinces. His expedition thus became an important factor in opening the St. Louis, Santa Fe, and Chihuahua trade and served as a spearhead for Anglo-American expansion in the Southwest.

During the fourteen-year interval between the return of the Pike expedition from Chihuahua and the overthrow of Spanish rule in New Mexico, a number of trading expeditions left the Missouri settlements for Santa Fe. Nine or ten of these merchant adventurers, including Robert McKnight, James Baird, and Samuel Chambers, were seized by the Spaniards and kept in prison in Chihuahua from 1812 to 1821.[3] The incident was described in an article,

[2] Dr. John Hamilton Robinson joined the expedition as a volunteer surgeon. Ostensibly he entered Mexican territory to collect Le Land's unpaid debt to William Morrison. For the relation of the expedition to James Wilkinson's intrigues and the Aaron Burr conspiracy, see Isaac Joslin Cox: "Opening of the Santa Fe Trail," *Missouri Historical Review,* Vol. XXV, No. 1, pp. 30–66.

[3] For an official account of this incident, see *A Message from the President of the United States Relative to the Arrest and Imprisonment of*

based on a letter by Ezekiel Williams, one of the principal trappers of the Missouri Fur Company, that appeared in the *Missouri Gazette* of October 9, 1813. Williams wrote that "whilst trapping beaver on the headwaters of the Arkansas, he met with a Spaniard, who informed him that ten Americans were taken up by the Spanish troops at an Indian village in the neighborhood of Sta. Fe, and sent prisoners to the mines."

The article then went on to say:

The date and number of men alluded to in Mr. W's statement corroborate with the time that ten men left this place, with the intention of visiting the internal provinces of Mexico, and endeavor to open a trade with them by the way of the Missouri &c. We are asstonished at the barbarity exersised by the officer who commands at Sta. Fe towards these men; for we know that they bore letters and other evidences of their pursuits being purely commercial. A strong hope is indulged here, that government will do something towards their liberation. For the information of their friends, we annex a list of these unfortunate men. Messrs. Baird and Shrieves were from Pennsylvania — Knight, Cook, Mines & Chambers from Virginia — Allen from Massechusetts — Baum, a hatter, from Kentucky, and an Irishman of the name of Michael McDonough, with a Spanish interpreter, a denizen of St. Charles.

In 1817 the Spanish authorities also seized Auguste P. Chouteau, Julius De Munn, and Joseph Philbert and con-

---

Certain American Citizens at Santa Fe . . . April 15, 1818 (Washington, 1818). The other members of the party were Benjamin Shrive, Michel McDonough, William Mines, Peter Baum (or Brown), Thomas Cook, and Charles Miers. *Ibid.,* pp. 10–11.

fiscated a large quantity of goods and furs — the proceeds of three long years of danger and privation — from the unfortunate traders. Chouteau was a member of one of the most famous families of St. Louis, an organizer of the Missouri Fur Company, and a dominant figure in the western fur trade for half a century. In later years he lived in a large stone house, with walls two and a half feet thick, which stood in the midst of spacious, park-like grounds. A stone wall, two feet thick and ten feet high, pierced with port holes for defense, surrounded the entire property. Philbert was one of the earliest American trappers to visit the mountains near the headwaters of the Arkansas. De Munn, like Chouteau, was a man of property and standing in the Missouri settlements.

A statement signed by eleven of the members of the Chouteau-De Munn party gave the following version of the episode:

United States, Territory of Missouri
County of St. Louis, sct.

The undersigned having been first duly sworn on the Holy Evangelists, severally, depose and say: that in the beginning of September, 1815, they were engaged by August P. Chouteau and company, at St. Louis, in the territory of Missouri, for a trading expedition with the Indians of the headwaters of the rivers Arkansas and Platte. The party conducted by the said Auguste P. Chouteau, proceeded to their grounds on the head waters of the Arkansas, and continued the trade until the spring of 1817; at which time, our encampment was visited by a guard of Spaniards, two hundred or more in number; the commanding officer of which guard, was the bearer of an order from the governor of New Mexico, to conduct our whole party to Sant Fé. This order was executed.

Auguste P. Chouteau, together with the whole party, consisting of twenty one persons, accompanied the troop or guard, and on their arrival at Santa Fé, was reviewed by the governor, and immediately put into close confinement. At the time of the arrest of our persons, within the limits of the United States, Mr. Chouteau, conscious no doubt, that he had violated none of the Spanish regulations, took with him a part of his property, to defray expenses; none of which he was permitted to retain, to exchange, or to make any use of. Not only that, but also the whole stock of the company *cached* or concealed in the ground, near our camp, east of the mountains, and on the head waters of the Arkansas, was seized by the Spaniards under special order from the governor, and taken to Santa Fe. We remained in prison (some of us in irons,) forty-eight days, during which time we were dieted in a very coarse and meagre manner, with boiled corn or beans, without salt. . . .

Long previously to our arrest, M. Chouteau had equipped several parties for different parts of the upper country, all, as we constantly understood, within the acknowledged limits of the United States. . . . As well as we recollect, Mr. Chouteau's party, on leaving St. Louis, amounted to forty-six.

JEAN BATISTI BRIZAR, his x mark.
BAPTISTI FICIO, his x mark.
CHARLES BOURGUIGNON, his x mark.
JOSEPH CISDELLE, his x mark.
ETUNNE PROVOTT, his x mark.
FRANCOIS MAUANT, his x mark.
PIERRE LEGRIS, his x mark.
FRANCOIS PAKET, his x mark.
FRANCOIS DERPORT, his x mark.
ANTOINO BIZET, his x mark.
JOSEPH BISSONET, his x mark.[4]

---

[4] *Message from the President,* April 15, 1818, pp. 14–15.

The proceedings against Chouteau and De Munn at Santa Fe followed a pattern that the Anglo-American frontiersman increasingly resented. For one reason or another the Governor lost his head, accused the Americans of bringing twenty thousand armed men into Spanish territory, and declared that they had erected a fort equipped with cannon and ammunition on the Rio de los Animas, presumably as a base for an invasion of the country. Later in the trial the Governor fell into a fit of rage that left him temporarily speechless. Regaining a measure of self-control, he pounded the table with his fists and finally shouted to his colleagues that the Americans must be taken out and shot.

Though the traders escaped this drastic penalty, they nevertheless spent forty-eight days in irons and lost thirty thousand dollars in goods and furs to the Spaniards.[5] Nearly thirty years later Chouteau's estate collected a substantial part of this sum from the United States government, which, in the Florida Treaty of 1819, assumed the claims of American citizens against Spain.

Four years after the Chouteau and De Munn affair a company led by Jacob Fowler, a well-known surveyor of Covington, Kentucky, and Colonel Hugh Glenn, of Cincinnati, found its way into New Mexico by a seldom used route from the Arkansas Territory. Fowler's journal of the expedition is an extremely valuable historical document, but its "preposterous orthography" led Chittenden to describe

---

[5] De Munn to Governor William Clark, November 25, 1817. *Message from the President,* op. cit., pp. 11–12.

it as "the best example of poor spelling and punctuation in existence." [6]

Both Fowler and Glenn represented the Western frontier at its best. The class to which they belonged was characterized by frankness, cordiality, independence, and openhanded hospitality. To these virtues, according to a contemporary writer, they added initiative and enterprise, a "disposition to go ahead and make a fortune; a readiness to embark in large and hazardous operations, with borrowed means, or even with no means at all." They had a complete disregard for trifles, "by which they meant anything short of positive ruin"; cherished "a sovereign contempt for prudence and small change!" — a term applied to any sum less than five thousand dollars — and subscribed to the creed of a western gentleman that his word was even better than his bond. [7]

The Glenn-Fowler party of twenty traders, trappers, and adventurers started at Fort Smith in the Arkansas Territory on September 21, 1821 and "meandered the whole course of the Arkansaw," from the mouth of the Little Arkansas to the base of the Rocky Mountains. Here Glenn and three others left the main party and made their way to Santa Fe. Fowler continued up the Arkansas as far as the site of the present city of Pueblo. [8]

---

[6] *History of the American Fur Trade of the Far West,* Vol. II, p. 503 n.

[7] Thomas James: *Three Years among the Indians and Mexicans* (St. Louis, 1916), p. 109 n. Reprinted by permission of the Missouri Historical Society.

[8] According to Elliott Coues, Fowler built the first "habitable and inhabited house on the spot where Pueblo now stands." *Journal of Jacob Fowler,* pp. xx–xxi.

There he received word that Glenn had obtained permission from the New Mexican authorities to trap in Spanish territory and rode south through the famous Sangre de Christo Pass to the mountain-girt pueblo of Taos to join his partner. After a brief reunion Glenn returned to Santa Fe, while Fowler made a spring hunt on the Rio Grande and some of its tributaries, trapping as far north and west as the San Juan Mountains. Upon Fowler's return to the Spanish settlements, he and Glenn again joined forces, and the reunited party started back to the American frontier. They reached Fort Osage, about forty miles below the mouth of the Kansas River in Missouri, after a journey of some thirty-five days. In its explorations, adventures, and personnel, the expedition played an important part both in the opening of the Santa Fe trade and in the beginning of the American fur trade in Colorado, New Mexico, and California.[9]

The opening of caravan traffic between Missouri and the "interior provinces of Mexico" — in other words, the historic Santa Fe trade — was begun by a Missouri frontiersman named William Becknell in 1821. To obtain recruits for his venture, Becknell advertised in the *Missouri Intelligencer* of June 25, 1821 for "a company of men destined to the westward for the purpose of trading for Horses and Mules, and catching wild animals of every description." Each volunteer was required to provide a horse, a good rifle, a three months' supply of ammunition, adequate

---

[9] At least one member of the expedition, a frontiersman named Isaac Slover, later joined the trapping party made famous by the pen of James Ohio Pattie and reached California in 1828.

clothing, and at least ten dollars in cash for the purchase of merchandise. Every eight men were also to furnish a pack horse, a tent, and an ax. The profits of the venture were to be divided equally among the participants, and each volunteer agreed "to be bound by an oath to submit to such orders and rules as the company when assembled" should impose.[10]

George C. Sibley, probably as well qualified to speak on the early Santa Fe trade as any man of the period, thus described Becknell's original venture:

It is not necessary to go into a very particular account of the trade from Missouri to Ste. Fee in N. Mexico . . . ; the first adventurers were hardy enterprising men who being tired of the dull and profitless pursuits of husbandry & the common mechanical arts of the frontier, determined to turn merchants or Traders, and in the true spirit of western enterprise directed their steps westward to the settlements of New Mexico, from whence [came] many strange and marvelous stories of inexhaustible wealth in the precious metals. . . . I believe the honour of the first enterprise of this sort belongs to William Becknell, a man of good character, great personal bravery, & by nature & habit hardy and enterprising — His pursuit immediately previous to his first trip to Ste. Fee was, as I am informed, that of a salt maker — He certainly had no knowledge of mercantile concerns, & tho' very shrewd & intelligent, was very deficient in Education.[11] His outfit consisted of a few Hundred Dollars worth of coarse cotton Goods — His followers . . . all of the same description of Persons or nearly so, & fitted out in the same manner.

---

[10] F. F. Stephens: "Missouri and the Santa Fe Trade," *Missouri Historical Review*, Vol. XI, Nos. 3 and 4, pp. 291–2.

[11] As evidence of this, see Becknell's letter to Governor Baca, p. 131.

. . . They left our frontier at Ft. Osage, in [blank] and after suffering many hardships reached the settlements of Taos in N. Mexico. . . . Becknell & his party returned home, having disposed of their merchandise to some advantage, the proceeds of which they brought home in specie, mules, Asses & Spanish coverlids or Blankets.[12]

Independence from Spain, the year of Becknell's original expedition, brought about a liberalization of Mexico's commercial policy, and that in turn led more and more of the venturesome Western merchants to extend their trading operations as far south as the Mexican capital itself. St. Louis occupied a dominant position in this rapidly expanding business, just as it served as the center of the growing fur trade with the Rocky Mountains and the Pacific coast. It was a raw, crude, boisterous, self-confident, adventurous, juvenile metropolis, this "little village under the hill," with fifteen physicians, twenty-three lawyers, forty-nine grocers and tavernkeepers, two printing offices, a gristmill, a sawmill or two, one or more hotels of consequence, and a population of 4,600.[13]

Franklin, the actual starting-point of the Santa Fe expeditions, at this time was directly across the Missouri River from the little settlement of Booneville. In 1819 it was a town of "about one hundred and twenty log houses of one story, several framed dwellings of two stories, and two of brick, thirteen shops for the sale of merchandise, four tav-

[12] Letter of May 1, 1825, to "Owen," Missouri Historical Society, MSS. (Sibley Papers).

[13] The figures are for 1820. I am indebted to LeRoy R. Hafen and W. J. Ghent: *Broken Hand, the Life Story of Thomas Fitzpatrick, Chief of the Mountain Men* (Denver, 1931), p. 16, for this description.

erns, two smiths' shops, two large steam mills, two billiard rooms, a court house, a log prison of two stories, a post office and a printing press issuing a weekly paper." [14]

In 1824 William Becknell, Augustus Storrs, M. Marmaduke, and other "gentlemen of intelligence from Missouri" organized the first of the great wagon caravans to the Mexican settlements. The party consisted of eighty-one men, each of whom was equipped with rifle, pistol, four pounds of powder, eight pounds of lead, and twenty days' provisions. Twenty-five wagons, thirty thousand dollars' worth of merchandise, and over a hundred and fifty horses and mules completed the caravan. [15]

Leaving Franklin on May 15, the expedition reached Santa Fe the 28th of July. [16] On the 29th of October, Becknell wrote to "His Excelannce" the Governor of New Mexico that he was at Santa Cruz with ten other Americans and expected to return to the United States in the spring. He added that there were other Americans at Taos "with sum trapes" but he had "Nothing to Dew" with them. [17] Beck-

---

[14] Edwin James: *Account of an Expedition from Pittsburg to the Rocky Mountains* (Philadelphia, 1823), Vol. I, p. 88.

[15] M. M. Marmaduke: "Journal from Franklin to Santa Fe in 1824," *Missouri Historical Review*, Vol. VI, No. 1, p. 3. See also Chittenden, op. cit., Vol. II, pp. 505–6. For an entirely different version of the opening of the caravan trade, in which Jedediah S. Smith is made to play the leading role, see E. D. Smith, Mead, Kansas, to J. M. Guinn of Los Angeles, August 18, 1910. MS. in my possession.

[16] According to George Bent, a man named Aubray once rode from Independence to Taos in five days. See Bent to George E. Hyde, December 19, 1916. Coe Collection of Western Americana, Yale University Library. (Huntington Library, Microfilm.)

[17] Becknell to Governor "Barlota Marie Barker" (i.e., Bartolomé Baca). Huntington Library, RI 80.

nell's "gentlemen traders" brought back $180,000 in gold and silver and $10,000 in furs. According to Chittenden, William Becknell thus deserves the credit of "having made the first regular trading expedition from the Missouri to Santa Fe; of being the first to follow the route direct to San Miguel instead of by way of Taos; and the first to introduce the use of wagons in the trade. This last achievement was four years before Ashley took his wheeled cannon to the Salt Lake valley, eight years before Smith, Jackson, and Sublette took wagons to Wind River, and ten years before Bonneville took them to Green river." [18]

Senator Thomas H. Benton and other advocates of Western development took advantage of the success of the Becknell expedition to persuade Congress to authorize a survey of a road from the Missouri River to New Mexico and the negotiation of a treaty with the Osage Indians to permit American traders to cross their territory.[19] B. H. Reeves, George C. Sibley, and Thomas Mather were appointed to carry out both commissions. The treaty was negotiated at Council Grove, a "luxuriant, heavily timbered bottom," about fifty miles southwest of present-day Topeka, Kansas, and a hundred and fifty miles from Independence. The text of the treaty was as follows:

Whereas the Congress of the United States of America being anxious to promote a direct and friendly intercourse between the citizens of the United States and those of the Mexican Republic and to afford protection to the same, did at their last Session pass an act which was approved the 3rd of March 1825 "To authorize the President of the United

[18] Chittenden, op. cit., Vol. II, ⸱p. 504.

[19] For a discussion of the survey see Chittenden, op. cit., Vol. II, p. 401.

States to cause a road to be marked out from the Western frontier of Missouri to the confines of New Mexico," and which authorizes the President of the United States to appoint Commissioners to carry said act of Congress into effect and enjoins on the Commissioners so to be appointed that they first obtain the consent of the entervening Tribes of Indians by Treaty to the marking of said road, and to the unmolested use thereof to the citizens of the United States and of the Mexican Republic. And Benjamin H. Reeves, George C. Sibley and Thomas Mather duly appointed as aforesaid, and being duly and fully authorized, have this day met the Cheifs [sic] and Head Men of the Great and Little Osage Nations, who being duly authorized to meet and negotiate with the Commissioners upon the premises, and being specially met for that purpose by the invitation of said Commissioners, at the place called the Council Grove on the River Nee-azho one hundred and Sixty Miles south West from Fort Osage, Have after due deliberation and consultation agreed to the following Treaty, which is to be considered binding on the said Great and Little Osage, from and after this day.

Article 1st. The Cheifs and Head Men of the Great and Little Osages for themselves and their nations respectively, do consent and agree that the Commissioners of the United States shall and may survey and mark a road in such manner as they may think proper, through any of the Territory owned or claimed by the said Great and Little Osage tribes of Indians.

Article 2nd. The Cheifs and head men as aforesaid do further agree that the road authorized in Article 1st. shall when marked be forever free for the use of the citizens of the United States and of the Republic of Mexico, who shall at all times pass and repass thereon without the hindrance or molestation on the part of the said Great and Little Osages.

Article 3rd. The cheifs and headmen as aforesaid in consideration of the friendly relations existing between them and the United States do further promise for themselves and their people, that they will on all fit occations [*sic*], render such friendly aid and assistance as may be in their power to any of the citizens of the United States or of the Mexican Republic, as they may at any time happen to meet or fall in with on the road aforesaid.

Article 4th. The Cheifs and headmen as aforesaid do further consent and agree that the road aforesaid shall be considered as extending to a reasonable distance on either side, so that travellers thereon may at any time leave the marked track for the purposes of finding subsistance and proper camping places.

Article 5th. In consideration of the privileges granted by the cheifs and head men of the said Great and Little Osages in the three preceeding articles the said Commissioners on the part of the United States have agreed to pay to them the said Cheifs for themselves and their peoples the Sum of *Five Hundred Dollars*, which sum is to be paid them as soon as may be in Money or Merchandize at their option at such place as they may desire.

Article 6th. And the Cheifs and head men as aforesaid do acknowledge to have received from the Commissioners aforesaid at and before the signing of this Treaty, articles of Merchandize to the value of Three Hundred Dollars, which sum of Three Hundred Dollars and the payment stipulated to be made to the said Osages in the 5th Article shall be considered, and are so considered by the said Cheifs and head men as full and complete compensation for every privilidge [*sic*] herein by the said Chiefs.

In Testimony whereof, the said Benjamin H. Reeves, George C. Sibley and Thomas Mather commissioners as aforesaid, and the Chiefs and Head Men of the Great and Little Osage tribes of Indians have hereunto set their hands

and Seals, at Council Grove this tenth day of August in the
year of our Lord One Thousand Eight Hundred and Twenty-
five, in the presence of

Signed   B. H. Reeves
Geo C. Sibley
Thomas Mather

Pa-hu-sha — (White Hair). Head Chf: G. Osages
Ca-he-ga-wa-tonega — Foolish Chief, Head Chf: Little
    Osages
Shin-gawassa, — (Handsome Bird), chf: Great Osages
Ta-ha-mo-nee, — (Good Walker), Chf: Little Osages
Ca-he-ga-wash-im-pee-she, (Bad Chf:) — chf. Great Osages.
Wee-ho-je-ne-fare, Without ears — Warrior Little Osages
Ca-he-ga-shinga, Little Chief Great Osages —
War-Bur-cou, Warrior of the Little Osages —
Maw-sho-hun-ga, Warrior Great Osages —
Waw-lo-gah, The Owl, — Little Osage
Maw-she-to-mo-nee, Great Osage
Che-he-kaw, Little Osage
Ne-ha-wa-she-tun-ga, Great Osage
Ho-no-possee, Little Osage
Waw-hun-chee, Great Osage
Pwa-ne-no-pushre, Little Osage.

I Archibald Gamble Secretary to the Commissioners do cer-
tify the above to be a copy of the Treaty made this 10th day
of August 1825 with the Great and Little Osage Tribes of
Indians at Council Grove. Given under my hand the date
above

[signed]   Archibald Gamble, Secretary
The Witnesses names are omitted in this copy.

A. G.[20]

---

[20] An original of the treaty is in the Ritch Collection of Manuscripts
(3983) of the Huntington Library.

After signing the treaty and carving the name Council Grove "in large and legible characters on the trunk of a venerable White Oak tree" that stood near the tent in which the council was held, the commissioners mapped out a route as far as the Arkansas River and marked its course by a line of dirt mounds. According to Gregg, however, the caravans continued to follow the tracks left by previous expeditions and made little if any use of the new route. In any case, by the mid-twenties the Santa Fe trade was a firmly organized, highly important branch of Western commerce, which followed a well-established routine and conformed to a clearly defined pattern.

Many important merchants of New Orleans and the Atlantic coast consigned their shipments for the West and the Santa Fe trade to St. Louis houses such as Chouteau, Pratte & Company. Much of the goods came up the Mississippi from New Orleans or down the Ohio from Pittsburgh and Louisville. The cargoes, extraordinarily mixed and varied, included:

oil, cherries, vinegar, gunny-bags, oranges, lemons, pimientos, rhinestones, sperm candles, alum, gloves, indigo, collars, soap, rice, plug tobacco, hair pencils, seidletz powders, suspender buttons, shaving brushes, almanacs, flannel, "congress" knives, bedcords, saws, files, wrapping papers, willow baskets, washboards, marble, Young Hyson and Imperial tea, casks for figs, bales of candlewick, saleratus, herring, codfish, salmon, tar, salt, pickles and mackerel. Other shipments included: molasses, hickory nuts, apples, cider, flour, glass, wheat, loaf sugar, spades, trunks, shovels, potatoes, deer skins, beaver and bear pelts, stone jugs, cheese, barrels of beef, candy, scythes, hops, whisky, nails, wool, starch, coffee, pepper, claret, drugs, tea kettles, stoves, sofas, peaches, spanish saddle trees and side saddle trees. Still other manifestos listed: writing and wrapping papers, bedcords, saws, epsom salts, sugar of lead, straw hats, bombazine, beer, ribbons, tape, silk handkerchiefs, rum, madeira, venetian red, Manila cordage, spanish brown, lamp black, black sand, champagne, silk handkerchief, ribbons, tape, brooms, shoes, white lead, almonds, wool, feathers, bacon, cherry-wood joists, shad, porter, raisins, carpets, butter, and buffalo and beef hides. Pails were: common, eared, painted, varnished, patented or fancy.[21]

Franklin, Independence, and Westport, the predecessor of the modern Kansas City (which Edward Kern described in the mid-forties as "a dirty place filled with Indians, Spaniards, Jews and all sorts and sizes of folks" [22]), successively served as the starting-point of the trading expedition.

Among the more important border merchants who either sent their own wagons to Santa Fe or supplied goods for other traders were Samuel C. Lamme & Company with stores at Franklin, Liberty, and Independence; and James and Robert Aull, pioneer merchants of Lexington, Richmond, Liberty, and Independence.[23]

---

[21] From the bills of lading and receipts of Henry P. Chouteau in the A. Chouteau Collection, Missouri Historical Society MSS.

[22] Fort Sutter Papers, Seymour Dunbar MSS., Huntington Library No. 7.

[23] Lewis E. Atherton: "Business Techniques in the Santa Fe Trade," *Missouri Historical Review,* Vol. XXIV, pp. 335–41. Samuel Lamme was killed by Indians in 1829.

San Miguel, the first New Mexican settlement encountered by the caravans, was 727 miles from Independence; Santa Fe itself lay perhaps fifty miles farther on.[24] About forty miles from Independence the later traders came to the junction of the Santa Fe and Oregon trails. The dividing place was marked by a rough signboard that bore the laconic inscription: "Road to Oregon" — to which, as one traveler remarked, the words "to Japan, China, and the East Indies might have been added." "Surely," Chittenden commented, "so unostentatious a sign never before nor since announced so long a journey."

The caravans usually left the Missouri settlements in small parties and effected their final organization for the long trip through hostile Indian country and across the plains at Council Grove. Here, too, the traders made needed wagon repairs from the hard woods growing along the stream. The caravan got under way with much shouting and some confusion. This is Gregg's description of the early morning start:

"All's set!" is finally heard from some teamster — "All's set" is directly responded from every quarter. "Stretch out!" immediately vociferates the captain. Then, the "heps!" of the drivers — the cracking of whips — the trampling of feet — the occasional creak of wheels — the rumbling of wagons — form a new scene of exquisite confusion, which I shall not attempt further to describe. "Fall in!" is heard from headquarters, and the wagons are forthwith strung out upon the

24 Chittenden, op. cit., Vol. II, p. 542. The following accounts of landmarks, etc., are mostly from Chittenden. For an extended account of Sapling Grove and Franklin, see *Mississippi Valley Historical Review*, Vol. IX, pp. 78, 269–82.

long inclined plain, which stretches to the heights beyond Council Grove.[25]

Pawnee Rock, 143 miles farther on, like El Moro on the old Spanish trail in New Mexico, or Independence Rock on the California-Oregon Trail, served as a gigantic register or directory for the hunters and traders of many races of the Southwest. The ford of the Arkansas lay approximately halfway between Independence and Santa Fe.

Here the trail divided. The longer, or so-called "mountain route," continued up the Arkansas to Bent's Fort, some 530 miles from Independence, where the caravans had their first view of the high, cloud-wrapped Spanish Peaks, which the Indians called Wah-to-Yah, or the Breasts of the World. The trail then crossed the river near the site of the present city of La Junta and ran south through Raton Pass, the gateway by which both Santa Fe Railway and transcontinental highway now cross the Continental Divide.

On the shorter but more dangerous route, the caravans forded the Arkansas, about twenty miles above modern Dodge City, plunged immediately into a sixty-mile desert or semi-desert region that lay between the Arkansas and Cimarron rivers, and struck the latter stream at the uncertain watering-place called Lower Spring. Scarcity of landmarks and a greater scarcity of water made the passage of this so-called Cimarron desert an ordeal of the first magnitude.

After reaching the Cimarron — the Bull River of the Indians — the trail ran about eighty-five miles up the val-

---

[25] Josiah Gregg: *The Commerce of the Prairies* (New York, 1844), Vol. I, p. 52.

ley to a familiar camping-place known as Cold Spring. Here it left the river, crossed the mountains by way of Rabbit Ear Pass to Santa Clara Spring, about 113 miles from Santa Fe and less than 50 miles from the nearest Spanish outpost, and united again at Wagon Mound with the Bent's Fort or mountain-route trail.[26]

The best of the Santa Fe wagons were made in Pittsburgh and had a cargo capacity of two or two and a half tons. Double canvas tops, with a heavy Mackinaw blanket in between, protected the merchandise from rain and incidentally reduced the Mexican customs charges on the blankets. Each member of the caravan was expected to have fifty pounds of flour, a like amount of bacon, ten pounds of coffee, twenty pounds of sugar, a little salt, and some beans, crackers, and other "trifles."

Horses, mules, and oxen were used for draft animals in the Santa Fe trade. Oxen were poor grazers and their feet frequently had to be protected by moccasins of raw buffalo hide against the sand and rocks of the plains. But the traders preferred the reliable, slow-moving beasts to mules or horses. From four to six yoke were used on each wagon.

A typical Santa Fe wagon train, like the New England hide and tallow ships on the California coast, carried a wide variety of merchandise, ranging from glass beads to rifles, from jew's-harps (of which there were many) to silk stockings and brightly colored ribbons. Calicoes and domestic cottons also bulked large in every cargo. In addition

---

[26] The traveler on the Santa Fe Railway idly reads the names of these landmarks, giving little thought to their historical significance or the rugged frontiersmen who first saw and named them.

to these items, a typical manifesto listed plain and fancy prints, handkerchiefs, velvets, Scotch ginghams, bed ticking, kid gloves, bleached muslins, cashmeres, "paint stuffs," "Bass balls," blue jeans, Tyrodese shanks, satins and satinettes, Pittsburgh cord, nankeens, cravats, shirtings, trick and ivory combs, thread, buttons, candlesticks, needles, razors, ink powder, files, coat molds, butcher and barlow knives, looking glasses, scissors, and medicines of various kinds.

Much of this merchandise found its way far beyond the New Mexican settlements of Taos and Santa Fe into the rich mining districts of Chihuahua, Durango, and San Luis Potosí; eventually part of it might be carried as far west as Sonora and California. The direct trade from New Mexico to California, discussed at length in a later chapter, began in 1829 with a little-known venture under Antonio Armíjo and became an established branch of Mexican-American trade with the William Wolfskill expedition of 1830.

In contrast to the wide variety of goods carried by the outbound caravans from Missouri to Santa Fe, the returning expeditions brought back primarily furs, silver, gold, and mules. The furs came chiefly from the trapping-grounds of the Rocky Mountains, the Sierra Nevada, and the lower Colorado; the silver from Chihuahua and other mining districts of Mexico; and the mules from Chihuahua, Sonora, and California.

In transporting specie the traders used an ingenious method to compress the mass of coins into a smaller bulk. Making a large bag of green bull or buffalo hide, they

filled it with silver pesos, shook the contents down as com-
pactly as possible, and sewed the mouth of the bag tightly
together. As the hide dried, it shrank into an iron-hard re-
ceptacle and squeezed the specie into a solid mass. Gregg
transported 27,500 pesos from Chihuahua to Santa Fe,
presumably in this fashion, in July 1830.[27]

The personnel of a typical caravan was as varied as the
cargoes it carried. Merchants and trappers predominated;
but invalids, scientists, travelers, fugitives, curiosity-seek-
ers, amateur hunters, and restless spirits of all sorts rode
in the white-topped wagons or accompanied the procession
on horseback. The equipment of a Santa Fe party "was
likewise of no common pattern, and there were as many
varieties of dress, saddles and firearms as there were of
men, wagons and animals." A writer in the *Missouri Intelligencer* appropriately described the traffic as "one of
the most curious species of foreign intercourse which the
ingenuity and enterprise of American traders ever originated."

In addition to the normal risk of accident from gunshot
wound or some similar misadventure of frontier travel, a
member of a Santa Fe train was exposed to the danger of
prairie fires, Indian attacks, and occasionally death from
thirst or hunger.

Under favorable conditions — a heavy growth of dry
grass and a brisk wind — a prairie fire traveled faster than
the fleetest horse and destroyed everything before it. Seen

---

[27] Josiah Gregg to the Collector of Customs, Chihuahua; Huntington
Library RI 170. The bullion, increased to 16,000 silver and 17,000 gold
pesos, was apparently carried on from Santa Fe in seven carts; ibid., 171.

at night from a place of safety, however, such a fire offered one of the most magnificent displays that the traveler was privileged to see: "The long sweeping line of fire stretching from one part of the horizon to the other, the lambent flames soaring high into the air, the flitting forms of animals driven suddenly from cover, and the reflection of the brilliant light in the clouds, composed a scene of truly terrible sublimity." [28]

The Santa Fe trail ran through territory occupied by at least five important Indian tribes — the Osage, Kiowa, Pawnee, Comanche, and Apache. Of the five, the Comanches were the most warlike and pre-eminently the most feared. "They are a people so numerous and so haughty that when asked their number, they make no difficulty of comparing it to that of the stars," wrote Athanase de Mézières shortly after the middle of the eighteenth century. "They are so skillful in horsemanship that they have no equal; so daring that they never ask for or grant truces; and in the possession of such territory that, finding in it an abundance of pasturage for their horses and an incredible number of cattle which furnish them raiment, food, and shelter, they only just fall short of possessing all of the conveniences of the earth, and have no need to covet the trade pursued by the rest of the Indians whom they call, on this account, slaves of the Europeans, and whom they despise." [29]

---

[28] Chittenden, op. cit., Vol. II, p. 756.
[29] *Athanase de Mézières and the Louisiana-Texas Frontier, 1768–1780*, ed. by Herbert Eugene Bolton (Cleveland, 1914), Vol. I, pp. 24–5, 218–19.

Gregg probaby had the Comanches specifically in mind when he spoke of the Indians as the *"unconquered Sabaeans* of the Great American Deserts"; and Thomas Jefferson Farnham called them the "Spartans of the Plains." When conducting a party through the Comanche country, even after the Mexican War, an experienced trapper such as Thomas Fitzpatrick protected his tents and wagons each night by a strong enclosure of fallen trees and interlaced branches.

Two examples must serve to illustrate the constant Indian menace to which the trading caravans were exposed. In 1826 the Kiowas killed two Americans and ran off a herd of 460 mules belonging to a company returning from Santa Fe.[30] In 1829 Charles Bent, Samuel Lamme, David Waldo, and Colonel M. M. Marmaduke applied to President Andrew Jackson for a military escort to the Arkansas River. Jackson ordered Major Bennett Riley, later Military Governor of California, and four companies of infantry to accompany the caravan. After crossing into Mexican territory on the left bank of the Arkansas River, the caravan, which consisted of sixty men and thirty-six wagons, engaged in a desperate fight with the Comanches, losing a number of men, including Samuel Lamme.

Later the caravan was joined by a relief force under Ewing Young "with ninety-five hunters who might be considered equal to five hundred inexperienced men." As a result of the attack, the train changed its destination and proceeded to Taos instead of Santa Fe. When the traders

---

[30] W. P. May to General William P. Clark, August 1826. Missouri Historical Society MSS., Clark Papers.

started back to Missouri, the Mexican government sent a military escort under General Vizcarra to accompany the party to the Arkansas; but the escort suffered serious losses in a disastrous Indian attack on the Cimarron River after it parted from the caravan.

On the sixty-mile waterless stretch between the crossing of the Arkansas and the Cimarron River the caravans dreaded death or suffering from thirst even more than they feared the Indians. More than one large, well-organized party almost perished for lack of water on this grim *jornada,* and the story of individual sufferings became part of the tradition of the trade.

Gregg recounts how the half-crazed men of Captain Becknell's pioneer expedition, tantalized and mocked by the "false-ponds," or mirages, finally killed their dogs and cut off the ears of the mules in a vain effort to satisfy their intolerable thirst with the hot blood. But the salty liquid "only served to irritate the parched palates and madden the sense of the sufferers." [31] Eventually one of the company killed a large buffalo, just returning from a hidden water-hole, and Gregg drove his knife into the beast's swollen stomach and drank the "filthy beverage" that spurted out, with indescribable delight.

But in spite of all these potential dangers — thirst, accident, prairie fire, and Indian attack — the actual loss of life on the Santa Fe Trail was surprisingly low.

The financial hazards of the trail were as threatening and varied as the dangers to life and person. Storms damaged or ruined the trader's merchandise; Indians looted

---

[31] *The Commerce of the Prairies,* Vol. I, p. 8.

his caravans; New Mexican officials confiscated his goods; large catches of furs and excessive imports of goods from St. Louis often broke the market. "With a blindness unaccountable, men still continue rushing to Santa Fe, as if fortunes were to be had there for the asking," wrote Albert Pike in 1834. "Men, who by hard and incessant labor have amassed a little money, laying that out to the last farthing and in addition, mortgaging perhaps their farms to obtain farther credit, convey the goods thus obtained to Santa Fe, hoping thus and there to gain a fortune, notwithstanding they have seen members returning poor and impoverished, after starting, as they are doing, with high hopes and full wagons. Here and there an individual, by buying beaver or trading to Sonora and California for mules, returns home a gainer, but generally the case is far otherwise." [32]

But despite hazards and depressions the trade grew both in volume and value till it became an important outlet for goods of American manufacture, a significant factor in Western commerce, and the basis of many a St. Louis fortune. After the Mexican War it expanded still more rapidly. "Murphy wagons" of St. Louis manufacture, with a capacity of nearly four tons, displaced the lighter Pittsburgh wagons. The value of the trade reached four or five million dollars annually. By 1860 nearly 17,000,000 pounds of freight had left Kansas City over the old trail. The business employed nearly 10,000 men and required over 6,100 mules, 28,000 oxen, and 3,000 wagons to keep

---

[32] Albert Pike: *Prose Sketches and Poems* (Boston, 1834), p. 10.

it moving. J. Evarts Greene thus described some of the picturesque features of the caravan operations:

The most peculiar part of their equipment was the formidable whip, its stock a good-sized, tough ash or pecan sapling nearly ten feet long, with a lash somewhat shorter, but fully two inches in diameter, ending in a buckskin thong. To wield this tremendous implement required all the strength of a man's loins. The driver did not flog his beasts with it, but cracked it with a heavy flourish and a smart jerk. You would hear a sound like a pistol shot, and see a little mist of hair and blood start where the cruel thong had cut like a bullet.

The day's drive was from fifteen to twenty miles. At the appointed stopping-place the wagons were driven up in such order as to form a square enclosed space or corral, an entrance to which could be closed by stretching chains across it. At halting, often early in the afternoon, the cattle were watered and turned out to graze under the charge of herders. At night they were driven into the corral and the entrance was closed. In the early morning for some hours before starting they were turned loose again to graze. The men camped for the night outside the corral, but retreated to it for defence in case of a formidable attack by Indians.[33]

From the beginning of the trade till the Mexican War, ill feeling between New Mexican officials and American traders was endemic. The Mexicans inherited the Spaniards' fear and suspicion of the northern interlopers and laid imposts on American goods that often seemed to the St. Louis merchants arbitrary and unwarranted. Sometimes, also, to satisfy a personal grudge or fatten his own purse,

[33] J. Evarts Greene: *The Santa Fe Trade: Its Route and Character* (Worcester, Massachusetts, 1893), pp. 15–16.

a governor at Santa Fe seized the goods and even the persons of the foreigners and denied them recourse to the basic remedies provided by the common law, which Americans took for granted.[34]

But though the arbitrary acts of Mexican officials sometimes led to serious consequences for the foreign traders, at other times the enforcement of the law at Santa Fe or Taos, viewed at least across the vista of a century and a quarter, took on the flavor and characteristics of pure *opéra bouffe*. Such an incident occurred when the first Alcalde of Santa Fe arrested four Americans [35] for gambling, and the greatly outraged four protested their innocence.

"This is the case," they wrote. "Last night the deponents were enjoying themselves playing cards. . . . About eleven or twelve o'clock there was a knocking at the door of the store, which none of the deponents answered. The outcome of this procedure was that at seven o'clock this morning, as they were about to leave the store, they were apprehended by the said Alcalde who, after fining them 150 pesos — which the deponents do not consider just — sent them to the public jail, where they are at present."

Commenting at length on the flimsy evidence on which the Alcalde acted, the prisoners then pointed out that there were only four players, two of whom had never taken part in illegal games, as any Mexican would testify, and that the four were only enjoying the well-known game of "Brag," which was played publicly in New Mexico and Chihuahua

---

[34] For an excellent example of "shake-down" and graft see the case of D. Francisco Robidoux v. D. Juan Bautista Vigil, New Mexican Archives MSS. (Huntington Library Microfilm.)

[35] John J. Lanham, Gentry Flood, Joseph Sutton, and John Morrison.

and thought of by no one as "a gambling game or game of chance." Then the spokesman for the four got down to serious business. "It may be contended that the players admitted their guilt by not opening the door," the protest added,

and this is probably the only charge that may be made against them; but this accusation may be entirely ruled out if the door in question, and the hour, are considered. It may be a civil duty to answer a knocking at the door, but it is certainly unwarranted to knock at an hour when the street is deserted and everyone is aware of the many abuses committed by wicked men. The door in question was that of a store, and no merchant is obliged to open his store if he apprehends that some unpleasant surprise may be awaiting him. The deponents would have opened the door and welcomed the Alcalde had he announced himself; but since he did not do this, they did not feel bound to open the door. . . . Under such circumstances the deponents are not to blame . . . and less still deserved the fine and imprisonment imposed on them. . . .

The Americans protested, in conclusion, that the Alcalde was "unlawful and intemperate," that he had violated the fundamental laws of the Mexican Republic in arresting them and "openly assailed the personal liberty of the deponents," and that the four now found themselves in a gloomy cell, grossly insulted because of the public nature of the place of their confinement and even more humiliated because the Alcalde had locked the door with a key!

When the Governor ordered the Alcalde to give him a speedy and detailed report on the incident, the latter replied that the Americans had been detained only to afford him an opportunity to determine whether or not they had been engaged in an illegal game of chance, that he had taken immediate steps to clarify the matter, that he was able to inform His Excellency that the prisoners were now free, and that he was satisfied that "circumstantial evidence alone had led to their arrest." [36]

But if the authorities were sometimes mercenary or arbitrary, the Mexicans, with good reason, often complained that the Americans themselves did not come into court with clean hands. In return for skins, they traded guns and ammunition to the gentile Indians of Chihuahua and Sonora, hunted beaver without permits or licenses, smuggled goods across the border, obtained passports to leave the country and then disappeared into the wild trapping regions of the Gila and Colorado rivers, encouraged Mexican citizens to violate the laws of their country, treated all Mexican institutions and Mexican laws with open and irritating contempt, and showed themselves "alien to every sane policy, strangers to reason itself, and Mexican tolerance." [37]

Drunken brawls with each other and with Mexican citizens were also frequent causes of complaint, especially when the Americans settled their bloody scores in the presence of Mexican officials and other onlookers. In one notorious case an American stabbed a Mexican who refused

[36] Santa Fe, July 12, 1832. Huntington Library, RI 136. See also Luciano Thursten to "The Political Chief of the Territory," July 24, 1832. Ibid., 137.

[37] Albino Pérez, Superior Political Chief and Principal Commandant of the Territory of New Mexico, Proclamation, October 16, 1835. Ibid., 153.

to give him a watermelon; on another occasion a number of ruffians, angered by the conduct of a certain trial, set upon and nearly killed the Alcalde before some of his countrymen came to the rescue. Nearly every American who visited New Mexico while the Santa Fe trade was in progress and who wrote of its people and government felt called upon to disparage and criticize.

"There are no people on the continent of America, whether civilized or uncivilized, with one or two exceptions, more miserable in condition or despicable in morals than the mongrel race inhabiting New Mexico," wrote Rufus Sage.

Next to the squalid appearance of its inhabitants, the first thing that arrests the attention of the traveller on entering a Mexican settlement, is the uninviting mud walls that form the rude hovels which constitute its dwellings.

These are one story high and built of *adobies*, with small windows, (like the port-holes of a fortification,) generally without glass. The entrance is by an opening in the side, very low, and frequently unprotected by a door. The roof is a terrace of sod, reposing upon a layer of small logs, affording but poor protection from the weather.

The interior presents an aspect quite as forbidding; — the floors are simply the naked ground, — chairs and tables are articles rarely met with. In case of an extra room, it is partitioned off by a thin wall of mud, communicating with its neighbor through a small window-shaped aperture, and serves the double purpose of a chamber and store-house.

A few rags, tattered blankets, or old robes, furnish beds for its inmates, who, at nightfall, stow themselves away promiscuously upon the ground or in narrow bins, and snooze their rounds despite the swarms of noxious vermin that infest them. . . .[38]

"The militia of Santa Fe when on parade beggared all description," wrote James. "Falstaff's company was well equipped and well furnished, compared with these troops of Gov. Malgaris. Such a gang of tatterdemalions, I never saw, before or since. They were of all colors, with all kinds of dresses and every species of arms. Some were bareheaded, others were barebacked — some had hats without rims or crowns, and some wore coats without skirts; other again wore coats without sleeves. Most of them were armed with bows and arrows. A few had guns that looked as if they had been imported by Cortez, while others had iron hoops fastened to the ends of poles, which passed for lances." [39]

In July 1827 the Governor of New Mexico reported that eighty-four foreigners came into his territory from the United States in a single month. Many of these immigrants stayed on and married, even though they had no passports. Others, without legitimate means of livelihood, smuggled goods in and out of the country and induced newly arrived Americans "to behave rudely and commit other offenses." The harassed official closed with the pertinent request: "I wish to be advised as to how to proceed with such foreigners — should I let them be or request that they return to their country?" [40]

Chittenden justified the Mexican War because of the

---

[38] Sage: *Scenes in the Rocky Mountains,* p. 174.

[39] James: *Three Years among the Indians and Mexicans,* pp. 150–1.

[40] Huntington Library, RI 196.

indignities, thefts, imprisonments, and even murders (connived at by the Mexican government) that Americans suffered for twenty years at the hands of Mexican citizens and officials. Such ill feeling between the two peoples, as many New Mexicans appreciated, hurt the residents of Santa Fe as well as the St. Louis merchants. On the eve of the Mexican War a member of the Legislative Assembly pointed out that trappers shipped some two hundred thousand dollars' worth of beaver skins annually from Abiquiu and Taos, and that the trade in horses, supplies, and provisions at the latter pueblo alone amounted to fifty or sixty thousand dollars a year. When the New Mexican officials interfered with this trade and confiscated the foreigners' furs and merchandise, the delegate continued, the American merchants retired into the interior beyond the reach of Mexican law and there established fortified posts from which they continued their trapping and trading operations to the great loss and impoverishment of New Mexico.[41]

Bent's Fort, on the north bank of the Arkansas, near the present-day city of La Junta, was by far the largest and most important of the American trading posts to which the New Mexican lawmaker referred. The fort was built jointly by Charles and William Bent (sons of Silas Bent of Charleston, Virginia, and St. Louis), and Céran St. Vrain, one of the ablest of the Santa Fe traders and a mountain man whose name was respected from the Snake River to Chihuahua. Known as "Black Beard" to the Cheyennes, St. Vrain was described as shrewd, enterprising, impetuous, choleric, intrepid, courteous, and charming. The part-

[41] Captain Donaciano Vigil, May 16, 1846. Ibid., 231.

ners carried on their extensive operations under the name
of Bent & St. Vrain, but the management of the fort was
largely left to William Bent.

As a result of the latter's marriage to Owl Woman, the
daughter of White Thunder, one of the principal chiefs of
the Cheyenne Indians, a large branch of that powerful tribe
left its former home and moved south into the valley of the
Arkansas. The tribe's traditional allies, the Arapahoes,
followed the lead of the migrating Cheyennes. The southern Cheyennes and the Arapahoes brought their furs to and
traded in the main with Bent's Fort, while the northern
Cheyennes and the Sioux carried on most of their business
at St. Vrain's Fort on the South Platte.

The Bents and St. Vrain also had a ranch or post at the
mouth of the Purgatoire. Here William Bent, known to the
Indians as Small White Man, kept large herds of horses,
mules, and oxen, baled thousands of beaver, deer, and
buffalo skins, and carried on an extensive caravan trade
with the Cheyennes, Arapahoes, Comanches, Kiowas,
Apaches, and a number of other tribes. From here he also
sent long lines of ox-drawn wagons to St. Louis for goods
for the Indian and Santa Fe trade.[42]

Charles Bent, whom the Cheyennes called White Hat,
was a man of light complexion, stockily built, independent,
fearless, and an able trader. "In all my dealings with him,"
wrote James Hobbs, "I always found him perfectly upright
in his dealings, both with his party and the Indians. He
commanded the confidence and respect of all the tribes he

---

[42] George Bent to George E. Hyde, May 19, 1914. Coe Collection, loc.
cit.

dealt with, and his honorable treatment of them prevented violence on their part." [43] Charles Bent opposed the sale of liquor to the Indians and never made use of it in his trading operations. William Bent, resembling his older brother in uprightness and integrity, commanded perhaps even greater respect among the trappers and Indians.[44]

Bent's fort was begun in 1828, but the size of the building, the ravages of smallpox among the workmen, and the difficulty of obtaining men and materials delayed the completion until 1832.[45] The fort was rectangular in shape and

[43] *Wild Life in the Far West* (Hartford, 1872), p. 18. Charles Bent, appointed Military Governor of New Mexico by Philip Kearny, in command of the Army of the West, was killed and scalped in the Taos uprising of January 19, 1847.

[44] George and Robert Bent were called Little Beaver and Green Bird respectively. All four of the brothers were named by Chief Yellow Bird of the Cheyennes. See George Bent to George E. Hyde, May 13, 1914. Coe Collection, loc. cit. See also George Bird Grinnell: "Bent's Old Fort and Its Builders," *Collections of the Kansas State Historical Society,* Vol. XV, p. 31.

[45] In the summer of 1829 Major Bennet Riley addressed the following letter to Don José Antonio Chavez, Governor and Commandante of New Mexico:

Near Chartern Island

10th July 1829

To His Excellency the Governor of Santafe
Sir

This will be handed to you by my friend Mr. Charles Bent he is a gentleman of the first Respectability in our country and has been elected to comd the company of traders that is with him any attentions or Assistence you may afford him will be thankfully Recvd by me

I have the honor to be with
Great Respect and Esteem your
Excellen   obt Sert
B Riley
Major U. S. Army

extended something over a hundred feet from east to west and between a hundred and fifty and a hundred and eighty feet from north to south. Its walls, built of adobe bricks in which wool, brought by wagons from New Mexico, took the place of straw, were fifteen feet high, six or seven feet thick at the base, and two feet wide at the top. In a passage remarkable for its accuracy, detail, and vividness, Arthur J. Flynn thus described Bent's historic outpost of trade and civilization on the farthest American frontier:

The main entrance was thirty feet in width through the east wall by means of two massive plank doors, which were plated with nail heads to insure them against fire. Above this entrance was a square watchtower, surmounted by a belfry, which in turn supported a flagstaff. Reaching upward to the height of thirty feet and bulging out from the building in the usual fashion stood two bastions, or round towers, fitted into the walls at the northwest and southeast corners. They were ten feet in diameter within walls and on the lower floor of each were large loopholes for cannon, and on the upper floor smaller ones for ordinary firearms. Since these towers stood out many feet away from the walls, with the exception of each narrow line of contact at the corners, an opportunity was given for observing and firing upon an enemy coming from any direction. It can be seen that, with such an arrangement, an enemy was in as great danger lurking under the shadow of the wall as if he stood out in the open. Under such conditions wall-scaling would also be impossible. For further efficiency in the matter of observing an approaching foe a

---

To his Excellency the
Governor and Commander in Chief
of the Province of New Mexico.

Huntington Library, RI 331.

long, powerful telescope, balanced on a pivot, stood in the watchtower, which had windows on every side. Here also swung a little mealtime bell. Within easy reaching distance along the walls were hung weapons. The outside walls were pierced by loopholes. At vital points throughout the building were stationed cannons and other ordnance to be used at a moment's notice in case of attack.

Fort Bent was much more than an ordinary trading post. It was an institution, standing like a castle in the middle ages far away from the stirring, throbbing world on the outside. Within the thick, outlying protective walls was an isolated community, enjoying many blessings of civilized safety and hospitality in contrast to the dangers and hardships that loomed up immediately when the outside world was reached. In the busy time of year there were a hundred employees, consisting of many classes and conditions of servitude; clerks, traders, trappers, mechanics, herders, teamsters, common laborers, and several children. A resident physician cared for the health of the inmates and ministered to travellers. . . .[46]

Robert Campbell, one of the largest merchants of St. Louis, furnished much of the goods sold at the fort; but caravans of Mexican traders, bringing flour, corn, beans, onions, dried pumpkin, salt, and pepper, frequently came from Taos to barter their simple products for guns, ammunition, tobacco, coffee, cloth, calico and other wares from the outside world.

For the most part the Bents were on good terms with the

---

[46] "Furs and Forts of the Rocky Mountain West," *Colorado Magazine* (March 1932), Vol. IX, pp. 51–5. Reprinted by permission of The State Historical Society of Colorado, Denver. For an earlier description of the fort, see Thomas Jefferson Farnham: *Travels in the Great Western Prairies,* pp. 34–5.

Mexicans, both officials and private citizens, but in 1841 Governor Manuel Armíjo denounced their fort, together with all similar American posts near the Mexican border, as "shelters" of thieves and contraband, instigators of Indian forays against Mexican citizens, and a constant menace to the welfare and independence of New Mexico.

In 1852, during the California gold rush, the federal government sought to buy the fort from William Bent, but the price offered was so low that Bent blew up the fort with gunpowder and built another trading center farther down the Arkansas. For twenty years, however, the old post had been the most important outpost of American life and civilization in the Southwest.

"In the early and middle forties, when traffic on the Santa Fe Trail was at its height," wrote Flynn, "Bent's Fort assumed the combined proportions of a great Oriental caravansary and an Occidental mercantile house. Here it stood on the plains, the central point of interest, the isolated refuge of wanderers on a widespread danger-abounding region. Here dwelt the scout, guide, and protector of travelers in a strange land. Here, at intervals for several years, Kit Carson was a resident hunter, supplying the Fort with buffalo meat. Here, in 1846, General Kearny, on his memorable march from Fort Leavenworth to Santa Fe, halted for several days to arrange supplies for his soldiers." [47]

[47] Arthur J. Flynn: "Furs and Forts of the Rocky Mountain West," loc. cit., p. 35.

CHAPTER 5

Perils of the Wilderness:

The Wanderings of James Ohio Pattie

To the adventurous Americans who poured into Taos and Santa Fe in the mid-twenties the Mexican settlements were merely a temporary resting-place for still more extensive trading and trapping ventures to the west and south. So while Jedediah Smith made his slow way across the Great Basin, through the interior valleys of California, and along the Oregon coast, traders and trappers from Taos and Santa Fe followed the old Spanish trail through the Paso del Norte to Sonora and Chihuahua, or penetrated the wild isolation that lay between the narrow fringe of civilization along the Rio Grande and the sheer, deep chasms of the Colorado.

The surviving accounts of most of these early trapping expeditions into the lower basin of the Colorado and other parts of the Far Southwest are either hopelessly tangled and confused or so fragmentary and laconic as to be of little value. The names of most of the trappers — Ewing Young, William Wolfskill, Miguel Robidoux, "Peg-leg" Smith, George Yount, "Old Bill" Williams, Céran St. Vrain, and a dozen others — are familiar to every student of the fur trade; but the exact dates, itineraries, incidents, and other vital details of their several expeditions are either unknown, disappointingly vague, or as crisscrossed and interwoven with each other as deer trails in a mountain meadow.

Fortunately, an extensive contemporary account of the wanderings and adventures of one of the first of these Southwestern pioneer fur traders has survived. The title of the narrative, like that of the immortal collection that Richard Hakluyt styled *The Principal Navigations, Voyages Traffiques & Discoveries of the English Nation Made by Sea or Over-land to the Remote and Farthest Distant Quarters of the Earth at any time within the compass of these 1600 Yeeres,* offered the reader a general preview of the contents of the book. It read: *The Personal Narrative of James O. Pattie, Of Kentucky, During An Expedition From St. Louis, Through The Vast Regions Between That Place And The Pacific Ocean, And Thence Back Through The City Of Mexico To Vera Cruz, During Journeyings Of Six Years; In Which He And His Father, Who Accompanied Him, Suffered Unheard Of Hardships And Dangers, Had Various Conflicts With The Indians, And Were Made Captives, In Which Captivity His Father Died; Together With A Description Of The Country, And The Various Nations Through Which They Passed. Edited By Timothy Flint.*[1]

---

[1] The book was copyrighted by John H. Ward in Cincinnati in 1831. Only a few copies of this small edition survive. Flint's edition was issued in 1833. The edition now most widely used was published by the Arthur H. Clark Company (then of Cleveland, Ohio, now of Glendale, California) in 1905.

Unfortunately Pattie's narrative contains few of the names of his companions, shows little more respect for accurate dates than a present-day "progressive" schoolteacher, and at times makes the author or his father the leading figure in other men's adventures and accomplishments.

Yet with all these admittedly serious limitations, Pattie's volume gives an authentic, over-all picture of the early days of the fur trade in the extreme Southwest and a true account of some of the dramatic incidents connected with it. Though Pattie himself may not have taken the leading role in all the adventures he describes, it is gratuitous to assume that such adventures did not actually take place or that he was not at least a witness to them. His descriptions of the country through which he passed are also too accurate and detailed (as the author can attest from personal observation in many instances) to be based on borrowed accounts or spurious experience.

James Ohio Pattie was foreordained to the trapper's calling. The boy's grandfather, a carpenter by trade who sometimes diversified his occupation by teaching school, migrated to Kentucky from Virginia in 1781. The Revolutionary War was still in progress; and the title "Dark and Bloody Ground" then belonged to Kentucky by right and not as yet only by tradition. Pattie volunteered to serve under Colonel Benjamin Logan in a distant campaign against the Shawnees, and during his absence his wife gave birth to a son. The boy, named Sylvester, grew to manhood on the Kentucky frontier and acquired the Kentucky frontiersman's skill with rifle, ax, and plow — "part of the fundamental knowledge of every man." He also received a reasonably good education and possessed that deep piety which characterized so many settlers of the Virginia-Kentucky frontier.

Like many of his fellow Kentuckians, Sylvester Pattie later moved to Missouri and there, following the example his father had set in the American Revolution, distinguished himself for his bravery and resourcefulness against the British and their Indian allies in the War of 1812. When the war closed, Sylvester Pattie moved his household to southern Missouri and established a prosperous saw and grist mill on the isolated Gasconade River.

James Ohio, the eldest of Sylvester Pattie's sons, was eight years old when the family left Kentucky. Like his father and grandfather, the boy was taught to shoot, read, and worship, and the lonely forests and hostile Indians of the Missouri frontier furnished an environment similar to the Kentucky wilderness in which Sylvester Pattie had spent his own boyhood days.

But population and civilization were rapidly moving westward, and in a few years the transient settlers on the Gasconade found that the frontier had reached and passed their clearings in the forest. Sylvester Pattie was ready for another change. The death of his wife from tuberculosis led his restless feet to turn even more eagerly toward the wilderness.

So the bereaved husband and father left the younger children with obliging relatives and, taking James Ohio as companion, sought to reconstruct his life in the solitude and excitement of the unpeopled West. His first and most natural objective was the Rocky Mountains. Well equipped with traps, trapping utensils, guns, knives, tomahawks, provisions, ammunition, blankets, and some surplus arms, the Patties and three companions set out in 1823 for the upper Missouri on a trading and trapping venture.

Crossing the river sixty miles above St. Louis, the expedition followed the usual route to Council Bluffs. Here the Patties met the first of many disappointments. Ignorant of the requirement, the company had neglected to obtain the necessary license to trap and trade within the Indian country and could not obtain permission to travel farther toward the Rocky Mountains.

Abandoning its original plan, the party then turned to the other great theater of the fur trade, the Mexican provinces of the Southwest, and joined a large trading caravan commanded by Sylvester Pratte that left Cabanne's Post, some nine miles above the present site of Omaha, for the distant pueblo of Santa Fe.

During the next seven years James Ohio Pattie suffered a constant succession of accidents, reversals, and misfortunes and gambled repeatedly with death. Eventually his travels carried him as far west as San Francisco, as far north as the Yellowstone, and as far south as Mexico City. Like Job's persecutor of old, he wandered up and down in the earth and to and fro in it, and his adventurous trails through the solitary and waste places of the West formed an endless and confusing maze.

The expedition to Santa Fe with which the young Kentuckian's Odyssey began was organized on a semimilitary basis and included a number of men who had served under

Sylvester Pattie in the War of 1812. As the party passed
through the territory of the Republican Pawnees, its leaders smoked the peace pipe with the Indians, and the chief
gave them "a stick curiously painted with characters,"
which he promised would ensure safe passage through any
of his tribal lands. The Pawnee Loups proved less hospitable and the Americans, who prevented them from tortur-
ing a boy captured from another tribe, were lucky to come
out with whole skins and nothing worse than the gruff advice of one of the chiefs to keep peace with friends and
save their powder and lead to kill buffalo and destroy their
enemies.

The journey enabled James Ohio Pattie to serve his apprenticeship as a mountain man and introduced him to
some of the common hardships and dangers of his new
calling. The traders showed him how to make moccasins
of buffalo hides to save the horses' hoofs from being cut
to pieces by the dry, rocky plains. He had his baptism of
Indian warfare when a band of Arikara Indians suddenly
attacked the camp. A little later two trappers were scalped
and mangled by a marauding band of Crows. The Indians
paid heavily in return, but a third American lost his life in
the melee. As the expedition neared Taos, the Arab-like
Comanches, most crafty and powerful of the Plains Indians, offered a new menace to the constantly alerted
caravan.

On the Arkansas River, in a region so infested with
grizzly or white bears that the company saw over two hundred in a single day, the younger Pattie witnessed one of
the familiar tragedies in the trappers' business. One night

a large bear stampeded the grazing stock, seized a luckless horse, and began to devour the helpless animal while it was still alive. Pattie, who was doing guard duty at the time, wounded the grizzly with a rifleshot. The infuriated beast charged the camp and caught one of the fleeing men. Pattie ran to the rescue, placed the muzzle of his gun directly against the side of the bear, and pulled the trigger. The grizzly fell dead, but the man was mangled beyond hope. "Our Companion," wrote Pattie, "was literally torn in pieces. The flesh on his hip was torn off, leaving the sinews bare, by the teeth of the bear. His side was so wounded in three places, that his breath came through the openings; his head was dreadfully bruised, and his jaw broken. His breath came out from both sides of his windpipe, the animal in his fury having placed his teeth and claws in every part of his body." [2]

Trapping on a small scale for beaver and sometimes trading with the Indians, the expedition finally reached the small but historic town of San Fernando de Taos. This mountain-girt outpost of Spanish settlement and culture, like other frontier pueblos of its time and origin, was small, primitive, and crude. Its houses were built of adobe — thick-walled, flat-roofed, dirt-floored. Its inhabitants were almost wholly mestizo or Indian, its life a fluctuating

---

[2] Reprinted by permission of the publishers, The Arthur H. Clark Company, Glendale, California, from *Personal Narrative during an Expedition from St. Louis to the Pacific Ocean*, by James O. Pattie, being Volume 18 of Early Western Travels series, edited by Dr. Reuben Gold Thwaites (Cleveland, 1905), p. 63. A number of other extended notations from the same volume appear in this chapter. For permission to use these I am also indebted to The Arthur H. Clark Company.

contrast between inertia, monotony, and tranquillity, and the red violence of Indian attack or drunken brawl; and here James Ohio had his first contact with Mexican frontier society — a bewildering contrast of simplicity, erratic justice, and brutal violence.

After a brief stay at Taos the company went on to Santa Fe. Snow-covered mountains in the distance and the nearer green of irrigated fields made an attractive setting for this isolated Spanish capital whose adobe walls the centuries had not yet beaten down. As for the pueblo itself, the strangers found it somewhat novel, perhaps, but neither very attractive nor imposing.

"The houses and business buildings were uniformly of one story; of mud bricks smeared with a thin plaster of more mud, and in rare cases whitewashed with *tierra blanca,* or white earth," wrote Edwin L. Sabin.

The mud roofs were flat, windows were protected by wooden shutters, iron bars, or, here and there, with sheets of thin, laminated gypsum in lieu of glass. Mud front joined with mud front, around the central plaza, in monotonous line, until at irregular intervals a winding lane, for a street, cut through. Dirt and squalor, refuse, dogs, and beggars predominated; nevertheless there was much to interest the visitor from the Missouri frontier.

The blanket-enveloped Mexican, smiling in the American's face and scowling at his back, indolent, graceful, eternally smoking his cornhusk cigarette, and ever a *caballero,* or gentleman; the shawled Mexican woman, her face stained crimson with the juice of the *alegria* plant, or coated with a paste of chalk, to preserve her complexion for the fandango; the burros, piled high with enormous loads of cornshuck for

166

fodder, or with wood from the mountains, or with parcels of melons, or balanced with casks of that whiskey termed "Taos lightning"; supplies of *chili colorado* and *chili verde*, vegetables, baked piñon nuts, peaches from the orchards of the Pueblos and Navajos, native tobacco or *punche*, grapes, bunches of *hoja* or husk for the rolling of cigarettes, and other products strange or appealing — or, to a newly arrived caravan, both; the constant gambling, principally at *el monte*, with Mexican cards, by high and low, rich and poor, alike, in open room and upon the street; the religious processions, at which everybody must uncover; aye, there was much to see.[3]

For some of the interlopers Santa Fe was journey's end; for many others the pueblo was only a resting-place, the starting-point for further adventure in the strange, perilous, alluring lands that lay beyond.

There, while the Americans awaited the Governor's permission to trap in Mexican territory, the Patties had a novel, highly melodramatic experience. For generations the outlying ranchos along the upper Rio Grande had been subject to Indian forays. Comanches, Navajos, and Apaches all alike raided the small, exposed settlements for cattle, sheep, and horses, girls and women, rapine and massacre. One of these raids occurred while the trappers were still in the pueblo.

Attacking in considerable force, a band of Comanches killed several rancheros, drove off some hundreds of sheep, and carried away four or five unfortunate women. The raid

---

[3] Reprinted by permission of the publishers, A. C. McClurg & Co., Chicago, Illinois, from Edwin L. Sabin: *Kit Carson Days* (Chicago, 1914), pp. 26–7.

gave rise to a rumor that the Indians were moving against Santa Fe itself and caused a wild night of terror in the city. The following morning a force of trappers (composed chiefly of the members of the Pattie company), augmented by a body of ill-equipped government troops, started in pursuit. Sighting the Comanches on the morning of the fourth day, the rescue party concealed itself in a mountain pass through which the trail of the marauders led.

Of the outcome of the ambush, Pattie wrote:

My post was in the centre of the line. We waited an hour and a half behind our screens of rock and trees, before our enemies made their appearance. The first object, that came in sight, were women without any clothing, driving a large drove of sheep and horses. These were immediately followed by Indians. When the latter were within thirty or forty yards of us, the order to fire was given. The women ran towards us the moment they heard the report of our guns. In doing this they encountered the Indians behind them, and three fell pierced by the spears of these savages. The cry among us now was, "save the women!" Another young man and myself sprang forward, to rescue the remaining two. My companion fell in the attempt. An Indian had raised his spear, to inflict death upon another of these unfortunate captives, when he received a shot from one of our men, that rendered him incapable of another act of cruelty. The captives, one of whom was a beautiful young lady, the daughter of the governor before spoken of, both reached me. The gratitude of such captives, so delivered, may be imagined. Fears, thanks and exclamations in Spanish were the natural expression of feeling in such a position. My companions aided me in wrapping blankets around them, for it was quite

168

cold; and making the best arrangements in our power for their comfort and safety.[4]

After this romantic interlude the trappers returned to their posts and engaged the Comanches in a brief but bloody skirmish. The Indians finally broke and ran, but ten of the trappers were lost in the affray and the surviving Americans charged their New Mexican allies with cowardice, inefficiency, and lack of co-operation. This ill feeling was intensified by a quarrel over the disposition of the two women whom the trappers had rescued from the Indians.

One of the two, a girl of unusual charm and beauty, whom Pattie called Jacova, was the daughter of a former Governor of New Mexico. She formed a warm attachment for the young trapper who had aided in her rescue and expressed her affection and gratitude in many ways. Her father owned a house in Santa Fe and a ranch on the Pecos River. His gratitude to the two Patties was as deep and sincere as that of his daughter, and he gave them hospitable welcome whenever their later wanderings brought them back to Santa Fe.

When the expedition that had gone in pursuit of the Comanches returned to Santa Fe, the Governor honored the Americans with an elaborate dinner and fandango and later issued licenses (under which five per cent of the furs were to be allotted to the Governor) that permitted them to trap in Mexican territory.[5] Organizing in small bands,

---

[4] Pattie: *Personal Narrative*, pp. 79–80.

[5] The Spanish name for beaver is *castor*, but in the north Mexican provinces the animal was called *nutria* (otter). This confusion in terms some-

the Americans then struck out for different parts of the beaver country.

The Patties joined a company, ultimately consisting of fourteen men, that had the Gila River of Arizona as its objective. The route to the trapping-grounds followed the course of the Rio del Norte to Socorro and then turned westward to an important *minería* known as Santa Rita. In *A History of American Mining*, T. A. Rickard, dean of Canadian and American mining engineers, gives the following description of this famous mining district and early trappers' landmark:

The first information concerning the occurrence of copper in the Southwest was derived from the Indians, who, in the latter part of the eighteenth century, found native copper at Santa Rita, now in the State of New Mexico. One account says that this mine was acquired by the Mexicans from the Indians in 1780; another asserts that in the year 1800 an Indian, grateful for an act of kindness, showed the place to a Mexican officer, Colonel José Carrasco, and he, in turn, mentioned the discovery to his friend Don Francisco Manuel Elguea, a merchant of Chihuahua, who thereupon obtained a concession of the district from the Spanish government in Mexico. Elguea bought Carrasco's interest in 1804, and soon thereafter made a contract to supply the government with copper for coinage, the common copper coin being the *tlaco*, which was an eighth of the *real*, itself an eighth of the *peso* of today.

The native copper of Santa Rita is found in the form of small lumps scattered through the matrix of granodiorite, but more commonly the metal occurs in flakes, leaves, and

times led to trouble over the trapper's license; but in California, Americans often claimed the right to hunt sea otter under such permits.

tabular masses sometimes more than two feet square. The Indians, before the Spaniards came, are said to have hammered the copper into rude ornaments, as was done contemporaneously by the aborigines in other parts of North America. The mining of the Indians, the Mexicans, and the Americans up to 1882 was based mainly on the extraction of this native copper, and not of any other ore. To the Mexicans the deposit was a *criadero de cobre*, or place where copper was generated. The native metal stuck out of a big outcrop, and it is reported that masses weighing as much as a ton were cut in pieces suitable for transport to Chihuahua.

Elguea made several visits to the mine. On the occasion of his second visit he built a triangular fort, with a martello tower of adobe at each corner, one of which survives. This fortification was meant to be a protection against the Apaches, and probably also to confine the convicts that had been loaned to him by the Mexican Government. Thus Elguea had the advantage of cheap labor; however, he was handicapped by the high cost of transport, on mules, over a rough trail for 300 miles. The ragged pieces of native copper were packed in wool, but even this made an awkward load, so a rudimentary furnace was built to melt the metal into ingots of 150 pounds, two of which made a fair load for a good mule. One of the old Mexican moulds for casting the copper has been found; it was cut in rock, and consisted of four recesses, 6 by 20 inches, side by side. Twenty ingots of copper were discovered in a clump of willows on Whitewater creek; these appear to have been dropped by persons in flight, probably at the time when Santa Rita was evacuated hastily in fear of an Indian attack soon after the Mimbres massacre, a horrible episode in frontier history. . . .

When Elguea died, in 1809, the Santa Rita copper mine was managed by Francisco Pablo de Lagera, by whom the property was leased to Sylvester Pattie, an American, in 1825. His son James Pattie shod his horse with the copper, which was hardly suited to the purpose, on account of its softness.[6]

The Pattie company spent the night at Santa Rita and then engaged two Mexicans to guide them to the headwaters of the Gila River. With the exception of the Colorado, the Gila is the most important river of the extreme Southwest. It rises in the Mogollon Mountains of western New Mexico, flows entirely across the state of Arizona, and finally empties into the Colorado River near the present city of Yuma.

In the high mountains of New Mexico and Arizona the river remains a clear, cool, well-timbered, lively stream; but gradually, as it reaches a lower altitude, the mountains grow rougher and more precipitous, the pine and aspen give place to manzanita and scrub oak, and at last the river drops down through a deep, tortuous gorge into the semi-desert country of central Arizona. In its long passage from the snow-fed springs of New Mexico to the silt-laden flow of the Colorado, the Gila receives the waters of the San Francisco, San Pedro, San Carlos, Salt, and several other important tributaries.

Of these numerous tributary streams, the Salt River and its branches offered the early fur-hunters their best trapping-grounds. The Salt, whose major tributaries rise in northeastern Arizona, joins the Gila a few miles below

[6] From *A History of American Mining* by T. A. Rickard (New York, 1932), pp. 252–5. Courtesy of McGraw-Hill Book Co., Inc. The Santa Rita, now an open-pit mine, is one of the large copper-producing properties of the Southwest.

the present city of Phoenix. Not far above this junction, it receives the waters of the Verde, a stream known alike to Spanish explorers, American fur traders, and early copper miners, which rises in the Colorado Plateau of central Arizona and meanders south for over two hundred miles to its union with the Salt.

When the Patties and their fellow trappers reached the headwaters of the Gila, they found themselves in good beaver country, but the party had no discipline or cohesion and soon fell apart. Seven trappers, late-comers who had joined the expedition west of Santa Rita, now brazenly pushed ahead and trapped the river so ruthlessly that their former companions, the members of the original company, found neither furs nor beaver meat.

The outlook grew brighter when the half-starved trappers reached the mouth of the San Francisco, a large tributary that joins the Gila near the present town of Clifton in eastern Arizona. The stream was virgin water, and the trappers took thirty-seven beaver the first night — a windfall that at once changed their former gloom and discouragement into unrestrained rejoicing.

The region, too, was one to delight the heart of any lover of the wilderness. Dark peaks rose high above the river, which there flowed through an open forest of aspen, oak, and tall, straight ponderosa pines. In places, moreover, as though to forestall any hint or suggestion of monotony, the trees gave way to long vistas of grassy swales and meadows and quiet beaver ponds. With the exception of buffalo — always first choice among the mountain men — the hunters were now able to obtain an almost endless variety of game

— turkeys, geese, deer, elk, bear, mountain lion, and, perhaps most welcome of all, Rocky Mountain sheep.

After a catch of two hundred and fifty beaver on the San Francisco, the men cached part of their furs and moved on down the Gila. There they were joined by four of the seven trappers who had deserted the parent company some weeks before. The story of the renegades was one of multiplied misfortune. Indians had attacked the party, killed one of their number, badly wounded a second, stolen all the horses, and forced the survivors to wander through the mountains for five days, destitute and half-starved. Realists if not saints, the Patties and their companions accepted the situation as they found it, overlooked the recent desertion of the intimidated and discouraged men, welcomed them back to the camp, and gave them food and blankets.

The two remaining survivors of the Indian attack, one suffering from a badly wounded head, straggled into camp the next day. The Patties then proposed to attack the Indians, regain the stolen furs and horses, and avenge the death of the slain trapper. But the six refugees had no stomach for another fight and announced their intention of returning to the copper mines at Santa Rita as soon as they were able to travel. A few days later, outfitted at the company's expense with three horses and a hundred and fifty pounds of food, they started back to the New Mexican frontier.

Meanwhile, James Ohio Pattie had been keeping his own private rendezvous with danger and excitement. One evening while on a solitary hunt for beaver streams, he made camp in a wood overrun with bear. "I placed a spit,

with a turkey I had killed upon it, before the fire to roast,"
he wrote. "After I had eaten my supper I laid down by the
side of a log with my gun by my side. I did not fall asleep
for some time. I was aroused from slumber by a noise in
the leaves, and raising my head saw a panther stretched
on the log by which I was lying, within six feet of me. I
raised my gun gently to my face, and shot it in the head.
Then springing to my feet, I ran about ten steps, and
stopped to reload my gun, not knowing if I had killed the
panther or not." [7]

Another morning, while looking for the company's
horses, James Ohio found a cave that a bear was using for
a den. Fastening a pine torch to his gun barrel, the fool-
hardy youngster entered the cavern. Suddenly a grizzly
gave a deep-throated growl and loomed up in the narrow
passageway ahead. The constricted space, the shadowy
form of the huge bear, the deep reverberating growls were
enough to terrify the bravest and most experienced hunter.
But for the moment Pattie kept his head. Raising his gun
and taking careful aim by the murky light of the pine torch,
he shot the bear squarely between the eyes. Then, as the lad
turned to run, he stumbled, fell, and dropped his gun.
Thinking the bear was hard on his heels, he scrambled
madly to his feet and fled in a mounting panic of fear to
the entrance of the cave.

Once in the open, however, Pattie regained breath, color,
and courage, borrowed his companion's gun, and re-entered
the den. The bear was stone-dead. He was the whitest
grizzly Pattie had ever seen and so huge that four men

---

[7] *Personal Narrative*, p. 88.

could scarcely drag the carcass from the cave. The heavy layers of fat yielded ten gallons of highly prized oil.

After the departure of the six trappers, referred to before this digression, the rest of the company continued down the Gila to the camp where the Indians had so recently attacked their companions. Pattie's account of the tragedy, in its wild and isolated setting, is grim, vivid, terse. "On the 30th . . . we found the man that the Indians had killed. They had cut him in quarters, after the fashion of butchers. His head, with his hat on, was stuck on a stake. It was full of arrows, which they had probably discharged into it, as they danced around it. We gathered up the parts of the body, and buried them." [8]

A little below the site of this tragedy the trappers found it necessary to detour to the north around a deep canyon into which the Gila River suddenly plunged. Rough, frowning peaks, rising in every direction high above the clouds, created a scene of dreariness and desolation that did nothing to relieve the general gloom.

For almost two weeks the company wandered through this rough, heartbreaking region before it found an outlet to the plains and returned to the river. There, for the moment, their luck changed. Both the Gila and one of its southern tributaries, appropriately named the Beaver, were virgin streams, and the trappers soon loaded their horses down with furs, Then, as they were ready to break camp and return to civilization, misfortune suddenly struck again. Under cover of darkness a band of Indians crept in among the grazing stock, stampeded the horses, and left

8 Ibid., p. 94.

the party completely stranded. The situation was desperate: the trappers could only cache their furs and start back to the copper mines on foot.

The journey proved an ordeal of thirst, hunger, and exhaustion. Progress was slow, food ran short, game almost disappeared. One long-remembered day the seven half-starved refugees ate a raven for breakfast and a turkey buzzard for supper. But ragged, hungry, and exhausted though they were, the wanderers doggedly kept on until they finally reached the little settlement of Santa Rita.

Waiting only a few hours to recuperate, James Ohio left his father at the mines and set out alone for Santa Fe to obtain the supplies and equipment necessary to outfit a second expedition to the Gila. On the way he stopped for a brief visit at the home of the beautiful Jacova. In contrast to his brave appearance when he rode to the rescue of the naked captives, the young trapper now cut a sorry and bedraggled figure. The hunger and fatigue of the Gila expedition had reduced him to little more than skin and bones. His hair hung round his shoulders, matted and uncombed. His head was covered by an old straw hat. Leather hunting shirt and leather leggings, tattered, torn, and stiff with dirt and grease, completed his attire. But the girl's affection and her father's hospitality were proof even against such disreputable trappings, and the two welcomed him, probably literally as well as figuratively, with wide-open arms.

Pattie completed his mission successfully, returned to Santa Rita, and outfitted the new expedition to the Gila; but the expense and effort went for little. Upon reaching the site of the buried furs, the party found the principal cache broken open and its contents gone. So, except for a few skins in another hiding-place, the trappers had nothing to show for their many months of hunger, danger, and hardship.

After his empty-handed return to Santa Rita, James Ohio and his father remained several months at the copper works, overseeing the mining operations and protecting the settlement from raids by the Apache Indians. The latter, though almost constantly at war with the Spaniards and Mexicans along the Rio Grande, then looked on the Americans as friends, and the chiefs of the nearest tribe willingly agreed to meet with Sylvester Pattie to negotiate a treaty. Four chiefs and upwards of eighty tribesmen attended the palaver. When, after endless speeches, a simple peace had been agreed upon, one of the chiefs lighted a pipe and passed it twice around the circle.

"They then dug a hole in the ground in the center of the circle," wrote Pattie, in describing the ceremony, "and each one spat in it. They then filled it up with earth, danced around it, and stuck their arrows in the little mound. They then gathered a large pile of stones over it, and painted themselves red. . . . We asked them the meaning of the spitting. They said, that they did it in token of spitting out all their spite and revenge, and burying their anger under the ground." [9]

But, in spite of these friendly professions, the owner of the Santa Rita mines continued distrustful of the

[9] Ibid., pp. 114–15.

Apaches and finally proposed to lease the property to the Americans for five years at the low figure of a thousand dollars a year. Sylvester Pattie accepted the offer and took over the management of the mines.

The agreement offered the Patties the promise of a fortune. But James Ohio still had itching feet or, as Flint expressed it in his stilted language, the boy possessed an "irresistible propensity to resume the employment of trapping." So, in spite of his father's counsel and persuasion, James Ohio joined an expedition, which he designated simply as a party of "French trappers," to undertake the long trip down the Gila River to the Colorado.

A quarter of a century ago J. J. Hill cleverly put many scattered bits of evidence together to show that the actual leader of this company was Miguel Robidoux, a member of a famous fur-trading family of St. Louis and a mountain man of distinction in his own right. The expedition left Santa Rita on January 2, 1826, if Pattie's chronology is correct, crossed the high plateau lands of New Mexico and Arizona to the Gila, regained some of the horses, furs, and other property that the Pattie company had lost to the Indians the year before, and traveled on to the country of the Papagos. These Indians had a large village at the junction of the Salt and Gila rivers, and there the company prepared to spend the night.

Suspecting treachery on the part of the Papagos, Pattie opposed the plan and violently criticized Robidoux for his naïve confidence in the Indians' professions of friendship and hospitality. When his protests were ignored, he and another trapper, whom he had known in St. Louis, withdrew from the company and made camp outside the limits of the Indian village.

In a few hours Pattie's worst fears were realized. About midnight the Indians fell upon the visitors while they lay asleep or found their pleasure with the women of the village, and killed all but Robidoux. Badly clubbed about the head, the wounded leader managed to evade his attackers in the dark and escape into the open country beyond the village. The following morning, almost dead from thirst and fever, he wandered into the narrow defile in which Pattie and his companion had taken refuge.

Unknown to the three survivors, a second trapping party from New Mexico happened to be in the vicinity. Its leader, Ewing Young, was one of the two or three most competent mountain men who operated out of Santa Fe, and a number of such famous trappers as "Peg-leg" Smith, George Yount, and Milton Sublette were among the company's personnel. A dramatic passage in Pattie's *Narrative* tells of the meeting of the three refugees with this band:

When it became dark, we descried three fires close together, which we judged to be those of savages in pursuit of us. . . . We concluded that my companion and myself should leave our wounded companion to take care of the horses, and go and reconnoitre the camp, in which were these fires, and discover the number of the Indians, and if it was great, to see how we could be most likely to pass them unobserved. When we arrived close to the fires, we discovered a considerable number of horses tied, and only two men guarding them. We crawled still closer, to be able to discern their exact number and situation.

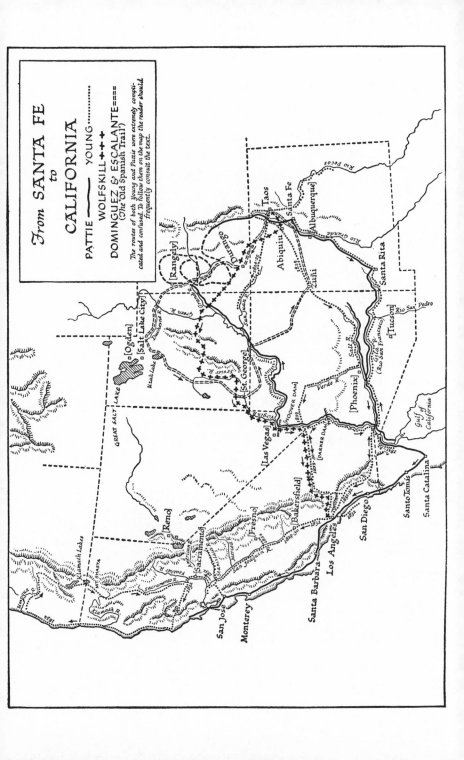

From SANTA FE
to
CALIFORNIA

PATTIE ——
WOLFSKILL +++
DOMINGUEZ & ESCALANTE ===
(The "Old Spanish Trail")
YOUNG ·········

The routes of both Young and Pattie were extremely compli-
cated and confused. To follow them on the map the reader should
frequently consult the text.

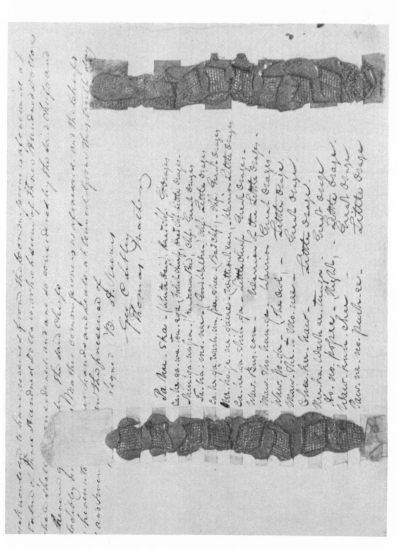

Treaty with the Osage Indians: August 10, 1825

In this way we arrived within fifty yards of their camp, and could see no one, but the two, any where in the distance. We concluded, that all the rest of the company were asleep in some place out of our view. We presumed it would not be long before some of them would awake, it being now ten at night. Our intention was to take aim at them, as they should pass between us and their fire, and drop them both together. We could distinctly hear them speaking about their horses. At length one of them called to the other, in English, to go and wake their relief guards. Words would poorly express my feelings, at hearing these beloved sounds. I sprang from my couching posture, and ran towards them. They were just ready to shoot me, when I cried "a friend, a friend!" One of them exclaimed, "where in God's name did you spring from." "You seem to have come out of the earth." The surprise and joy upon mutual recognition was great on both sides. I gave him a brief sketch of the recent catastrophe of our company, as we followed them to camp.[10]

Young's company, now numbering some thirty-three men, immediately made plans to attack the Papago village. By a simple strategem the trappers enticed the Indians into an ambush, killed many of their warriors, burned the village, recovered much of the plunder the savages had taken, and buried the dismembered and horribly mutilated bodies of Robidoux's men. "A sight more horrible . . . I have never seen," wrote Pattie of the victims. "They were literally cut in pieces, and fragments of their bodies scattered in every direction."

The trappers now left the Gila River and turned up the Salt, a stream bordered on both sides by rich, arable land

---

[10] Ibid., pp. 127–8.

and well supplied with beaver. At the junction of the Verde and the Salt the company divided. One party, passing through a region that was to yield fabulous riches in copper to the pioneers of a later generation, trapped the Verde to its source in the high mountains southwest of the present town of Williams, Arizona. The rest of the trappers, including Pattie, followed the Salt River to its headwaters in the White Mountains of northeastern Arizona, near the present New Mexican boundary line.

As the latter company moved up the river, the alluvial bottom lands, with their inviting stretches of cool, green cottonwoods, gave place to bold, rough mountains, criss-crossed by innumerable barrancas and covered with chaparral, mesquite, and juniper. Above these arid, semi-desert levels the character of the country again changed, and the trappers found themselves in a magnificent forest of pine, oak, spruce, and aspen, a region of green meadows, clear running streams, and cloud-reflecting lakes.

After a successful hunt both parties returned to the junction of the Verde and Salt rivers. The reunited company then followed the Salt to its near-by union with the Gila and trapped down the latter to the Colorado. Here the Americans had their first contact with the Yuma Indians, a people whom Pattie describes as "the stoutest men, with the finest forms I ever saw, well proportioned . . . as straight as an arrow," and "as naked as Adam and Eve in their birthday suit."

The trappers had no difficulty, apparently, on this visit with the Yuma Indians; but as they moved up the Colorado, taking sometimes as many as thirty beaver in a single night, the Americans reached the territory of the unpredictable Mojaves. If Pattie's chronology is correct, Young's arrival must have antedated by several months the visit of Jedediah Smith in the fall of 1826. But many of Pattie's dates are contradictory and unreliable, and there is reasonable ground to believe that Young's company, instead of preceding Smith, reached the Mojave villages *between* the latter's first and second California expeditions. In any event, Young's party enjoyed none of the hospitality that Smith received from the Mojaves on his initial visit.

Stopping three miles above the first of the Indian villages, Young saw signs of growing hostility among the Mojaves and erected a breastwork of cottonwood logs and packs of beaver skins to protect his camp. As the day wore on, the Indians became more and more truculent, until a defiant Mojave chief at last began hostilities by spearing one of the trapper's grazing horses. Four of Young's men immediately shot the Indian dead.

The grim battle was now on. Strengthening their barricade and posting lookouts in the tops of the highest cottonwoods, the trappers waited for the Indians to open the attack in force. But the enemy followed the characteristic Mojave pattern and reserved his assault for the hour before dawn. Young's men were prepared for this eventuality, however, and the Mojaves, with their bows, arrows, and war clubs, were no match for the expert riflemen. Sixteen Indians were killed in the attack.

Young then resumed his march up the river, unmolested further by the Mojaves. At the end of four days, assuming that they were well out of hostile territory, the weary men made camp and fell asleep without posting a sufficient guard. This was a tragic blunder. Keeping out of sight by day and creeping close to the enemy's camp at night, the Mojaves had followed the unsuspecting trappers all the long way, only waiting for their hour of revenge. Now their opportunity had come. Crawling within easy bowshot in the dark, they poured a shower of poisoned arrows into the sleeping and unguarded camp. The deadly flints killed two of the trappers and wounded two others. Pattie escaped death by something less than the skin of his teeth. His bed-fellow was killed beside him. Two arrows went through his own hunting shirt. Sixteen arrows transfixed his blanket and pinned it fast to the ground.

When daylight came, a force of eighteen grim-faced trappers set out to avenge their dead companions. A little before dark they caught up with a band of the Mojaves who had killed a horse and stopped to have an evening feast. Warned of the enemy's approach, the Indians broke and ran for the brush; but the mounted trappers overtook many of the stragglers before they could find cover and rode or shot them down without mercy. The whites then hung the bodies of the slain Mojaves on the limbs of the cottonwood trees and left them "to dangle in terror to the rest."

To prevent further Indian attacks, Young divided his men into two groups. The first was given sole responsibility for trapping, the second for keeping guard. The plan not only lessened the risk of massacre but materially increased the catch of furs, and this, as Pattie once sagely remarked, was after all "the grand object of the enterprise.

Farther up the Colorado the trappers came to a stream,

later known as Bill Williams Fork, that flowed into the river from the east.[11] Three of Young's men undertook to reconnoiter this stream for signs of beaver. When the scouts failed to return, Young put a searching party on their trail. But the three were beyond all human aid. "At mid-day," wrote Pattie, "we found their bodies cut in pieces, and spitted before a great fire, after the same fashion which is used in roasting beaver. The Indians who had murdered them, saw us as we came on and fled to the mountains so that we had no chance of avenging the death of our unfortunate companions. We gathered the fragments of their bodies together and buried them."

Above Bill Williams Fork, near the site of the present Hoover Dam, the company was forced to keep along the crest of the stupendous Cañon of the Colorado, and for the next three hundred miles the weary men contended against snow, hunger, discouragement, and the appalling desolation of a region still best described as "a land where no man comes or hath come since the making of the world."

The route is too confused, uncertain, and contradictory for one to attempt to follow it with any degree of assurance or satisfaction. Apparently it ran along the south rim of the Colorado, and the trappers, unable anywhere to descend the almost sheer walls, looked down into the breath-taking cañon where, far, far below, the river shone like a ribbon of moving silver — tantalizing, inaccessible, lonely as the frozen surface of the moon. "A march more gloomy and heart-wearying," Pattie wrote in retrospect, "to people

---

11 Not far from the famous Parker Dam of the Metropolitan Water District of Southern California.

hungry, poorly clad, and mourning the loss of their companions, cannot be imagined."

At the place now known as Lee's Ferry, where the Mormon fugitive John D. Lee went into hiding after the Mountain Meadows Massacre, the walls of the Colorado gorge break down and for several miles it is possible to approach the river either by horseback or on foot; but the trappers apparently detoured around this accessible stretch of the Colorado without being aware of its existence.

A hundred miles above Lee's Ferry the turbulent San Juan — a river of sand waves, silt, and weird and lonely beauty — enters the cañon of the Colorado.[12] Unable to reach the junction of the two streams because of the sheer cañons and rough mountains, the trappers presumably turned east along the crest of the San Juan gorge and attempted to return to the settlements in New Mexico that they had left so many months before. But friendly Navajo Indians soon warned them not to attempt the passage of the rugged, snow-covered range that loomed like a wall against the eastern sky. So the trappers presumably crossed the San Juan, returned to the Colorado, and resumed their slow march along its rugged course.

Pattie's description of the route from this point on is almost worthless. He speaks vaguely of crossing the Rocky Mountain Divide through "a low gap" in the mountains — a gateway to the east that may or may not have been the

---

[12] A little above Lee's Ferry, at the Crossing of the Fathers, Domínguez and Escalante forded the Colorado on their return to Santa Fe in 1777. See Chapter 7 of this volume. Even now there are many beaver in the San Juan, but the half-starved trappers found it impossible to descend to the river.

famous South Pass — and finding it filled with hard-packed snow, higher than a rider's head, so that the trappers' horses were thankful to use a trail that wallowing buffalo had made through the deep drifts. From the *Narrative* it appears that the company then wandered over half the Rocky Mountains and set its traps on streams as widely separated as the South Fork of the Platte, the Big Horn, the Yellowstone, Clark's Fork of the Columbia, and the headwaters of the Arkansas.

A fight with roving Blackfeet on the Arkansas resulted in the death of four trappers and sixteen Indians. The company then crossed to the upper reaches of the Rio Grande and reached Santa Fe without further serious misadventure. All in all, the expedition had traversed some thousands of miles of wilderness, lost nearly a third of its number in conflicts with different Indian tribes, and brought back perhaps twenty thousand dollars' worth of beaver skins.

Again, however, official avarice at Santa Fe proved financially more costly to the trappers than all the vicissitudes and perils of the wilderness. The trouble rose when Don Manuel Armíjo, a newly appointed Governor with a marked anti-foreign bias, seized the party's hard-earned catch of furs (on the charge that the Americans had trapped without a license), and thereby raised a great hullabaloo in the city and created a *cause célèbre* whose echoes were faintly heard in both Mexico City and Washington.[13]

The Governor's action, like the Indians' earlier raid on

13 For further details of this incident, including Young's arrest, see Chapter 6.

his cache of furs on the Gila, left Pattie with nothing to show for his months of danger and privation on this second expedition. But the hospitality and affection of Jacova and her father, as he rode down the trail from Santa Fe to Santa Rita, provided a measure of compensation. Then, too, when he reached the copper mines everything was running smoothly. Production had increased, his father "was making money rapidly," and the outlook, from all standpoints, was encouraging.

The young trapper had every prudent reason to remain at Santa Rita and join his father in the enterprise; but his spirit was as restless as that of any desert nomad and he had no depth of root, even on the outskirts of the wilderness. Yielding to his roving instincts, he soon undertook a combined sightseeing and trading expedition into the Mexican provinces of Chihuahua and Sonora.

The venture carried him from the city of Chihuahua, the epitome of so much of the history, culture, economic life, and tradition of New Spain, through the rough borderlands of Chihuahua and Sonora, into the country of the Yaqui Indians (from whom he bought gold in lumps and bars for ten dollars an ounce), and as far west as the port of Guaymas on the Gulf of California. Pattie was a close observer, and the intimate contact he enjoyed with the country and its people gave his comments on Mexican life, customs, and institutions, though tinged by the characteristic prejudices of the American frontiersman, remarkable detail and understanding. His picture of the northern Mexican provinces less than a decade after Independence is not surpassed by any contemporary observer. Of Chihuahua, he wrote:

It is the largest and handsomest town I had ever seen, though the buildings are not so neat and well arranged as in our country. The roofs are flat, the walls well painted, and the streets kept very clean. Here they smelt and manufacture copper and silver, and several other metals. They have also a mint. The terms of their currency are very different from ours. They count eight rials, or sixteen four pence half pennies, to the dollar. Their merchandize is packed from Ymus, or Mexico. . . . During a stay of only three days here, ten dead bodies were brought into town, of persons who had been murdered in the night. . . . No inquest of any sort was held over the bodies. They were, however, paraded through the streets to beg money to pay the priests for performing funeral rites at their burial. This excited in me still more disgust, than the murders. . . . On the evening of 16th, I left this city, and travelled through a fine country, thickly inhabited by shepherds, who live in small towns, and possess a vast abundance of stock. It is well watered, but thinly timbered. The most magnificent part of the spectacle is presented in the lofty snow covered mountains, that rise far in the distance, and have their summits lost in the clouds, glistening in indescribable brilliance in the rays of the rising and setting sun.[14]

Like other Americans interested in such matters, Pattie found the Mexicans poor farmers and their farming implements "clumsy and indifferent." "They use oxen entirely in their agriculture," he wrote.

Their ploughs are a straight piece of timber, five feet long and eight inches thick, mortised for two other pieces of timber, one to be fitted to the beam, by which the oxen draw, and another to the handle, by which the man holds the plough.

---

[14] Pattie: *Personal Narrative,* pp. 153–4.

)oint that divides the soil, is of wood, and hewed sloping
⌄⌄ such a point, that a hollow piece of iron is fastened on it
at the end. This is one inch thick, and three inches broad at
top, and slopes also to a point.

Their hoes, axes and other tools are equally indifferent;
and they are precisely in such a predicament, as might be
expected of a people who have no saw mills, no labor saving
machinery, and do everything by dint of hard labor, and
are withal very indolent and unenterprising.[15]

Pattie's trading venture into the interior Mexican provinces proved profitable as well as interesting. Much of the
country was wild and lawless, but luck, courage, and precaution carried him safely through. Then, soon after his
return to Santa Rita, he had another characteristic hairs-
breadth escape. While hunting, he and a companion came
upon a large grizzly bear. Pattie's companion fired, but
the powder was damp, the gun "made long fire," and the
bullet hit the animal in the belly instead of in the head.
When the wounded bear charged, Pattie took careful aim
and fired. The powder flashed in the pan. The bear, then
only six feet away, rushed on with open mouth. Pattie
leaped desperately to one side, tumbled headlong over a
hidden precipice, struck his head on a large rock, and
cracked his jawbone. He regained consciousness to find
that his fellow hunter, in the role of amateur surgeon, had
cut "a considerable orifice" in his arm with a hunting knife
to bleed him. This treatment, Pattie dryly remarked, "I
deemed rather supererogation; for I judged, that I had
bled sufficiently at the chin." Having survived the fall, the

---

15 Ibid., p. 145.

broken jaw, and the bleeding, Pattie managed to regain enough strength to track down and kill the wounded bear!

But despite such injuries and excitement, the indefatigable adventurer grew tired of what he called "the stationary and unruffled sort of life" of the copper mines and soon joined a party of fifteen Americans in a trapping expedition to the Puerco River, one of the upper branches of the Rio Grande. A generation later, one of the members of Lieutenant Beale's expedition described the Puerco as "a small stream some five yards across, and the dirtiest thing that runs. Mules would not drink it." [16]

The river ran through the territory of the Mescalero Apaches — a matter of more importance to the trappers than its unattractive appearance — and the company soon found itself engaged in a serious engagement with those warlike people. Early in the fight an arrow struck Pattie in the hip. The shaft broke off, but the flint head shattered against the bone, and the fragments remained deeply embedded in the flesh. A few minutes later a second arrow buried its point in the muscles of Pattie's chest. He broke off the shaft, left the arrowhead in the wound, and continued in the fight.

Any American who cherishes the delusion that the Indian had a monopoly of the savagery of border warfare might profitably read Pattie's blunt account of the trappers' conduct when the Indians finally broke and ran. "They left their dead and wounded at our mercy," he grimly wrote. "Truth is, we were too much exasperated to

[16] [W. P.?] Floyd: "Diary of a Trip with Beale's Expedition," September 27, 1858 to May 1, 1859. Huntington Library, Grabhorn MS. No. 36.

show mercy, and we cut off the heads of all indiscriminately." [17]

According to Pattie, the Mescalero bows were the most powerful used by any of the Western Indians. The staves were made of a flexible wood and backed with buffalo or elk sinews. The arrows were of cane or reed, with an insertion of hard wood, tipped by an extremely sharp, inch-long flint arrowhead. As Pattie knew from his own experience, one of these arrowheads almost invariably shattered when it struck a large bone, and the removal of the splintered fragments was often too difficult an operation for the crude surgery of the plains to undertake.

Soon after their engagement with the Mescaleros, Pattie and his companions returned to the settlements, reaching Santa Fe in time to attend the grand fandango traditionally held on New Year's Eve. The Americans were dressed in the usual trapper style — deerskin hunting shirts, leggings, and moccasins, with red flannel loincloths, "not an article of which," wrote Pattie, "had been washed since we left the Copper Mines."

"It may be imagined," he continued, "that we did not cut a particular dandy-like figure, among people, many of whom were rich, and would be considered well dressed any where. Notwithstanding this, it is a strong proof of their politeness, that we were civilly treated by the ladies and had the pleasure of dancing with the handsomest and richest of them. When the ball broke up, it seemed to be expected of us, that we should each escort a lady home, in whose company we passed the night, and we none

[17] *Personal Narrative,* p. 163.

192

of us brought charges of severity against our fair companions."

It is not necessary to describe Pattie's further experiences in New Mexico in detail. He went on a mission for his father to purchase wine and whisky for the mines, and again almost lost his life when a friendly Apache, mistaking the sleeping American for a Spaniard, drove his spear into the ground so close to the unconscious man's neck that Pattie woke to feel the cold steel resting against his skin. Sylvester Pattie's mining, trading, and ranching operations proved so profitable that the far-traveled adventurers began to look forward to an early return to Missouri as well-to-do or even wealthy men. Then, without warning, their fortune, "like snow upon the desert's dusty face, lighting a little hour or two," was gone.

To meet the needs of the rapidly growing market at the mines, Sylvester Pattie entrusted thirty thousand dollars to his confidential clerk and manager (a versatile Spaniard who spoke Russian and English as well as Spanish) and instructed him to go to Santa Fe, or if necessary to St. Louis, to buy a large additional supply of goods.

Time went by and the accomplished gentleman did not return. More time went by, but there was still no word from the missing and now obviously defaulting agent. As a last resort, James Ohio followed the fugitive to Santa Fe, but there the trail vanished. Neither the Spaniard nor the money was ever seen by the Americans again.

The loss of their working capital compelled the Patties to give up their mining and trading activities at Santa Rita and return to trapping. With a passport, *guía* (or license), or perhaps merely a customs-house certificate from Santa Fe, permitting them to hunt in Mexican territory, the two joined an expedition that left New Mexico, probably in the fall of 1827, for the Gila-Colorado trapping-grounds. The Gila, by that time a familiar thoroughfare to American companies operating in the Southwest, was no longer the rich beaver stream of former years, so the party determined to push on directly to the Colorado.

Before leaving New Mexico, all the members of the expedition had signed a formal agreement to stay together, obey the decisions of the majority, and impose the death penalty, if necessary, on anyone who violated the terms of the compact. But friction and conflicting opinions now split the party. According to Pattie's *Narrative*, twenty trappers refused to follow his father and started at once for the Colorado, while the remaining eight continued down the Gila and reached the Yuma villages without serious misadventure. A somewhat different account of the incident, by an anonymous correspondent living in Los Angeles (probably J. J. Warner), appeared in the *Alta California*, a San Francisco newspaper, of July 2, 1865. This version read:

In the fall of 1827 a party of about 15 men, under Pattie as their leader, was made up in Taos, to trap the Gila river from its sources down to the Colorado. In this party was Mr. William Workman, a young Englishman, then and until 1841, living in New Mexico, and now of La Puenta rancho, in this county, and Mr. Yount of Napa. The elder Pattie was elected Captain of this party. Before reaching the mouth of the Gila, a majority of the men became so dissatisfied with their leader that a separation took place. A majority withdrew, and elected Mr. Workman as their leader. The two parties continued on down the Gila until they reached the Colorado, trapping beaver upon it for some distance above the mouth of the Gila, and downstream to tide-water. The party commanded by Mr. Workman returned to New Mexico. The Pattie party consisted of the eldest and youngest Pattie, Nathaniel Pryor, a silversmith, who for some time previous had been one of the lessees of the Santa Rita copper mines on a tributary of the Gila . . . and Richard Laughlin, both of whom settled, married and died in Los Angeles . . . Jesse Ferguson who settled and married in this place, but removed to Lower California where he died . . . Mr. Slover who subsequently returned to New Mexico, but afterwards came to California . . . and settled in San Bernardino, where he . . . lost his life in a private encounter with [a] . . . grizzly bear. . . .

After referring to the division of the party, Pattie made no further reference to the trappers under Workman who separated from his father's command, but continued the account of his own party's rapidly changing fortunes.

The Yuma Indians, who were in a friendly mood on his former visit, now showed themselves openly defiant. Taking advantage of the wind, rain, darkness, and thunder of a stormy night, they crept in among the tethered stock and stampeded the frightened horses. The loss was irreparable and left the trappers only one faint outlet of escape. Misled by signs and scraps of information gathered from the Indians into believing that the Colorado would carry them to the Spanish settlements of California, the refugees hastily hollowed out two cottonwood logs for canoes, put their furs and equipment on board, and started off down the muddy current.

But the last state of the imperiled men was worse than the first. Instead of bringing them to California, the river took them into an almost hopeless cul-de-sac. To the south lay the utterly lonely waters of the Gulf of California; the way to the east was barred by a wide, desolate waste; a desert even more terrible separated the Colorado delta from the Western coast.

Temporarily, however, the exiles' prospect was more encouraging. Running through a low, marshy delta, the river furnished such an ideal breeding-ground for beaver that the trappers took from thirty to sixty skins a night. The Indian menace, too, apparently had been left behind; but by accident one morning the trappers detected two Yuma bowmen concealed in the tops of some cottonwood trees overlooking the stream, waiting to pick off the canoemen as they floated past. "We betrayed no signs of having seen them," wrote Pattie, "but sat with our guns ready for a fair shot. When we had floated within a little short of a hundred yards, my father and another of the company gave them a salute, and brought them both tumbling down the branches, reminding us exactly of the fall of a bear or a turkey. They made the earth sound when they struck it." [18]

Shortly after this incident the trappers entered the territory of a friendly but unusually backward tribe that Pattie called the Cocopa. These Indians had no knowledge of whites, clothes, or firearms, and the arrival of the trappers threw them into a wild hysteria of fear. When this subsided, the savages welcomed the strangers with every sign of friendship and offered them a feast of stewed dog meat

---

[18] Pattie: *Personal Narrative*, p. 193.

as a special mark of hospitality. The Cocopa men, burned a dark brown by the fierce sunlight, were quick and alert, though much smaller in stature than the Yumas. Men and women alike went naked and the girls and younger women had figures of exquisite symmetry and grace. The night that the trappers spent in the village "passed away pleasantly," according to Pattie, "and to the satisfaction of all parties."

Down the river from the friendly Cocopas, the trappers found a village of hostile natives whom Pattie called the Pipi. These Indians, possibly members of the Piman family, had six-foot bows made of a tough, elastic wood, and used the usual cane arrow, carrying an inserted shaft of hard wood and a flint arrowhead.

Eighty miles below the mouth of the Gila, as Pattie estimated the distance with surprising accuracy, the inland voyageurs encountered the huge tidebore that drives up from the gulf with race-horse speed. The onrushing flood caught the inland-born trappers unaware, submerged their camp, soaked their baggage, nearly overturned their canoes, and threatened to drown the lot of them out of hand.

Unable to make further headway down the river, the trappers turned about and attempted, by paddling, poling, and the use of a makeshift cordelle, to fight their way upstream. But the crest of a late winter flood caught the canoes and made it impossible for the refugees to overcome the angry, silt-laden current. With all hope of escape either up or down the river thus cut off, the trappers cached their large supply of furs and set out on foot toward the west.

It is doubtful if the men had any conception of the extent or nature of the country that lay ahead. It was in truth an awful land. Even to this day most of it is shunned by human beings. Waste, waterless, and savage, it was then as lonely as chaos, as grim as Milton's Hell. To the forlorn wanderers who found themselves at the mercy of this land, the earth soon turned to iron and the sky to brass. Once, when they could go no farther, a spring of good, sweet water saved their lives. Then the sand and thirst grew worse. As a desperate expedient, some of the men began to drink their urine — thick, hot, and salt. Still the thirst grew worse, and still the eight went on.[19] Their tongues swelled, their lips turned black, their eyes sank back into their sockets, their bodies grew dry as sun-tanned beaver skins.

A painful blindness, induced by the blazing sun and white-hot sand, increased their misery. Sylvester Pattie and Isaac Slover lay down to die. One of the party attempted suicide. For miles, with the exception of one lone, thorny, shriveled little tree, they saw no life or sign of any living thing — bird, bush, animal, or grass. But "the Eternal Power," as Pattie gratefully wrote, "who hears the ravens when they cry, and provideth springs in the wilderness," had mercy upon the thirst-crazed men. At the foot of a hill they found a running stream.

Here the wanderers met a group of Christian Indians from the Mission of Santa Catalina, on the headwaters of the San Quentín River, in Lower California. It was only four days' travel to the site, but the trail ahead was still

---

[19] The party consisted of the two Patties, Richard Laughlin, Nathaniel Pryor, William Polk, Isaac Slover, Jesse Ferguson, and James Puter.

beset by tribulation. The trappers' deerskin moccasins were almost worn out, and as a result one of James Ohio's feet was badly bruised by the rocks and stones of the rugged trail. Infection set in, and the injured man became too lame to walk. So he was left behind to spend the night as best he could, though the region was badly infested with rattle-snakes, mountain lion, and grizzly bear. Fortunately the mission was not far away and the trappers reached it in a few hours and obtained help for their incapacitated com-panion. Two Indians, sent from the mission on foot, found James Ohio about midnight. Having no other means of con-veyance, the simple natives turned themselves into pack horses and carried the grumbling trapper home on their backs.

If the half-dead trappers expected a royal welcome at Santa Catalina, they were quickly disillusioned. Both civil and ecclesiastical authorities regarded the strangers as spies and interlopers and placed them under arrest. After a week's confinement in the guardhouse, the trappers were sent under military escort to the Mission of San Sebastian, about a day's journey from Santa Catalina. There, after they had suffered some preliminary unpleasantness at the hands of subordinate officials, the sergeant of the guard took them in charge, treated and fed them well, and made life in general rather comfortable in what Pattie called that "strange and charming country." Early in April 1828, according at least to Pattie's calendar, the company started under military guard over the rough trail dignified by the name of El Camino Real for San Diego. Brief stops were made en route at the Mission Santo Tomás, the port of

Todos Santos, the Mission of San Miguel, and several intermediate ranches.

José María Echeandía, whose recent dealings with Jedediah Smith left something to be desired, was still Governor of the province and unluckily then at San Diego. Pattie portrayed him as an arbitrary, cruel, vacillating, and cowardly official. The picture was doubtless overdrawn, but the Governor's unsavory reputation among the Californians themselves lends some color to the charges.

According to Pattie, Echeandía looked upon the Americans as "worse than thieves and murderers," charged them with spying on the land for Spain, tore up their passports, took away their arms, and confined them in separate cells in the guardhouse. "My prison," wrote Pattie, "was a cell eight or ten feet square, with walls and floor of stone. A door with iron bars an inch square crossed over each other, like the bars of window sashes, and it grated on its iron hinges, as it opened to receive me. On the external front of this prison was inscribed in capital letters *Destinación de la Cattivo.*"

As a partial alleviation of Echeandía's harsh treatment, a sergeant of the guard named Pico substituted decent food for the usual loathsome prison fare and allowed the prisoners to keep their blankets. But imprisonment, despite these special favors, was galling enough, both physically and psychologically, to the younger trappers. For Sylvester Pattie it was fatal. Worn out by long-sustained hardships and suspense, still suffering from his collapse in the desert, and now confined in a wretched Mexican jail, the elder Pattie sickened presently and died.

With his father's death, James Ohio's cup of grief, hatred, and bitterness overflowed. The kindness of Captain
John Bradshaw and Rufus Perkins, master and supercargo
respectively of the New England ship *Franklin,* and frequent visits of a charming and devoted California señorita,
probably the sister of Sergeant Pico, whom the *Narrative*
refers to simply as "Miss Peaks," were almost his only
source of comfort.

Week succeeded week, while James Ohio wrangled with
Governor Echeandía; and Captain Bradshaw, moved by a
mixture of Yankee shrewdness and generous instincts, tried
to persuade the Governor to allow the trappers to recover
the valuable cache of furs they had left on the Colorado.[20]
Echeandía finally agreed to Bradshaw's proposal, but in-
sisted on keeping Pattie in prison as a hostage for the good
faith of his companions.

The quest for the skins was futile. By the time the trappers reached the Colorado, the spring rise, against which
they had repeatedly warned Echeandía, was at its height
and the river had overflowed the site of the cache and
ruined the furs. According to the *Narrative,* two members
of the party that went to salvage the skins deserted at the
Colorado, but the rest returned to San Diego.

Pattie, whom Echeandía still kept in jail, finally obtained his freedom in a curious and unexpected fashion. A
devastating plague of smallpox — one of the periodic
curses of early California — had recently broken out in
the province, and the Indians of the missions, ranchos, and

---

[20] Bradshaw presumably had arranged to buy the furs from the trappers
for shipment to New England in the *Franklin.*

pueblos (with almost no inherited or acquired immunity to the disease) were dying off in alarming numbers. The mestizo Californians were also hard hit, and neither provincial nor mission authorities were able to combat the epidemic. In the midst of this crisis, Echeandía learned that Pattie had a limited supply of smallpox vaccine, which his father had brought with him from the copper mines, and that the trapper knew the technique of vaccination.

Alternating threat with persuasion, Echeandía then tried to induce Pattie to immunize the inhabitants of San Diego; but the prisoner refused to perform a single vaccination until he and his companions were guaranteed their liberty. One stormy interview followed another, while the plague drew nearer and nearer to San Diego and week by week the reports of its virulence grew more alarming. Unwilling to risk the danger of a province-wide calamity any longer, Echeandía finally agreed to Pattie's not unreasonable terms and let the last of the Americans, most of whom were probably already at liberty, go free. The trappers then separated, but a majority elected to remain in California.

With Echeandía's blessing, and the promise of a fee of a dollar a head for each vaccination, Pattie assumed the role of surgeon extraordinary to the Governor and set out on his novel medical crusade. His *carta de seguridad,* or letter of safe conduct, read:

Whereas, Santiago Ohio Pattie, who came into this territory hunting beaver in company with other foreigners, without any license whatever, in March of the past year, appears to be a North American according to a custom-house permit given in New Mexico; and whereas, the commandante of this place reports him not to be vicious but of regular conduct, in the petition presented by Pattie on the 27th of this month for permission to travel and remain in the country, there being no consul nor mercantile agent of his nation, nor any Mexican bondsman, therefore I have determined to grant him provisionally this letter of security, that he may remain and travel in this territory for one year. . . .[21]

Pattie's commission took him to every mission, presidio, and pueblo between San Diego and the Russian fort of Bodega north of San Francisco. In each of these centers of population, patients came to him by the hundreds, so that his grand tour resulted in the inoculation of nearly twenty-four thousand persons. His descriptions of California scenes and places, though unreliable in many details, are surprisingly accurate in their essential features. Two of these will serve as examples of the rest. He wrote of the Mission of San Luis Rey:

This is said to be the largest, most flourishing, and every way the most important mission on the coast. For its consumption fifty beeves are killed weekly. The hides and tallow are sold to ships for goods, and other articles for the use of the Indians, who are better dressed in general than the Spaniards. All the income of the mission is placed in the hands of the priests, who give out clothing and food, according as it is required. They are also self constituted guardians of the female part of the mission, shutting up under lock and key, one hour after supper, all those, whose husbands are absent, and all young women and girls above nine years of age. Dur-

---

[21] H. H. Bancroft: *History of California,* Vol. III, p. 168 n.

Pattie's supply of vaccine was of course replenished from some of his inoculated patients.

ing the day, they are entrusted to the care of the matrons. Notwithstanding this, all the precautions taken by the vigilant fathers of the church are found insufficient. I saw women in irons for misconduct, and men in the stocks. . . . They are taught in the different trades; some of them being blacksmiths, others carpenters and shoe-makers. Those, trained to the knowledge of music, both vocal and instrumental, are intended for the service of the church. The women and girls sew, knit, and spin wool upon a large wheel, which is woven into blankets by the men. . . . This mission is composed of parts of five different tribes, who speak different languages.[22]

In a brief description of Los Angeles, "called the town of The Angels," Pattie wrote:

The houses have flat roofs, covered with bituminous pitch, brought from a place within four miles of the town, where this article boils up from the earth.[23] As the liquid rises, hollow bubbles like a shell of a large size, are formed. When they burst, the noise is heard distinctly in the town. The material is obtained by breaking off portions, that have become hard, with an axe, or something of the kind. The large pieces thus separated, are laid on the roof, previously covered with earth, through which the pitch cannot penetrate, when it is rendered liquid again by the heat of the sun. In this place I vaccinated 2,500 persons.[24]

Pattie's career as a doctor ended in a grand financial debacle. Instead of the substantial monetary payment he expected to receive from the California mission authorities,

---

[22] *Personal Narrative*, pp. 275–6.
[23] The famous "brea pits" of Hancock Park, near Wilshire Boulevard, now known to paleontologists throughout the world.
[24] *Personal Narrative*, p. 278.

he was tendered a tract of land, a thousand head of cattle, and some other livestock; and the offer was made only on condition that he become a Mexican citizen and a member of the Catholic Church. These unexpected terms exhausted the small remnants of the trapper's patience and touched off his hair-trigger temper. In a violent outburst he denounced priest, church, and government, rejected the offer of the father-president of the missions, and returned in a great huff to Monterey. There he boarded an American ship and spent the next several months sailing up and down the coast.

In the meantime popular discontent against Governor Echeandía had culminated in the first of California's many revolutions. The leader of the movement, an ex-convict named Joachím Solís, had little to commend him either to native Californians or to Americans; but Pattie's hatred of Echeandía led him to join the movement and march with the tatterdemalion band of *insurrectos* as far south as Santa Barbara. By the time the company reached that presidio, however, he had come to the conclusion that Solís was as much of a petty tyrant as Echeandía and even more hostile toward all foreigners in California.

So he and his fellow Americans had a change of heart, incontinently abandoned Solís, and went over to Echeandía. They next proceeded to render their recent comrades-in-arms completely *hors de combat* by a generous distribution of free rum throughout the insurgent ranks and finally wound up by capturing Solís and his personal bodyguard and handing them over to the Governor.

Following the collapse of the Solís revolution, Pattie returned to Monterey and there found John C. Jones, the American Consul at Honolulu, who had befriended him during his prison days in San Diego. On Jones's advice, Pattie decided to visit Mexico City and present a claim for damages to the Mexican government.

"He advised me to make out a correct statement of the value of furs I had lost by the general's detention of me," wrote the stranded trapper, "and also of the length of time I had been imprisoned, and to take it with me to the city of Mexico, where the American minister resided, and place it in his hands. It was probable, the consul continued, that he would be able to compel the Mexican government to indemnify me for the loss of property I had sustained, and for the injustice of my imprisonment." [25]

While waiting for a vessel to take him down the coast, Pattie found time to attend a fiesta at the Mission of San Carlos and later to engage in a profitable sea-otter hunt with an unnamed Portuguese companion. This, so far as we know, was Pattie's last venture after furs. He eventually sailed for San Blas in the *Volunteer*. The ship carried a number of other passengers whom Pattie had known at a more auspicious time. Below decks, fastened to a long iron bar in the vessel's hold, Joachím Solís and sixteen miserable fellow conspirators meditated on the fickleness of fortune and speculated on the outcome of their fate at the hands of the Mexican officials.

Pattie reached Mexico City in June 1830, and placed his claims in the hands of Anthony Butler, American Chargé

[25] Ibid., pp. 298–9.

d'Affaires in the troubled republic. Butler presented his countryman to President Vicente Guerrero, and the latter gave him a courteous and attentive interview. Showing genuine surprise when Pattie described his experiences in California, the President replied that he had already recalled Echeandía because of his arbitrary conduct in the province.

Whether Guerrero's sympathies for Pattie's wrongs were really sincere or a mere expression of Mexican courtesy, the tangible outcome was the same. The chronically bankrupt Mexican treasury had no funds, Guerrero himself was soon to become a victim of another revolution, and Pattie never received a farthing in satisfaction of his claims.

Before sailing from Mexico, Pattie wrote this simple but revealing letter to his former companions in suffering and misfortune who had chosen to remain in California:

Mexico
June 14th. 1830.
Dear friends I arived at St. Blas on the Eighteenth of may In good health and obtain [retain] it till this date and hope these linse will find you all enjoying the Same I Still remain with capt. Hinkley we Start to morrow to barrercruss [Vera Cruz] to embark for New York as I find kernal Butler only a charge of affars and cannot do any thing in our behalf tho advise [he advised] me to go on to the united States and Seek redress thar her they think it is imposable for us to recover any thing tho the charge of affairs advise[s] me to lay it befor the presidin of the united States

M: Lothlin [Laughlin] kernal Butler said that your parrants had herd of your arrest in the California and was much affected and was Desirous to See or hear from you Capt.

cooper you will pleas to forwed this Letter on to M.ʳ pryor in the puavlo [pueblo]

Give my respects to all in quiring friends may god bless you all

Your evr well-wisher

James O Pattie [26]

Pattie finally took ship at Vera Cruz for New Orleans and reached his family's old home in Kentucky, an impoverished, bitter, lonely man.

With the publication of Pattie's remarkable *Narrative* by Timothy Flint of Cincinnati, the far-venturing Kentuckian drops almost completely out of sight. According to William Waldo, he was a student for a time at Augusta College in Kentucky. To this brief statement Waldo adds: "This man . . . left my camp in the Sierra Nevada Mountains, amidst the deep snows of the terrible winter of 1849–50; and his sister, whom I met in Missouri eleven years after, said that was the last account she ever received concerning him. I suppose he perished in the deep snows, or was killed by Indians." [27]

It was fitting that darkness and oblivion should thus mark the hapless adventurer's tragic end.

[26] Photostat reproduction from the Bancroft Library: Vallejo Documents 30:85 (new styling).

[27] William Waldo: "Recollections of a Septuagenarian," loc. cit., p. 80.

CHAPTER 6

"Joaquin Yong" and the Men of Taos

THE PERIOD between 1825 and 1832, covered so dramatically in James Ohio Pattie's narrative, witnessed a rapid expansion of the trade between Missouri, Santa Fe, and Chihuahua; the heavy exploitation of the beaver streams of the Southwest; and the opening of an extensive traffic between New Mexico and California.

Hundreds of traders and trappers — the exact number will never be known — crossed the Mexican border with or without passports, paused for a few days (or a lifetime) at Taos or Santa Fe, continued their traffics and discoveries into Chihuahua, Sonora, and Durango, fanned out to the west as far as the Pacific; or, turning to the north, completed the grand circuit back to the Missouri settlements by way of the Green River Valley, the headwaters of the Missouri, the Platte, and the Missouri.[1] Many of these for-

[1] The Huntington Library has an original MS. record book of the passports presented by foreigners coming to Santa Fe between August 1828 and October 22, 1836, and the passports issued at Santa Fe to traders and trappers during the same period. There were over 170 passports, but many of them applied to groups or small companies rather than to individuals. The names of many prominent fur traders and merchants are on this list. Others equally well known are conspicuous by their absence. There is a similar list prepared at Taos for November 1825. RI 108 and 113.

eigners became Mexican citizens. The list included Juan Rowland, distinguished later in the history of southern California, Carlos Beaubien, Antoine and Louis Robidoux, José Ricardo Campbell, one of the most important of the trapper merchants, William Wolfskill, mentioned at length in a later chapter, "Dr. Ceran Sambrano," better known as Céran St. Vrain, David Waldo, "of Efigenia," or Virginia, and various and sundry gentlemen "from Quintoqui," or Kentucky. Naturalization, at least as illustrated by the case of David Waldo, one of the most important of the Santa Fe traders, involved a long and somewhat burdensome procedure.

In a petition addressed to the Illustrious Ayuntamiento of San Geronimo de Taos, Waldo declared that he left his native state, "Efigenia," in 1828, and the same year reached Taos with some fellow Americans, properly equipped with passports, to engage in trading-operations. Before the end of the year he had developed such a profound admiration for the Mexican government that he desired to settle in Taos and live permanently under the laws, customs, and manners of the republic. With these objects in view, he appeared before the Ayuntamiento of Taos and orally announced "to their Excellencies" that it was his intention to establish residence in the country. "That I am a Roman Catholic — a fact of which I am proud," Waldo added, "may be ascertained through the declaration made by the reverend father, for I was baptized this year of 1831 in this curate (parish) of San Geronimo."

The declaration then went on to say that, after taking the above steps, Waldo, like other Mexican citizens, had "helped preserve the security of the nation and the upkeep of an ecclesiastical minister" and that he had reliable witnesses to testify to the truth of his statements.

"I, of course, renounce allegiance and obedience to any other nation or foreign government, especially the one to which I belonged," Waldo then affirmed, "as well as any title, decoration, or award, which I may have received, and bind myself to support effectively the constitution, decrees, and general laws of the United States of Mexico." In conclusion he requested the Ayuntamiento to send the necessary documents, including a statement as to his character and means of livelihood, to the Governor and ask His Excellency to issue the desired naturalization papers.

A special session of the Ayuntamiento was held in the public hall on July 12, 1831 to consider Waldo's request and receive the testimony of his supporting witnesses. At the conclusion of the hearing, the council drafted a report declaring that the statement of the reverend father proved that Waldo was a Christian; that his ability and industry as a merchant, attested by reliable witnesses, assured him of a decent livelihood; and that "his character and the way he has conducted himself and conducts himself is generally known to be politically, socially, and religiously upright and restrained." In the light of these facts, the Ayuntamiento authorized the president and secretary to send a formal report approving Waldo's application for Mexican citizenship to the Governor.[2]

Trapping, as distinct from trading, remained a major

---

[2] Huntington Library, RI 234. Waldo's petition to the Governor is dated June 12, 1831. RI 126.

activity of the Americans in New Mexico until at least the mid-thirties. As early as 1826, James Baird, companion of the 1812 adventurers Robert McKnight and Samuel Chambers, and now a Mexican citizen, indignantly protested against the encroachments of the foreign interlopers on Mexican territory. Declaring that beaver skins to an estimated value of one hundred thousand dollars were taken annually from Mexican territory by Anglo-American trappers, he charged that these trappers disregarded the laws of the republic, defied its authorities, treated the Mexican nation with arrogance and contempt, and said openly that, in spite of laws and regulations to the contrary, they would hunt beaver wherever they pleased.

In conclusion Baird protested that he made his complaint not primarily to protect his own interests as a trapper, though these were being jeopardized by a flood of lawless Americans, but for the sake "of the honor and general welfare of the nation" of which he had gratefully become a part. He therefore besought His Excellency to take steps to see that the national laws were protected, that foreigners were held within prescribed bounds, and that "we Mexicans may peacefully profit by the goods with which the merciful God has been pleased to enrich our soil. . . ." [3]

Baird's protest stirred up a hornets' nest. Letters were dispatched from Mexico declaring that the Governor of New Mexico had no authority to issue trapping licenses to aliens, warning local frontier officials to be on their guard against the illegal entry of foreigners into their ter-

---

[3] Thomas Maitland Marshall: "St. Vrain's Expedition to the Gila in 1826," *Southwestern Historical Quarterly*, Vol. XIX, No. 3, pp. 256–7.

ritory, and advising them to take new measures to prevent beaver-trapping by the Americans.

Manuel Armíjo, Governor of New Mexico, pointed out that these interlopers had already taken most of the beaver from the rivers of the country without contributing a cent of profit to the nation; that Pratte and other Americans who were engaged solely in trapping had invested thirty thousand pesos in the business, "which must offer them great profit if they are willing to risk an initial outlay of such magnitude"; and that he had certain Americans under surveillance against whom he would move as soon as they left Taos or Santa Fe.

Armíjo added that one of the suspects, Tomas Boggs, was planning to hunt beaver on the rivers of California; but that he, the Governor, would send men to overtake the law-defying alien and seize his traps as soon as he started for the forbidden territory. In the end, however, Armíjo's plan misfired. Boggs disappeared into the wilderness and the commander charged with making the arrest came back empty-handed.[4]

Boggs became involved with the law a second time for trapping the Gila and Colorado without a license and in this case a number of skins were confiscated by the Santa Fe officials. But Boggs had a good alibi, as the following document attests:

At San Geronimo de Taos, on the 16th day of May, 1828, there appeared before me, Vicente Truxillo, Alcalde . . . the North American citizen, naturalized in this jurisdiction,

---

[4] Mexico, General Archives, Secretariat of Government, Expediente No. 45.

Jose Tomas Bo[ggs] requesting that I take down a deposition from the citizen Ramon Vigil, whom I summoned . . . and on being asked if he knew how the said Tomas Boggs had acquired the beaver skins which they confiscated from him at Santa Fe . . . he said that he joined the above-mentioned gentleman at the junction of the Gila and Rio Grande and he noticed that Boggs was bringing horses which he had bought in Sonora . . . that Boggs did not have with him any traps or other instruments with which to catch beaver . . . that the skins seized from him were bought from . . . Manuel Hurtado, six from him and six from Juan José Garcia . . . and another four from Julian. . . . The witness then stated he had nothing further to declare.

[Signed]   Ramon Vigil
[Attested by]   Vicente Truxillo.[5]

In the light of the above facts, the Alcalde of Santa Fe decided that Vigil and Boggs had come by the skins lawfully, through purchase from Mexican citizens rather than by their own efforts, and that the confiscated furs should be restored to them.

As a result of these and many other unpunished violations, local officials hastened to point out that the prohibition on beaver-trapping was useless without sufficient troops to pursue the foreigners and that the Americans laughed at government regulations and mocked at Mexican officials because the department's military force was too weak and poorly equipped to make the law respected.

Even the Sonoran frontier was alerted against the foreign intruders. From Arispe, José Figueroa, later Governor of California, warned the commandant of the presidio of

---

[5] New Mexican Archives (Huntington Library, Microfilm).

Tucson to be on guard against their coming and to advise the Indians of the Gila River that they must notify Figueroa if the trappers visited their villages. As to his own procedure, Figueroa was decidedly in the dark. "I inform your Excellency of all this," he wrote to the Secretary of State, as well as to the Secretary of War, "for your better knowledge and also that you may advise me as to what I must do in case the aliens should penetrate furtively into our Territory." [6]

Though Baird's protest against the activities of his sometime fellow citizens thus led to the writing of many letters and the circulation of numerous warnings, the American trappers continued their activities on the Gila, the Colorado, and other rivers of the Southwest, with additional caution possibly, but apparently with no lessening of activity or zeal.

Among such trappers — indeed, among all those who engaged in the Santa Fe trade or visited the beaver streams of the Southwest — none deserves more favorable recognition at the hands of the historian than Ewing Young. In one respect, however, Young did history a great disservice. He apparently kept no journals of any of his expeditions, left nothing in the way of a biographical sketch, nor dictated a line of reminiscences. None of the traders and trappers out of Santa Fe traveled farther or to better purpose than this "intelligent, industrious, and scrupulously honest" representative of the Tennessee frontier. But our knowledge of his character and activities comes only from fragmentary personal letters, a few public documents, and the writings

---

[6] Ibid.

and reports of others. Because of this incomplete and shadowy background, Young's fame has been eclipsed by that of lesser men, and the literature of the Southwest deprived of an extraordinarily colorful, important, and adventurous chapter.

Young went to Santa Fe with the original Becknell expedition of 1821 and for the next fourteen years served as merchant, trapper, trader, and explorer in the wild border provinces of Mexico. He died in 1841 in the midst of the great forests and green fields of western Oregon — an honored citizen whose influence on the fate of that disputed land was second only to the zeal of the missionaries and the impact of the great company whose charter ran to the "Governor and Company of Adventurers of England Trading into Hudson's Bay."

A powder-maker named Ferrel probably persuaded Young to make his first trip to Santa Fe to manufacture powder for the Mexican government. Because of lack of niter in the country, the venture failed and Young abandoned the undertaking and returned to Missouri. A year later, however, he joined Becknell's second expedition, and for the next few years made frequent trips between the American frontier and the Mexican settlements.

One of Young's companions in the second Becknell caravan was William Wolfskill, a young Kentuckian, destined to become almost as distinguished in the annals of the Southwest as Young himself. Upon reaching Santa Fe, the two formed a partnership to trap the Pecos River, a comparatively near-by tributary of the Del Norte or Rio Grande, which had not as yet been overrun by trappers.

A few months later the partners extended their trapping-operations as far west as the San Juan River. Formed by two major tributaries, one of which rises in New Mexico and the other in Colorado, the San Juan flows from the eastern boundary of Utah across a brooding, desolate waste, to enter the still older channel of the Colorado. Cut through timeless ages by silt-laden waters — "too thick to drink, too thin to plow" — the gorge of the San Juan and its rapids are only less spectacular than those of the Grand Cañon. Quick-forming sand waves, three or four feet high, the peculiar possession of this strange, sinister, but fascinating stream, add still another hazard to the river's perilous navigation.[7]

After reaching the San Juan, the Young-Wolfskill party broke up into small bands, and as the trapping season progressed, these continued to divide still further until at last only Wolfskill and Isaac Slover remained with Ewing Young.[8] At the end of the season the trappers returned to Santa Fe with furs worth approximately ten thousand dollars. Young immediately organized a second company to return to the same region. The party consisted of some sixty men, an unusually large venture for that early date, but no further record of the expedition is available.

Upon his return from this expedition Young apparently made a hurried trip to St. Louis to replenish his stock of

---

[7] The trappers followed the crest of the gorge, descending to the water only at long intervals, instead of attempting to navigate the river.

[8] Slover was an important member of the Santa Fe expedition of Colonel Hugh Glenn and Jacob Fowler in 1821. His part in the Pattie expedition and his subsequent death in California are mentioned in Chapter 5.

merchandise. On April 11, 1825, according to the records of the customshouse of Santa Fe, he paid duty on four bundles, or mule-loads, of goods with an appraised value of over fifteen hundred pesos.[9] His activities from 1826 to 1834 can be conjectured (but not definitely traced) from occasional items in official Mexican documents and references in the accounts of other trappers.

Young's part in avenging the massacre of Miguel Robidoux's party on the Gila and his subsequent leadership of the so-called Pattie expedition of 1827, whose itinerary included so large a part of the Great Basin and the Rocky Mountains, have already been briefly described. This expedition involved Young in long and serious difficulties with New Mexican officials, which had both tragic and comic aspects. The company returned to Santa Fe apparently unaware that it had anything to fear from Mexican law or New Mexican officials. But this happy illusion was quickly dispelled. Asserting that the Americans had violated a decree, issued by the central government in 1824, that forbade citizens of the United States to hunt beaver in Mexican territory, Governor Manuel Armíjo confiscated the party's entire catch of furs, valued at twenty thousand dollars, and brought about the death of one of his own countrymen in the proceedings.[10] This latter phase of the

---

[9] Huntington Library, RI 81. I am indebted to Mr. Joseph J. Hill for the pioneer account of Ewing Young's activities in the Southwest. His article appeared in the *Oregon Historical Society Quarterly* in 1923, Vol. XXIV, No. 1, and is the starting-point for all subsequent studies of Ewing Young's career.

[10] James Ohio Pattie's statement relative to this incident is referred to in the preceding chapter.

incident is described at sufficient length for our purpose in the following official report:

> For the purpose of seizing a contraband of beaver skins which a citizen from the States of North America, called Yon [Young], had hidden in the house of Dn. Luis Maria Cabeza de Baca, in the village of Peñablanca, I provided as requested [the services] of the Substitute Commissary of this Territory, Dn. Agustin Duran, also one corporal and eight soldiers of this company, who, acting according to my instructions and those of the said Commissary and the Alcalde of Cochití, Dr. Juan Estevan Aragón, fulfilled their duties to my satisfaction by bringing to this Commissariat the above-mentioned contraband, which is here at present awaiting the outcome of the stubborn and unlawful armed resistance made by the above-mentioned Cabeza de Baca while trying to prevent the seizure of the contraband belonging to the American Yon and hidden in his house, [thus] forcing the auxiliary troop headed by its own Alcalde . . . to kill him, which death he brought upon himself by firing a number of shots, as the record of the examination of the corporal and soldiers, the original of which I am sending to your Excellency . . . will show. I beg you to declare the corporal and soldiers free of responsibility — which I consider just — of the charge which may be brought against them of having killed Cabeza de Baca . . . for in my opinion the deceased died while defending a violation of the usurped rights of the Nation. . . . Santa Fe, June 6, 1827.[11]

The aftermath of Armíjo's action is set forth in detail in numerous contemporary Mexican documents, but only a summary of the proceedings can be included here. They began with the following official statement:

---

[11] Archives of New Mexico (Huntington Library, Microfilm).

Territory of New Mexico   Year 1827

Initial proceedings against the Anglo-American Joaquin Young for the crime of disobedience to the Political Chief of the said Territory, and the part he took in the daring action of his fellow-citizen Soblet, in the robbery committed by the latter of a load of beaver skins, from the Commissariat of this Territory.

Prosecuting Judge
Lieutenant D. Felipe Griego

Court Clerk
Corporal José Tapia [12]

This new phase of Young's troubles began on July 11, 1827, when Armíjo permitted three of the trapper's men to air and dust the confiscated beaver skins, which were stored in the official commissariat in Santa Fe, to get rid of dust and moths. The furs were accordingly laid out on the plaza and the beating and dusting began.

Among the furs were two bundles belonging to Milton Sublette, sometimes called the "Thunderbolt of the Rockies," a well-known figure among the mountain men. Sublette asked Young to point out the skins that carried his mark or brand. Young obligingly showed him the two bales. Thereupon "the alien Soblet," as Armíjo habitually called him, "with the greatest audacity," picked up the skins, threw them over his shoulder, and ran off to a house belonging to one Don Cristóbal Torres, in which he and a number of other Americans had their quarters.

[12] Department of State, General Archives. Mexico City, Expediente No. 2721 — Year 1827 — Case against the Anglo-American Joaquin Young. I am indebted to Dr. Ralph Bieber for the use of the microfilm of this manuscript. The translation is by Miss Haydée Noya of the Huntington Library.

The whole pueblo was immediately in an uproar. Armíjo sent the municipal guard to regain the skins and arrest Sublette. The trappers seized their rifles and prepared to resist the guard. Finally the first Alcalde and the Governor's secretary, Don Santiago Abreu, searched the house, but found neither Sublette nor the furs.

Armíjo then summoned three leading Americans, including "the one they call Chief," told them that the dignity of the Mexican nation had been deeply offended, and announced that if they failed to find and surrender Sublette he would be forced to seize their property and even sacrifice his life, if the worst came to the worst, to make the Mexican nation and its legal authorities respected. The Americans tried to reply through an interpreter, but Armíjo declared that they said things, "I know not what, which I refused to hear," and closed the interview by requesting them "to leave at once, which they did."

After much further to-do and an official conference attended by Don Antonio Narbona, chief commandant of the province, Armíjo summoned Ewing Young and informed him that he proposed to put him under arrest for taking up arms against the authorities, conniving with Sublette in the theft of the furs, and concealing the names of his accomplices in the crime. The Governor then asked Young if he was ready to obey him "as Political Chief of the Territory and go at once to the jail." If not, would he at least be good enough to say so and thus enable the Governor to take "the necessary measures"? Young emphatically rejected Armíjo's first suggestion and hurriedly left the room, "notwithstanding that he was called two, three, or more times."

Bedlam then broke out. Armíjo and Narbona leaped to their feet and called the guard. But there were over a hundred Americans in the city, most of whom could be counted upon to take up arms in defense of their countrymen, and the municipal police were not equal to the crisis. So the commandant and the governor decided on sterner measures. "The Company of Santa Fe" was ordered to take up arms, aim two loaded cannon point-blank at the house of Don Cristóbal Torres, in which Young had taken refuge, and "at the cost of any sacrifice, to bring him out and put him in jail." Armíjo also ordered the guard to seize Sublette and bring him in, dead or alive.

Young then surrendered. "And when I asked him if he was ready to obey me," Armíjo complained in his account of the incident, "he answered me very rudely and with his hat on that he was, upon which I promptly ordered him delivered to the . . . guard, to be marched and locked up separately in a cell." Here Young was kept incommunicado until summoned for formal examination. The next day, when "the retired physician, Don Cristóbal Lorrañaga," certified that the prisoner was suffering from fever and constipation and required peace and quiet to effect a cure, Young was released in the custody of two bondsmen. As Armíjo afterward admitted, some of his measures found no justification in Mexican legal procedure, but the Governor excused his actions on the ground that he was driven to them "by imperious necessity."

At his formal examination, with an American named George W. West, "who said he spoke Spanish well," serving as interpreter, Young testified that he was born in

Thomas Boron, or Thomasboro, in the state of Tenesi, United States of North America; that he did not know why he was imprisoned; that when proper notice was served on him he surrendered voluntarily; and that, if Governor Armíjo in the first place had formally ordered him to surrender instead of merely asking "if he wanted to be arrested," Young "would not have answered that he did not wish to be arrested nor risen and gone to his own house."

The prisoner denied that he had instigated the seizure of the skins, had taken part in concealing them, or had the slightest knowledge of Sublette's whereabouts. Asked for the names of the Americans who had taken up arms against the Mexican officials, he naïvely replied that "he could not give their names because they were foreign names and he could not pronounce them."

As the examination proceeded, Young was urged to reconsider his testimony and indicate, even at the cost of contradicting his own word, where he thought "Soblett and the load have gone to." In doing this, he was assured, he would render a great public service, save his own skin, and enable the treasury to collect its just dues. But Young replied that if his very life depended on his ability to answer the question, "then he would have to lose it, because Sublette definitely did not advise him of his whereabouts, nor his plans."

When witnesses testified that they saw the prisoner, rifle in hand, among the other armed Americans in Don Cristóbal's house, and that they also watched him carry away the stolen skins, Young replied, in effect, (a) that while the witnesses may have seen him carrying a rifle, they misinterpreted his purpose; he had picked up the gun first to clean it and then to move it to another room, where there was less danger of its being stolen; (b) the charge that he was seen carrying the stolen skins was also a mistake. By a mere coincidence, he happened to be moving his baggage from one room to another when Sublette ran into the house, and this doubtless confused the witnesses and led them to say that they had seen him with the missing furs.

Whatever may have been Young's actual part in this affair, he apparently escaped further acquaintance with the guardhouse, but the final fate of the skins, with the exception of the two bundles that Sublette carried off, is problematical.[13] Official documents of the time, however, contain a few further interesting references on the subject. When Young and some of his fellow trappers protested that they had not violated any law of the Mexican Republic, Armíjo and his fellow officials were somewhat embarrassed because they failed to find, in the archives of Santa Fe, a copy of the federal decree of 1824 forbidding Americans to trap in Mexican territory, which they had cited as justification for the seizure. A great rain "that almost ruined all the houses in town" wet the furs and led the Alcalde to authorize their sale to protect the interests of the parties concerned. The skins went for two pesos each and brought a total of 2,328 pesos. Ewing Young was absent when the sale took place, but the Alcalde asked Elisha [?] Stanley, one of "the rich and well established foreigners," to rep-

---

[13] See Josiah Gregg: *The Commerce of the Prairies,* Vol. II, pp. 227–9.

resent him. Stanley proved a very loyal advocate, particularly in insisting that the assistant commissariat, the custodian of the skins, produce a copy of the federal decree giving legal sanction to their confiscation. At last the bedeviled official wrote that the requests of "the foreigner Estanley" were becoming such a nuisance "that they almost keep me from the important matters which burden this office."

There is little likelihood that either Young or any of his associates, always excepting "the thief Soblett," ever regained the skins that had cost them so many months of hardship and danger; but there is even less likelihood that either they or their fellows ever again voluntarily exposed themselves to the risk of a similar experience.

The year following the incident of the confiscated furs was an eventful one for Ewing Young. On April 26, 1828 he and four other Americans, including Richard Campbell and Julian Green, applied for Mexican citizenship; [14] in the summer of that year he formed a partnership with William Wolfskill, who had just returned from St. Louis with a valuable cargo of merchandise, to open a store in Santa Fe; and, finally, he outfitted a trapping expedition for the Gila River, which took a bad drubbing from the Apache Indians in the Arizona mountains, possibly because illness prevented Young from leading it in person.

In spite of this loss, Young soon undertook an even more extensive invasion of the trapping country west of the Rio Grande. With a party of forty men he left Taos in August

[14] Huntington Library, RI 99.

1829, ostensibly headed for the Missouri settlements.[15] But once beyond the reach of the Mexican officials, the Americans swung sharply to the southwest and traveled through Zuñi and the country of the Navajos to the headwaters of the Salt River. The route lay close to the lone sandstone mesa called El Moro, or Inscription Rock (the greatest of all American historical directories), which rises high above the juniper-dotted plains; and perhaps the trappers even camped where Don Juan Oñate, fellow explorer and lover of the wilderness, had built his own campfires more than two centuries before.

Young's party was made up almost wholly of seasoned trappers; but among them rode at least one apprentice to the business, a novice among the mountain men. He was a slight, modest, self-reliant youngster, with observant, penetrating, blue-gray eyes, silky flaxen hair that later was allowed to reach almost to his shoulders, a voice as gentle as a girl's, and muscles as tireless as those of the toughest of the wild creatures of the woods. His name was Kit Carson. Every factor — birth, tradition, training, environment, and opportunity — combined to make this undistinguished beginner the personification of the craft and courage of the West.

When he joined Young's expedition, Kit was between nineteen and twenty years of age. Some four years earlier he had been apprenticed to David Workman, of Franklin, Missouri, with the hope that he would learn the saddle and harness trade. But he was not ordained to bondage at a

---

[15] Young's rescue of the Bent-Waldo party, referred to on p. 41, must have occurred about this time.

saddler's bench or a merchant's counter; he was not intended to wear soft raiment and follow the ways of conven-
tional society. His birthright was the sun and sky, the wind
and stars, freedom and solitude, the mystery and hardship
and danger and beauty of the West.

So Kit ran off, in the fall of 1826, to join a caravan to
New Mexico; and his short-handed but not overgrieved employer offered the handsome reward of one cent for the
return of his missing apprentice.

The runaway spent the ensuing winter at Taos, in the
house of a hospitable trader named Kinkaid. During the
next two years and more, almost a runt in stature and too
poor to provide his own outfit for either trading or trapping, Kit traveled with the wagon-men who journeyed
south to Santa Rita, El Paso, and Chihuahua. Then Young
gave him leave to join his company of mountain men, and
Kit found a new life, with all that he had aspired to or
dreamed of, opening out before him.

Near the head of the White River or one of the other
headwaters of the Salt, possibly in what is now the Apache
or San Carlos Indian Reservation, the trapping party am-
bushed a force of Indians whom they suspected of partici-
pating in the attack on Young's men the year before, and
killed fifteen members of the band.

Then, as well as a generation later, the Apaches were
a formidable foe. They fought mostly with their native
weapons, the lance, bow, and arrow. According to Pike, the
bow of the Western Apache formed two demicircles, with
a shoulder, skillfully covered with the sinews of deer, antelope, or mountain sheep in the middle, which gave great

elasticity to the weapon. The Apache arrows, about three and a half feet long, consisted of a light reed or cane, in which a shaft of hard wood about a foot in length was inserted, and a head or point of iron, bone, or flint. It was extremely difficult to extract such an arrow from a wound because the shaft almost invariably pulled loose and left the head embedded in the flesh. The Apache bows were so powerful that an arrow would go through a man's body at the distance of a hundred yards, and it was not unusual for a good bowman to shoot as many as ten arrows a minute.

The other offensive weapon of the Apache warrior was a lance about fifteen feet long. The charging rider held this in both hands above his head and guided his horse with his knees. "With this weapon," wrote Worcester, "an Apache was considered more than a match for any Spanish dragoon in single combat, but because of a lack of knowledge of tactics they never could stand the charge of a body in concert. All carried shields, and a few had firearms. Only the lancers were mounted." [16] Even the rifles of the trappers had little margin of superiority over such weapons in a free fight.

After the engagement on the headwaters of the Salt, the Americans trapped down the river to the mouth of the Verde and meandered that stream to its source. Here the company divided. Twenty-two of the party returned to New Mexico, taking with them the furs already obtained, while Young and the rest of the party, including Kit Carson, set out for the Colorado, the half-fabled land of California

---

[16] D. E. Worcester: "The Weapons of American Indians," *New Mexico Historical Review*, Vol. XX, No. 3, p. 233.

that lay on the other side of the great river, and the waters of the western sea.

This was not an easy, Sabbath-day's journey. Young knew from the sign language of the Indians that a formidable desert lay between his pleasant camp, high up among the alpine meadows and pine and aspen groves of the Black Forest, and the Colorado River. But even he and his experienced companions underestimated the difficulties and hardships of the route.

Before many miles the company found itself in a region "shriveled to absolute barrenness," an implacable land of thirst and torment, "a rolling plateau with occasional thick growths of pines and cedars; with expanses of loose, porous soil wherein the mules sank to their fetlocks; with sharp slopes, forming small, higher plateaus, and unexpected, sheer, impassable *cañoncitas*, or ravines, sometimes so thickly intersecting that the plateau was shattered like a ruin; with an intensely hot sun streaming down through a dry, thin air that sucked moisture from the body; with not an animate thing encountered; and finally, with mules staggering along as if drunken, and men's brains afire with the scorching rays." [17]

Before beginning the long *entrada*, the trappers killed three deer, cased their hides with melted tallow so that they could be made into "tanks" or water-bags, and converted the venison into "jerky." "The first four days' march," Kit Carson wrote nearly thirty years later, "was over a coun-

---

[17] Edwin L. Sabin: *Kit Carson Days* (Chicago, 1914), p. 48. The quotation is from Sabin's paraphrase of Lieutenant J. C. Ives's description of the country in his *Exploration of the Colorado River of the West* (Washington, 1861), p. 49. The paraphrase is better than the original.

try sandy, burned up and not a drop of water. We received at night a small quantity of water from the tanks. . . . A guard was placed over the tanks to prohibit anyone from making use of more water than his allowance."

On the evening of the fourth day the company came to a little oasis, probably the place known today as Young Spring, fifteen miles northeast of the town of Truxon, Arizona.[18] Here the exhausted, dehydrated men drank and rested, rested and drank for forty-eight hours. Four days further across the waterless desert brought them to the Colorado, somewhere "below the great Cañon." There they encountered a band of wandering Mojaves, from whom they obtained a small quantity of corn and beans and a worn-out old mare, which they immediately killed and ate.[19]

Young forded the Colorado not far from the scene of the massacre of Smith's men two years before, and probably followed his predecessor's trail to the Mojave. Making its way along the course of this "sun-burned" river to the base of the San Bernardino Mountains, the party crossed the range either by the old Indian trail or through the Cajon Pass and reached the San Gabriel Mission early in the winter of 1830. Here the trappers traded butcher knives for steers, at the rate of four knives per head, and filled their gaunt bellies with the fresh meat.

Perhaps to avoid any difficulty with the California authorities, Young gave his trail-weary men only a day's rest

[18] An excellent description of this region is given in Floyd's "Diary," loc. cit., entries April 15, 1859 *et seq.*
[19] According to Carson, the mare was with foal, and the men ate both mare and foal.

and then pushed on, by way of Mission San Fernando, to the beaver streams of the San Joaquin and Sacramento valleys.

As the Americans traveled down the San Joaquin, they found traces of another trapping party that had preceded them along the river. Their rivals proved to be a Hudson's Bay brigade, commanded by Peter Skene Ogden, from Fort Vancouver, near the mouth of the Columbia. The two bands met without animosity on either side and trapped the region amicably together until they came to the delta region of San Francisco Bay. Ogden then turned north along the course of the Sacramento River, while Young retraced his steps and established a base camp, the site of which is still unidentified, in the San Joaquin Valley.

There the hunters found "elk, deer, and antelope in thousands," and since the season was too far advanced for trapping, the company settled down to a well-fed, lazy life. Twice during the ensuing weeks, however, the easy routine of the camp was interrupted by incidents arising from the activities of horse-stealing Indians from the Sierra. Hostility between the gentile Indians in the valley and the California settlements was endemic. From time to time the Indians raided the horse herds along the coast, and the government retaliated by sending punitive expeditions into the interior. Similar expeditions were also dispatched to bring back runaway bands of neophytes, or "Christian Indians," to the missions.

While the Americans were camped in the valley, Lieutenant Francisco Jiménez, Jedediah Smith's former benefactor, made an unsuccessful attempt to capture a body of these deserting neophytes who had left the Mission San José and taken refuge with their unregenerate kinsmen in the mountains. Unable to capture the runaways with the small force at his command, Jiménez appealed to the Americans for reinforcements.

Ten or eleven trappers, with Kit Carson in command, joined the Californians. The mixed body of soldiers and mountain men routed the Indians, killed a third of their number, and restored the remaining fugitives to the mission. In return for this assistance the fathers of San José invited Young to visit the mission and exchange his furs for horses, mules, and supplies — a striking contrast to the harsh treatment Smith had received four years earlier at the same mission.

A few nights after Young's visit to San José the valley Indians, now actively hostile to the Americans, raided the trappers' camp and drove off sixty horses. Kit Carson, with twelve companions, followed the trail for a hundred miles till he caught up with the raiders in one of the innumerable recesses of the Sierra Nevada. Taking for granted that they were beyond all danger of pursuit, the Indians had there killed five or six of the stolen animals and started their long-delayed feast. The situation was made to order for the mountain men. Creeping up unobserved, Carson and his men fired into the circle of unsuspecting savages, killed or wounded a considerable number, and recaptured all the surviving horses.

Soon after this, Young evidently laid out a new program. He decided to shift the scene of his fall trapping operations from the San Joaquin and Sacramento region to the Colorado, return to the coast at the close of the season, dispose of his furs to Captain Cooper (the hide and tallow trader who had earlier befriended Jedediah Smith and James Ohio Pattie in their difficulties with the Californians), invest the receipts in California mules, drive the mules halfway across the continent, and sell them in Missouri — a market the Santa Fe traders had supplied for a decade with mules from New Mexico, Chihuahua, and Sonora.

Young's proposal was typical of the temerity and rash imagination of a fur trader, and his plan soon became a major feature in the California, Santa Fe, and St. Louis trade. But Young himself never actually participated in it. For this he had to thank a tragic incident that occurred near the pueblo of Los Angeles while he and his men were en route from the San Joaquin Valley to the Colorado. Kit Carson's account of the affairs ran as follows:

On the first September we struck camp and returning by the same route which we had come, passed through San Fernando. We traveled to the Pueblo of Los Angeles, where the Mexican authorities demanded our passports. We had none. They wished to arrest us, but fear deterred them. They then commenced selling liquor to the men, no doubt for the purpose of getting the men drunk so that they would have but little difficulty in making the arrest. Mr. Young discovered their intention, directed me to take three men, all loose animals, packs, etc. and go in advance. He would remain with the balance of the party and endeavor to get them along. If he did not arrive at my camp by next morning I was directed to move on as best I could, and on my return to report the party killed; for Young would not leave them. They were followed by the Mexicans, furnishing them all the liquor they could pay for. All got drunk except Young.

The Mexicans would have continued with them till they arrived at the Mission of San Gabriel, then, being reinforced, arrest the party, only for a man by the name of James Higgins dismounting from his horse and deliberately shooting James Lawrence. Such conduct frightened the Mexicans, and they departed in all haste, fearing that, if men, without provocation, would shoot one another, it would require but little to cause them to murder them.[20]

The incident sobered Young's half-drunken men. Fearing that they would be arrested, or at least detained by the Californians, and probably having no great love for the bully, "Big Jim," the victim of the shooting, the trappers left his body lying in the dusty trail, hurriedly rode on toward the desert, and caught up with Carson and his two associates the next day. The combined company then backtracked for nine days over its old trail to the Colorado. Young trapped the lower course of the river to the gulf and back again to the Yuma villages. Probably fearing arrest if he returned to California, he took the route up the Gila to the copper mines of Santa Rita.

The company reached that frontier settlement with some two thousand pounds of beaver skins. Warned by his previous experience with Governor Armíjo, Young preferred to take no unnecessary chances, even though he was now a naturalized Mexican citizen, and hid the furs in the adits and shafts of the copper mines while he went on to Santa Fe to sound out the government officials. These proved ame-

---

[20] *Kit Carson's Own Story of His Life,* ed. by Blanche C. Grant (Taos, New Mexico, 1926), pp. 17–18.

nable to reason and issued him a permit to trade with the Indians in the vicinity of Santa Rita. Under the ægis of that obliging document, Young carried his beaver skins to Santa Fe and disposed of them without official interference.

The death of Jedediah Smith in 1831, described at the close of Chapter 3, left numerous traders and trappers of his large Santa Fe expedition temporarily at loose ends in New Mexico. Drawing on some of these for needed personnel, Young entered into a partnership with William Waldo and David E. Jackson to carry out his cherished idea of a combined beaver-trapping, mule-buying expedition to California.

Waldo was a naturalized Mexican citizen and a merchant of long experience in the Santa Fe trade. Unfortunately the known records of Jackson's life and activities, aside from the fact that he was a member of the famed triumvirate of Smith, Jackson, and Sublette and belonged in the inner circle of the mountain men, consist of only a few scattered, disconnected fragments.

But if historical records have proved so indifferent to Jackson's memory, the lake and valley among the Tetons that bear his name are monuments sublime and enduring enough for any man. And, as Russell correctly points out, Jackson's Hole epitomizes "the trappers' role in the winning of the West" better than any other place in the mountains.[21]

In keeping with the plans of the Young-Jackson-Waldo

---

[21] Carl P. Russell: "Trapper Trails to the Sisk-ke-dee," *Annals of Wyoming*, Vol. XVII, No. 2, p. 105.

partnership, Jackson left Santa Fe on August 29, 1831 at the head of a party of eleven men for the California settlements. In addition to the usual baggage train, the party took with it several pack mules loaded with Mexican silver pesos that were to be used for the purchase of mules and horses from the missions and rancheros on the coast.[22]

Two months later Young set out from Taos with thirty-six companions for the Colorado. At the close of the spring trapping season he intended to meet Jackson in California, purchase additional horses and mules with the proceeds from his furs, and drive the combined herd back to Santa Fe for eventual sale in New Mexico, Missouri, and Louisiana. The company included such well-known trappers as Moses Carson, Sidney Cooper, J. J. Warner, Benjamin and William Day, Isaac Sparks, James Green, Joseph Gale, Isaac Williams, and Job F. Dye.

En route to the Colorado the expedition encountered the usual quota of hardship, hunger, and Indian attack, added a murder and an accidental death for good measure, and ate twenty-three horses in one camp because of the lack of other food. In a private venture of their own, four of the trappers, attacked by over a hundred Apaches, fought for an hour and a half, killed fourteen of the enemy, and wounded at least as many more.[23]

The trappers found plenty of beaver on the Gila, but the

[22] On September 17, 1831 David Waldo and Antoine Robidoux requested a license to take twenty-five Mexican citizens and five foreigners "because of their dexterity in trapping" on a beaver-hunting expedition. New Mexican Archives (Huntington Library, Microfilm).

[23] Job F. Dye: "Recollections of a Pioneer of California," *Santa Cruz Sentinel,* May 15, 1869.

catch was disappointing because a slight defect in the traps, most of which had been bought in New Mexico, allowed the beaver to escape when the trap was sprung. The party worked down the Colorado to tidewater and then returned to the Yuma villages. There the company divided. Young and twelve companions, including Moses Carson (one of Kit's older brothers), Isaac Williams, J. J. Warner, Isaac Sparks, Isaac Galbraith, an escapee from the massacre of Smith's men on the Colorado, and John Turner, one of the four survivors of the Umpqua tragedy, set out across the Colorado desert for the coast. The party crossed what is now the lower end of the Imperial Valley, presumably entered the mountains near the present site of Warner's Ranch, and reached Los Angeles, by way of the fringe of the California settlements at Temecula, on March 14, 1832. About a month later Young kept his appointed rendezvous with Jackson at the Rancho La Sierra, on the Santa Ana River, near the present city of San Bernardino.

Jackson's mule-purchasing venture, which constituted one of the major features of the program, had been disappointing. Though Jackson traveled as far north as San Francisco, he returned to the rendezvous with only 500 mules and 100 horses instead of the 2,500 head that the company hoped to obtain. This required some alteration in the partners' plans. Upon breaking camp, however, the entire company returned to the Colorado. Here the trappers found the river in flood from the melting snows of the upper basin, and a number of animals were drowned in attempting to ford the treacherous current. On the east side of the river the partners again separated. Young and five of the trappers returned to California, while Jackson and the rest of the company continued to New Mexico with the mules and horses.

Young spent the off season in an unsatisfactory sea-otter hunt along the southern California coast; then, with eight or nine trappers added to the five who had come back with him from the Colorado, he again took the familiar trail to the San Joaquin and Sacramento valleys. The party trapped the lower course of the Kings; then, while three of his men continued down the San Joaquin River by canoe, Young and the rest of the company crossed overland to the Fresno River and trapped that stream to its junction with the San Joaquin.

There the three voyageurs reported that an unidentified band of trappers had preceded them down the San Joaquin and left unmistakable signs of their presence along the banks. In the light of this disturbing word, Young determined to strike directly for the Sacramento and cut in ahead of his unknown rivals. The company reached the river near the mouth of the American, only to find that its competitors were already on the ground. A large brigade of Hudson's Bay trappers, under Michel Laframboise, had come to California early in the spring, trapped most of the streams of the Sacramento and San Joaquin valleys before the close of the season, and were now camped a few miles below the junction of the American and Sacramento rivers.

Young's visit unfortunately occurred during the year of the great pestilence in the Sacramento Valley. Some idea of the ravages of the disease may be gained from the appalling description contributed by George C. Yount, one of Young's fellow trappers:

In the fall of 1833 the cholera broke out in California, and raged with terrible violence among the Indians; so great was the mortality that they were unable either to burn or bury the dead, and the air was filled with the stench of decomposing humanity. A traveler who passed up the Sacramento valley at this time, relates that on his way up he passed a place where there were about three hundred Indians, with women and children, encamped; when he returned, after an absence of three or four days, the ground was literally strewed with dead bodies, all having died except one little Indian girl; she occupied the camp alone, while around her lay the festering bodies of her dead companions, and the air was rendered noxious by the disgusting stench arising from the dead bodies which, not alone in this camp, but every where throughout the valley, strewed the ground.[24]

After his encounter with Laframboise's trappers Young's wanderings covered an amazing extent of territory. Writing from memory many years later, J. J. Warner thus described his activities:

Young and his party reached the Sacramento River in the evening of the first day of a long and continuous rainstorm which held him encamped some twenty days, and until flooded out of his camp by the river, which, after inundating all the land around about, overflowed its banks and forced him to make his way over and through sloughs, lakes, mud and mire to the unsubmergable bank of the American River. Here a

---

[24] George C. Yount: "Sketches of the Early Settlers of California," the *Hesperian*, Vol. II, p. 2. Yount's cholera was probably a virulent influenza.

rawhide boat was constructed with which the party was ferried to the opposite shore, and by a long and circuitous route succeeded in again reaching and crossing the Sacramento River at the mouth of the Feather River, in January, 1833. Finally, after a month's experience of amphibious life, the party reached the dry land of the Putah River, leaving behind a deluged world in which for weeks it had wallowed. Ascending the mountain and passing along the southern and western shore of Clear Lake, the party traveled northwesterly and struck the shore of the ocean about seventy-five miles north of Ross, a port of the Russian-American Fur Company.

Young followed along up the coast, searching with little success for rivers having beaver, and in fruitless attempts to recross the mountain range, until near the Umpquah River, where he succeeded in getting over the mountains and fell upon that river at the eastern base of the coast range of mountains. This river was followed up to its southeastern source, and then traveling Jedediah Smith's trail, he struck the Klamath Lake near its northern extremity. From thence he traveled southerly along its western shore and, crossing the Klamath and Rogue rivers and passing through the camp where McLeod lost his horses and valuable catch of beaver skins, crossed Pitt River and entered the Sacramento Valley, which he descended to the American River and then crossed the country to the San Joaquin River, up which he traveled to the great bend and then to the mouth of Kings River, where, striking the trail of the preceding year, he followed it southerly to Lake Elizabeth, where, leaving it, he traveled more easterly along the northern base of the mountain to the San Bernardino Cajon Pass, through which he entered the valley of San Bernardino in December, 1833, and passing on to Temecula, took the trail upon which he had come from the Colorado in the spring of 1832, and returned to that river to make a winter and spring season hunt upon it and the lower part of the Gila River.[25]

On the trip to the Colorado to which Warner referred, Young had indifferent or, at best, only fair success. On "14 March, 1834," he wrote from his camp on "Red River" to the well-known Los Angeles merchant Abel Stearns: "Dear Sir — if Capt Cooper has not got the Mill Irons from Mr Anderson I wish you would do me the favor to procure them for me I will be in the Pueblo some time in the month of may I am not Ketching much Beaver but doing the best I can I would have sent you two or three pack of beaver by Pedro Cordover to pay for the mill Irons and to get some other articles I stand in need of but he was so bad of for animals that I had to Lend him some pack mules to Carry his own baggage I would also write to Mr. Anderson but I do not know if he is yet on the Cost." [26]

So far as we know, this was Young's last expedition to the Colorado or to any other part of the Southwest. At the close of the trapping season of 1834 he went to San Diego and there fell in with the Oregon zealot and protagonist Hall J. Kelley, who persuaded him to transfer his interests

[25] J. J. Warner: "Reminiscences of Early California, 1831–1846," *Annual Publications of the Historical Society of Southern California, 1907–8,* Vol. VII, pp. 187–8. The Huntington Library also has a typescript of a paper entitled "Jedediah Smith and Early California Trappers," by J. J. Warner, which differs in some important particulars from the above article. The paper was read before the California Historical Society on April 17, 1888.

See also *Fur Brigade to the Bonaventura,* edited by Alice Bay Maloney (San Francisco, 1945).

[26] Huntington Library MSS., Abel Stearns Papers.

from New Mexico to the Oregon territory and from the Colorado River basin to that of the Columbia. Kelley was a curious mixture of sincerity, conceit, restless ambition, and crusading zeal. "Everything came from his pen," said Chittenden, "clothed with the beauty of a western sunset." But Alfred Robinson wrote: "If he should never be king of the Oregon, I think he may be called King of Beggars. I set him down as the greatest bore I ever knew." Kelley said of himself that he sought to plant "in the genial soil of Oregon the vine of Christianity and the germ of Civil Freedom."

As a first venture in the adopted field of his activities Young undertook to realize an old ambition in a new setting and drove a herd of horses from northern California to central Oregon, where the American settlers in the Willamette Valley provided a ready market. Unfortunately, General José Figueroa, Governor of California, anticipated Young's arrival in Oregon by warning Dr. John McLoughlin of Fort Vancouver that the American trapper was a rogue and a horse-thief, and to have no dealings with the rascal.[27] But the charge proved groundless. Young won McLoughlin's confidence, and his character and ability soon made him the recognized leader of the American settlers in the Willamette Valley.

In 1837 the former Santa Fe trader and trapper joined McLoughlin and a number of Americans in the organization of the "Williamet Cattle Company" and returned to

---

[27] One wonders if Figueroa's attitude toward Young might not have been the aftermath of some unrecorded clash between the two when Figueroa was an official on the Sonora and Gila River frontier.

California as the company's agent to purchase a herd of cattle for the Oregon settlements. One of Young's associates in the venture was Philip Leget Edwards, afterward a prominent Californian; while John Turner, survivor of the Umpqua massacre, probably served as a vaquero.

In a petition to Governor Juan B. Alvarado, Young thus set forth the purpose of the expedition:

To His Excellency Gov. of the State of Up. California.
Sir.

Your Petitioner would beg leave to inform your Excellency that there is on the Wallamette [*sic*] River south of the River Columbia a small settlement of Citizens of the United States. This community have from their origin laboured under many difficulties for want of horned cattle of which they have none. But knowing that your Excellency is aware of the advantages which they confer, your petitioner cannot think it necessary to express in detail the reasons why cattle are indispensible to the prosperity of Agricultural People. Under these circumstances a part of the citizens of said community on the 13 day of February A.D. 1837, formed themselves into a joint stock company for the purpose of procuring cattle from Upper California. The object of your Petitioner as well as that of said company, are expressed in the following extract from their Articles of association viz "Whereas we the undersigned Settlers upon the Wallamette River are fully convinced of the utility and necessity of having neat cattle of our own in order successfully to carry on our farms and gain a comfortable livelihood, and whereas we find it impossible to purchase them here as all the cattle in the country belong to the Hudson's Bay Company, and they refusing to sell them under any circumstances, and as we believe the possession of cattle will not only benefit us personally, but will materially benefit the whole settlement, we the undersigned do hereby agree etc., etc."

In pursuance of the object expressed in these articles, a Party of Ten American Citizens and three Indian Boys of whom I was chosen leader, took passage in the American Brig Loreat, Capt. Bancroft, of which vessel Wm. A. Slacum Esq of the United Navy was charterer.

In complaince with the wishes of said Association, Your Petitioner would pray your Excellency's permission to purchase Cattle to the Number of Five or Six hundred head of the Citizens of California for the purposes expressed above, And relying on the Friendly relations in which the Citizens of the United States have always stood to those of your Government and on your personal generosity he waits determination.

> I am Your Excellency's
> Hmbl & Obdnt Servt
> (Signed)   EWING YOUNG

San Francisco
10th March 1837 [28]

Young finally obtained some seven hundred head of cattle from the California rancheros and started on the long drive to the Willamette. The journey involved almost every conceivable hardship and misfortune — swimming hundreds of unruly cattle across swollen rivers; breaking a trail over seemingly impassable country and through almost impenetrable brush; endless hours of thirst, dust, aching bones, and lungs "painful from halloing"; constant vigilance against the Indians, made treacherous and vindictive by wanton acts of cruelty; and the cumulative fatigue of days of weary riding, and nights of broken sleep.

---

[28] Huntington Library, Walker Collection, MS. 2.

But the cattle got through, and the American settlers in consequence found their life on the Willamette a little more prosperous and secure.

Young died on his Oregon ranch in 1841. By that time the fur trade was spoken of in the past tense and the trappers were referred to as a fast disappearing race. Farms were more sought after than beaver, and settlers were rapidly crowding out the last of the mountain men. But the settlers reached the West over the trails Young and his fellow trappers had explored — from Tennessee to the Columbia, by way of Missouri, Santa Fe, the trails of Spanish explorers, and many trails of his own — a long, long way for a man to travel the Wilderness Trace in the space of a dozen years. But Ewing Young was more than wanderer and explorer. He was symbolic of the settler in the clearing, the westward-moving caravans of covered wagons, the impact of the Anglo-American on the Spanish, French, and even English borderlands.

CHAPTER 7

From Santa Fe to California

Dᴜʀɪɴɢ the period of Ewing Young's career in New Mexico, many other American trappers, known and unknown, followed the beaver to the deep recesses of the far Southwest. Antoine Robidoux, variously described as "the first American trapper out of Taos," and the "Kingpin of the Fur Trade of the Southwest," was one of Young's most distinguished contemporaries among these foreign intruders. Robidoux entered New Mexico in the early twenties and soon became favorably known to Mexicans and Americans alike. He was the fourth of six brothers, sons of a certain Joseph Robidoux who came to St. Louis from Canada before the American Revolution to found one of the West's most important frontier families.

Joseph Robidoux, oldest of the brothers, established a trading post on the Missouri that eventually grew into a city and gave rise to the saying that since its founder would never be a saint in any other way, it was only fair to add "Saint to his Joseph." Louis Robidoux, the third brother, was a trader in Santa Fe for many years and later became a familiar figure and landowner in southern California.[1]

---

[1] His name is perpetuated by the mountain overlooking the city of Riverside on which the custom of holding sunrise Easter services began in southern California.

Michel or Miguel, the youngest member of the family, led the party that figured so tragically in the Indian massacre on the Gila of which Pattie wrote. François and Isadore were traders of less importance in Santa Fe, Sonora, and Chihuahua.

As trapper, trader, and frontiersman, Antoine was more distinguished than any of his brothers. One of the earliest Americans to establish himself in New Mexico, he became president of the Junta del Ayuntamiento or town council of Santa Fe in 1830,[2] and took an active part in the business and political life of the province for many years. He was also one of the pioneer American trappers in the Green River Valley and erected the first trading post west of the main range of the Rocky Mountains, in what is now southwestern Colorado, on the Gunnison River. Later he built historic Fort Uintah at the forks of Uintah River (better known to the trappers as the Wintey) and White Rocks Creek.[3] His pass across the Sangre de Cristo Range, now called Mosca Pass, was long a familiar route to the "inner country."[4]

The route from Taos to Fort Uintah was thus described by Rufus Sage as he followed it in 1842:

---

[2] For the details of this contested election, see the official letters of José Antonio Chavez of December 5 and December 28, 1830, Archives of New Mexico (Microfilm, Huntington Library).

[3] For an interesting account of Denis Julien, one of Robidoux's almost unknown trappers who carved his name on a bluff near Fort Wintey in 1831 and left six inscriptions in the cañons of the Colorado, all dated 1836, see Charles Kelly: "Mysterious D. Julien," *Utah Historical Quarterly*, Vol. VI, No. 3, pp. 83–8.

[4] Edwin L. Sabin: *Kit Carson Days*, p. 121.

A small party from a trading establishment on the waters of Green river, who had visited Taos for the procurement of a fresh supply of goods, were about to return, and I availed myself of the occasion to make one of their number.

On the 7th of October we were under way. Our party consisted of three Frenchmen and five Spaniards, under the direction of a man named Roubideau, formerly from St. Louis, Mo. Some eight pack-mules, laden at the rate of two hundred and fifty pounds each, conveyed a quantity of goods; — these headed by a guide followed in Indian file, and the remainder of the company mounted on horseback brought up the rear.

Crossing the del Norte, we soon after struck into a large trail bearing a westerly course; following which, on the 13th inst. we crossed the main ridge of the Rocky Mountains by a feasible pass at the southern extremity of the Sierra de Anahuac range, and found ourselves upon the waters of the Pacific.

Six days subsequent, we reached Roubideau's Fort, at the forks of the Uintah, having passed several large streams in our course, as well as the two principal branches which unite to form the Colorado.[5]

Sage spent several days at Fort Wintey, from which Robidoux sent his trapping parties as far south as the Gila and Colorado and probably west and north to the Snake River country. "The trade of this fort," wrote Sage, "is conducted principally with the trapping parties frequenting the Big Bear, Green, Grand, and the Colorado rivers, with their numerous tributaries, in search of fur bearing game.

"A small business is also carried on with the Snake and Utah Indians living in the neighborhood of this establish-

---

[5] Rufus Sage: *Scenes in the Rocky Mountains,* p. 178.

ment. The common articles of dealing are horses, with beaver, otter, deer, sheep, and elk skins, in barter for ammunition, firearms, knives, tobacco, beads, awls, etc." [6]

While at the fort, Sage was completely taken in by the tall tales of some yarn-spinning trappers who solemnly assured him that they had once spent four pleasant weeks with the "Muncies," a white, highly civilized people, some eight hundred strong, plainly of European descent (though their complexions were fairer than those of most Europeans), who occupied a branch of the Gila River in the wilds of Sonora. They were a non-warlike people who lived under a simple democratic form of government and, on threat of invasion, retired to well-provisioned caves, barricaded the entrances, and patiently waited for the enemy to leave. Sage also accepted a fanciful tale of a lost city situated in an isolated valley, completely shut in by precipitous mountain walls. American trappers and Spaniards alike knew of the city, many had sought it, some had found it, but none had ever returned to describe it.

Even as late as 1840 a somewhat different version of the story of the "Muncies" received a measure of credence from scientific men. Lieutenant Charles Wilkes, who commanded the important government exploring expedition to the Pacific Ocean in 1838–42, included the following account in his lengthy report of the voyage:

Southwest of the Youta Lake live a tribe who are known by the name of Monkey Indians; a term which is not a mark of contempt, but is supposed to be a corruption of their name. They are said to differ remarkably from the other na-

[6] Ibid., p. 182.

tives of this country; and the description of them has the air of romance, though it appears to be well substantiated by persons who have travelled in the direction of their country. But few have seen them, except the hunters of Mr. Walker's party who were with Captain Bonneville. They are reported to live in fastnesses among high mountains, to have good clothing and houses; to manufacture blankets, shoes and various other articles, which they sell to the neighboring tribes.

Their color is as light as that of the Spaniards; and the women in particular are very beautiful, with delicate features and long flowing hair. They are said to be very neat in their persons, dignified and decorous in their manners, and exceedingly modest. The story goes that the hunters who saw them were so much pleased, that they determined to return and settle among them, but on their return to the Rocky Mountains, they were prevented by old associations. Some have attempted to connect these with an account of an ancient Welsh colony, which others had thought they discovered among the Mandans of the Missouri; while others were disposed to believe they might still exist among the Monkeys of the Western Mountains.[7]

Fort Uintah was destroyed by the Ute Indians in 1844. Robidoux then gave up his trading-trapping operations and removed from Santa Fe to St. Louis. In 1846 he served as interpreter and guide for Kearny's "Army of the West" and suffered a serious lance wound in the Battle of San Pasqual in California. He was later given a small pension by the United States government. "Well known and highly regarded," W. J. Ghent wrote of Antoine, "he was one of

---

[7] *Narrative of the United States Exploring Expedition, during the years 1838, 1839, 1840, 1841, 1842* (Philadelphia, 1845), Vol. IV, pp. 472–3.

the most energetic, daring, and adventurous of all the trader-trappers." [8]

Like Antoine Robidoux, Céran St. Vrain was a leading figure in the close-knit fraternity of the responsible traders and trappers of the Southwest. He led the party with which Young returned from St. Louis to Santa Fe in the spring of 1826; and in the fall of that year he took a company of trappers to the Gila and trapped the streams of Sonora, "to the known injury of our treasury and in infraction of our laws," as Governor Narbona sadly wrote.[9]

Following this venture, St. Vrain served as clerk of an expedition led by Sylvester Pratte, presumably from Taos, to the Green River country. Pratte died after a short illness at Park Kyack, Colorado, and in a letter written "with trembling hand" on September 28, 1828, St. Vrain communicated the sad news to "Messrs. B. Pratte & Co." in St. Louis. "All the assistance I could give him was of no youse his Pickup lasted but very few days, I have never yet experienced such feelings as I did at that moment, but it is useless for me to Dwel to long on that unfortunate subject, it was the will of God." [10]

After burying his employer, St. Vrain arranged with the men to continue the expedition at the same wages Pratte

---

[8] The best summary of the life of Antoine Robidoux is given by Joseph J. Hill: "Antoine Robidoux, Kingpin in the Colorado River Fur Trade, 1824–1844," *Colorado Magazine*, Vol. VII, No. 4, pp. 125–32. Substantially the same account appears in *Touring Topics*, Vol. XX, No. 12, pp. 26–7, 31.

[9] Thomas Maitland Marshall: "St. Vrain's Expedition to the Gila in 1826," *Southwestern Historical Quarterly*, Vol. XIX, No. 3, pp. 251–60.

[10] Missouri Historical Society Collection. See also Declaration of the Party of Engages, Taos, New Mexico, September 1, 1829. Ibid.

had agreed to pay them. The company accordingly moved on to the Green River and there spent a rigorous winter. St. Vrain planned to return to the Platte with some of the men in the spring and start to St. Louis with the furs when the trapping season closed; but lack of ammunition and the discovery of the trail of a large Indian war party led him instead to head for Taos. The company, now in possession of one thousand beaver skins, seven mules, eight horses, seventeen traps, and a miscellaneous collection of goods and guns, reached the pueblo of San Fernando on May 23, 1828, and there St. Vrain sold the skins for enough to pay off the men.

Early in 1831 St. Vrain formed a partnership with Charles Bent, and for the next twenty years his time was largely occupied with the affairs of "Bent, St. Vrain, and Company," builders of Fort Bent, and, next to the American Fur Company, the largest trading and trapping organization in the Rocky Mountain West. With Cornelius Vigil, St. Vrain received a multimillion-acre grant in New Mexico a few years before American troops occupied the province.

A record of the experiences and explorations of any one of the many trappers working out of Santa Fe or Taos would enrich our knowledge of the West and add a new saga to frontier tradition; but the chronicles of such men were seldom written, and if written, were even more rarely preserved for future generations. Thanks to contemporary interest, however, two of the number, both important enough to stand near the top of any category of mountain men, fared better than their fellows in having at least a partial account of their lives and activities rescued from oblivion. One of the two was Old Bill Williams; the other, William Wolfskill.

Old Bill, christened William Sherley by God-fearing parents, was born January 3, 1787, on Horse Creek, in Rutherford County, North Carolina. He died in March 1849, probably at the hands of a Ute Indian, in the snowy wastes of the Continental Divide, near the headwaters of the Rio Grande.

Like many another fur trader, Williams spent his boyhood in a log cabin on the Missouri frontier. In addition to his training in hunting and woodcraft, at which he became exceptionally adept, the boy had the advantage of devout religious upbringing and at least a year of schooling. The preaching of the Reverend John Clark, emigrant from Scotland, who had been in turn sailor, privateer, pirate, impressed seaman in the British Navy, deserter, and schoolteacher, seems to have turned the adolescent boy's thought to the ministry and at the age of seventeen he left home to become a Baptist preacher.

Some years later Old Bill took up his residence among the Osage Indians and for a time attempted to combine the callings of missionary and fur trader. But the Indian manner of life offered his restless nature what civilized society could not provide, so he married an Osage girl, became a member of the tribe, and added many of the Indian beliefs and superstitions to the Christian teachings of his childhood and the mysticism of his Welsh ancestry.

Among the Osage, Old Bill served as trapper, trader, interpreter, and government messenger. When the United

States commission undertook to survey the road to Santa Fe, he negotiated the necessary treaty with the Osage tribe, and accompanied the commissioner George C. Sibley to New Mexico in 1825.

At that time Williams was reputedly thirty-eight years old. During the remaining twenty-four or twenty-five years of his life he rarely ventured east of the Rocky Mountains. Occasionally he joined some favored company of trappers and lived for a time with his fellow mountain men. He accompanied St. Vrain on the expedition down the Gila in 1826, became a member of a company that trapped the Yellowstone in 1832, served in Joseph Reddeford Walker's famous California expedition of 1833–4, and started on a two-year hunt in 1843 that carried him and his party to the Columbia River, on into northern California, through the Great Basin, and back to Santa Fe.

Williams knew the Indians as few Americans have ever known them, and lived with many different tribes; but for the most part Old Bill went his shadowy, solitary way alone — the most eccentric, mysterious, unpredictable of the mountain men, a half-mythical figure who moved like some distorted phantom through the mountains and across the deserts of the Western hinterlands.

Coming out of nowhere, Old Bill delighted to appear at some fur trading post or roaring rendezvous of the Rocky Mountains, or in the Mexican settlements of Taos or Santa Fe, to confound his rivals with the wealth of furs supplied by one of his secret trapping grounds. But trappers of a certain type were said to envy his capacity for reckless gambling and appalling orgies as much as they envied his uncanny ability to locate virgin beaver streams and his consummate skill in trapping.

"This was Bill Williams, the divine, who having preached and taught all the religion he knew in the States, naturally appeared without any in the mountains of the West," wrote William Drummond Stewart, the Scotsman.[11] Williams was a shrewd trader who could outwit both Indians and whites, and an Indian-fighter whom one of his associates described as "the bravest and most fearless mountaineer of all." He was a man of powerful physique, as hard, tough, and weather-beaten as a sun-dried elk hide. He seemed immune to hardship and fatigue, shot with a curious double wobble and deadly accuracy, and walked with the peculiar lurch of a common drunk. Most writers who visited the Rocky Mountains during the heyday of the fur trade described Bill Williams, both because of his fame and eccentricities, either from hearsay or personal observation.

"Williams always rode ahead," wrote Frederick Ruxton,

his body bent over his saddlehorn, across which rested a long heavy rifle, his keen gray eyes peering from under the slouched brim of a flexible felt-hat, black and shining with grease. His buckskin hunting shirt, bedaubed until it had the appearance of polished leather, hung in folds over his bony carcass; his nether extremities being clothed in pantaloons of the same material (with scattered fringes down the outside of the leg — which ornaments, however, had been pretty well thinned to supply "whangs" for mending moccasins or pack saddles), which, shrunk with wet, clung tightly

---

[11] William George Drummond Stewart: *Edward Warren* (London, 1854), Vol. I, p. 159.

to his long, spare, sinewy legs. His feet were thrust into a pair of Mexican stirrups made of wood, and as big as coal-scuttles; and iron spurs of incredible proportions, with tinkling drops attached to the rowels, were fastened to his heel — a bead-worked strap, four inches broad, securing them over the instep. In the shoulder belt which sustained his powder-horn and bullet-pouch, were fastened the various instruments essential to one pursuing his mode of life. An awl, with deer-horn handle, and a point defended by a case of cherry-wood carved by his own hand, hung at the back of his belt, side by side with a worm for cleaning the rifle; and under this was a squat and quaint-looking bullet-mold, the handles guarded by strips of buckskin to save his fingers from burning when running balls, having for its companion a little bottle made from the point of an antelope's horn, scraped transparent, which contained the "medecine" used in baiting traps. The old coon's face was sharp and thin, a long nose and chin hob-nobbing each other; and his head was always bent forward giving him the appearance of being hump-backed. He appeared to look neither to the right nor left, but, in fact, his little twinkling eye was every where. He looked at no one he was addressing, always seeming to be thinking of something else than the subject of his discourse, speaking in a whining, thin, cracked voice, and in a tone that left the hearer in doubt whether he was laughing or crying.[12]

The trait, more than any other, that made Bill Williams the most colorful and intriguing of the mountain men was his confirmed practice of hunting and trapping by himself. He was as unpredictable as a vagrant wind, and no one knew when he might saddle his scarred, flea-bitten Rosi-

[12] George Frederick Ruxton: *Life in the Far West* (New York, 1859), pp. 124–5.

nante, pack up his traps, furs, and personal belongings, and disappear into the forest or set out for "tother side of the big hills." Men found the ashes of his campfires beside unmarked streams in the heart of the Rockies and in the depths of the desolate cañons that feed the lower Colorado. No valley was too hidden for him to find, no desert too remote for him to cross. A Ute Indian once said that he was as solitary as "the eagle in the heavens, or the panther in the mountains." [13]

When John Charles Frémont led his ill-fated exploring expedition into New Mexico in the winter of 1848–9, he engaged the famous trapper to guide the company across the forbidding Sangre de Cristo, San Juan, and La Garita mountains. Old Bill knew the country as well as any man could know it. But the cold was unprecedented; the valleys and passes were blocked and sealed by snow; the worst of the winter, already harder than any season the oldest trappers had previously experienced, still lay ahead. Williams was at fault in accepting Frémont's offer and attempting to guide the party through; but Frémont automatically assumed responsibility for the subsequent disaster when he stubbornly held to the route of his own choosing across the mountains and refused to follow Old Bill's advice to seek a safer way.

"His knowledge of that part of the country was perfect," Antoine Leroux wrote of Williams to "Don Commander de Taos" on August 22, 1850. "The course which was taken by Col. Frémont was an impracticable one in winter. No

---

[13] Chauncey P. Williams: *"Lone Elk,"* Part I, p. 32 (The Old West Series, No. Six. Denver, 1935).

sensible mountaineer would even for a moment entertain the idea of taking it, as no road ever existed there known either to the trapper or the Indians."

Eleven men paid for this folly with their lives through exhaustion and outright starvation. All too late, Frémont gave up the undertaking and left his baggage and equipment in the snow. Early in the spring, as soon as it was possible to travel, Bill Williams and Dr. Benjamin Kern, the scientist of the expedition, attempted to salvage the abandoned instruments and collections. But the two were shot, probably by a roving band of Utes, who mistook Old Bill, an adopted member of their tribe, for some other white.

Though he knew the hidden holes and corners of much of the Colorado basin even better than Joe Walker or Ewing Young, Williams kept most of his knowledge to himself and rarely shared the results of his explorations and discoveries with the outside world. He was a symbol of the return to the primitive, the strong-willed self-reliance, the passion for loneliness and solitude that characterized the mountain man.[14] His name is fittingly perpetuated by a major tributary of the Colorado River, a near-by mountain peak, and probably a flourishing Arizona town.

William Wolfskill, the last of the fur traders with whose activities this chapter deals, was the very antithesis of Old Bill. The one represented the rough, half-savage, licentious Ishmaelite among the mountain men. The other was a man of character and substance, in later years a distinguished

---

[14] See Alpheus H. Favour: *Old Bill Williams, Mountain Man* (Chapel Hill, North Carolina, 1936), *passim*.

and honored benefactor of California, the land of his adoption.

Another member of the long list of Virginia-descended frontiersmen who extended the Wilderness Trace to the Pacific, Wolfskill was born near Richmond, Kentucky, on March 20, 1798. Eleven years later the family moved to Howard County, Missouri, and there his father built a fort for protection against the Indians. At the close of the War of 1812 William went back to Kentucky to attend school. Five years later he returned to the family's new home in Boone's Lick, Missouri, and remained a member of the household until 1822. Then, at the age of twenty-four, "he started out in the world on his own account, to seek his fortune, to penetrate still further into the far west, and to find a better country in which to settle." [15]

Wolfskill's quest for "a better country in which to settle" led him first to New Mexico in the Becknell wagon train with Ewing Young. From Taos and Santa Fe, generally as Young's partner or associate, Wolfskill made a succession of trapping and trading expeditions that carried him into the Rio Grande, San Juan, and Gila river basins and some parts of the states of Chihuahua and Sonora. Twice, at least, the Indians attacked the parties, killed a number of the trappers, and carried off some of his belongings.

Once, while trapping on the Rio Grande, Wolfskill was treacherously shot in his sleep by a Mexican companion and left for dead; but the wounded man succeeded in reaching a Mexican village, twenty or twenty-five miles distant, where he was able to obtain a little crude medical

[15] *Wilmington Journal* (Wilmington, California), October 20, 1866.

attention. The next day his would-be murderer appeared in the same settlement with the report that a band of Indians had attacked the camp and killed the American. Wolfskill denounced the scoundrel, and the authorities placed him under guard and took him back to the scene of the attack. There the snow showed only two sets of footprints and thus completely disproved the Mexican's trumped-up story of the Indian raid. Even in the face of this evidence, however, the criminal escaped with a brief imprisonment, while Wolfskill carried the scars left by the wound for the remainder of his life.

In 1830 Wolfskill made an agreement with Ewing Young and William Waldo to lead a trapping expedition to California. The party of eleven men, including George Yount and Lewis Burton, later a prominent resident of Santa Barbara, left Taos in September. After reaching Los Angeles, his first objective, Wolfskill proposed to trap the rivers of the San Joaquin Valley and at the close of the season form a junction somewhere in California with a second company under Ewing Young. The combined party would then return to New Mexico by way of the Great Salt Lake. The last part of this plan was never carried out. When Wolfskill left Taos that September morning, he looked on the mountain-girt pueblo for the last time.

New Mexican traders had already opened a trail of sorts to Los Angeles; but with the hope of finding profitable trapping on the way, Wolfskill and his men took "a route further north than that usually adopted by the Spaniards in traveling between California and New Mexico." Roughly, the trail ran in a northwesterly direction from Abiquiu, crossed both the Grand and Green rivers above their junction, then struck westward to the Sevier River and perhaps followed Jedediah Smith's old trail along that stream into the wilderness of high, rough peaks in the heart of the Wasatch Range.

Here, the men suffered severely from cold and hunger; but when Wolfskill attempted to escape by the old "Spanish Trail" of the New Mexican traders, deep winter snows blocked his efforts and a howling blizzard brought all movement to an end. George Yount's account of the experience still makes real the trappers' sense of utter isolation and leaves the reader in the grip of the deadly, penetrating mountain chill. Graphically he wrote:

Our trappers, with much toil, reached a strip of table land upon a lofty range of mountains, where they encountered the most terrible snowstorm they had ever experienced — During several days, no one ventured out of camp — There they lay embedded in snow, very deep, animals and men huddled thick as possible together, to husband and enjoy all possible animal warmth, having spread their thick and heavy blankets, & piled bark and brush wood around & over them — The Blankets used by these travellers of the wilderness are of a peculiar kind; — very thick and almost impervious to water — A small stream of water, running directly through a corner of their camp, they found not difficult to keep open for the use of themselves and their animals, and a blazing fire was kept burning night & day in the centre — With their Beaver-skins they were enabled to cover themselves and provide a comfortable bed — Thus they lay, shut out from all the world, while the storm was howling around them, and the snow falling in astonishing profusion — The snowstorm ended with rain during several hours, and then followed a season of piercing cold; by means of which was formed, on the surface of the snow, a strong crust of ice, which would bear the weight of the heaviest animals — After the storm subsided and the weather had softened, Yount & Wolfskill ascended a lofty Peak of the mountains for observation — in the whole range of human view, in every direction, nothing could be discerned, in the least degree encouraging, but only mountains, piled on mountains, all capped with cheerless snow, in long and continuous succession, till they seemed to mingle with the blue vault of heaven and fade away in the distance — It was a cheerless prospect, and calculated to cause emotions by no means agreeable in the stoutest heart.[16]

The descent from the frozen, snow-covered heights of the Wasatch plateau to the valley of the Virgin River was a nightmare of cold, trackless mountains, impenetrable snowdrifts, and, slipping, sliding horses; but the hardships at last ended in a pleasant valley, filled with herds of elk, deer, and antelope, virtually unmolested by man and almost as tame as the sheep and goats of a farmer's barnyard.

Leaving this Elysium, Wolfskill traveled some distance down the Colorado and then struck off across the desert to the Mojave River. Following that "inconstant" stream to the San Bernardino Mountains, the company finally reached Los Angeles by way of the Cajon Pass. Once in the pueblo, the party rapidly disintegrated, leaving Wolfskill without money or equipment and heavily in debt to his creditors in New Mexico.

The expedition ended Wolfskill's career as a mountain man, but made him a permanent resident of Los Angeles

16 "The Chronicles of George C. Yount," ed. by Charles L. Camp, *California Historical Society Quarterly*, Vol. II, No. I, pp. 39–40.

and one of the two pioneers in "California's greatest industry, the production of wine and fruit." Wolfskill died in 1866, "leaving an enviable reputation as an honest, enterprising, generous, unassuming, intelligent man."

The Wolfskill expedition aided materially in the development of the important caravan trade between New Mexico and California, but the common belief that it opened the "Old Spanish Trail" between the two provinces is incorrect. As a matter of fact, no particular man or expedition deserves that credit. The trail represented the contributions of many rather than of one.

The story of the trail (east of the Colorado) began with a certain Spaniard named Juan María de Rivera, who led a party by way of the San Juan River and the Uncompagre Plateau to the Grand River basin in 1765 and piloted at least two other expeditions into the same region within the next decade. In 1776 two Spanish friars, Fray Francisco Anastasio Domínguez and Fray Silvester Valez Escalante, started from Santa Fe to open a route to California.

The trail ran north and northwest by way of present-day Durango, the great Rangely oil field, and the Duchesne River. Turning south at Provo, it later bent nearly due west, then changed its course again to run almost parallel to Highway 91, and finally crossed the Escalante Desert to St. George. From St. George the expedition swung back to the Colorado, fording the river at the Crossing of the Fathers, and returned to Santa Fe by Oraibi, Zuñi, Ácoma, and Albuquerque.[17] New Mexican trappers and Indian

17 Hubert S. Auerbach: "Father Escalante's Journal and Related Documents," *Utah Historical Quarterly*, Vol. XI, Nos. 1–4.

slave traders soon followed the footsteps of the padres as far as southern Utah.[18]

The explorations of Jedediah Smith and Francisco Garcés, pathfinder pre-eminent of the Colorado Desert, prepared the way for the extension of this pioneer trade route from the Indian villages of southern Utah to the remote pueblo of Los Angeles; but the opening of the rest of the trail is still obscure. History has not yet positively identified the trader who first drove his pack train over the entire route and thus joined together the pioneer explorations on the east and west.[19] The nearest approach to an answer is probably supplied by the brief record of a party of thirty-five New Mexican traders, accompanied by Richard Campbell, one of Ewing Young's associates and a leading figure in the commerce of the prairies both west and south of New Mexico, who made the trip from Santa Fe to San Diego in 1827.[20]

---

[18] Joseph J. Hill: "Spanish and Mexican Exploration and Trade Northwest from New Mexico into the Great Basin, 1765–1853," ibid., Vol. III, No. 1, pp. 3–4.

[19] Dr. LeRoy Hafen of Denver has an extensive study of the Los Angeles-Santa Fe Trail now in progress. The volume will undoubtedly clear up this and other doubtful matters.

[20] See Humphrey to Gwin, 1858, Bancroft MSS. Cited in Sullivan: *The Travels of Jedediah Smith,* p. 171 n. The reference is vague and the original letter cannot be found.

Richard Campbell (not to be confused with Robert Campbell, the well-known merchant of St. Louis) reached New Mexico at least as early as 1825. On April 27 of that year he entered six bales of mixed goods, valued at about 800 pesos, in the National Customs House at Santa Fe. A year later, in company with John Pearson, Julian Green, Lucas Murray, and Ewing Young, he applied for Mexican naturalization, and his name appeared frequently thereafter in New Mexican affairs. Huntington Library, RI 81, 86.

The trail of these early traders ran by way of Zuñi and the San Juan River almost to the Colorado. Beyond that point the route is problematical. Almost nothing further is known of the personnel, experiences, and results of the expedition, but presumably its members brought back such favorable reports of the attractions and resources of California and the possibilities of trade between that province and New Mexico that other traders of Santa Fe were induced to undertake further expeditions.

The first of such fully authenticated ventures left New Mexico in the fall of 1829 and reached the settlements of southern California the last of January. It was led by an adventurous trader named Antonio Armíjo. The expedition was described unofficially in the *Registro Oficial del Gobierno de los Estados-Unidos Mexicanos* (published in Mexico City on June 5, 1830), and in Armíjo's official diary, which appeared in the same journal two weeks later.[21]

The unofficial account began:

On the 6th of November of the past year, there left from the village of Abiquiu 31 men, including the commandant Citizen Antonio Armíjo, inhabitants of the territory of New Mexico, wishing to discover a route to Upper California and to sell therein some manufactures of their country, traveling towards the Northwest, and a month later reaching the Rio Grande, or Colorado, which they forded without difficulty,

[21] LeRoy R. Hafen, Director of the Colorado State Historical Society, discovered the documents in the *Registro Oficial* and published translations of them, with extensive editorial notes, in the *Huntington Library Quarterly*, Vol. XI, No. I, pp. 87–101. The New Mexican archives also contain vague reports of other trading and trapping ventures from New Mexico to California before 1828.

despite its being about 2,000 varas wide, and on the banks of the said river, which are of smooth stone, there are some inscriptions which they inferred to be made by the missionary fathers, who had long ago attempted and failed to discover this route.

From the official diary, which he characterizes in a noticeable understatement as "aggravatingly brief," Hafen worked out Armíjo's itinerary in considerable detail. In general, the route ran from Abiquiu by way of Cañon Largo, the Mancos River, and the southern border of Mesa Verde National Park, to the vicinity of the present little settlement of Mexican Hat and the famous Goose Neck Gorge of the San Juan River. Thence it traversed the rugged country crossed by Domínguez and Escalante, where at times the men had to unload the mules and carry the baggage on their own shoulders, till it reached "the edge of the mesa of the *Rio Grande,* known in the Californias as the Colorado, a day's journey without water." [22]

Armíjo reached the Colorado on or about the 6th of December. The next day he examined the ford, commonly known as the Crossing of the Fathers, which Domínguez and Escalante had used on their return journey from the western to the eastern side of the river. On the 8th of December the train lay by while the men repaired the steps that the friars had cut in a steep sandstone hogback on the western bank of the Colorado more than half a century before. "To lead the animals down by their bridles to the canyon," wrote Escalante of this incident, "it was necessary to hew steps with the ax in a rock for a distance of

---

[22] The entry is for December 5, 1829.

about three yards or a little less. The animals could go down the rest of the way, but without a pack or a rider."

One blazing day in June 1946 I left the small rowboat in which two companions and I — part of a company of nine members — were floating down the Colorado, and made an overland reconnaissance. Without trail or landmarks, we wandered over a high, barren mesa, climbed in and out of a deep cañon, crossed rough, naked ridges, and came at last to the crude steps that Father Escalante fashioned a hundred and seventy years before and Citizen Antonio Armíjo successfully used a long generation later. They were not steps in the ordinary sense of the word, but shallow grooves, makeshift devices that weary men had cut out of grudgingly yielding rock to check the momentum of their mules and let the slipping, sliding animals regain their balance.

As we looked at the ridge and river and walked up and down the roughly fashioned steps, the years fled away, and the past, with its sandaled priests and rugged, unlettered traders, became more real than the troubled world of wars and roaring machines and infinite anxieties that lay beyond the desert's farthest rim.

Not far from the Domínguez-Escalante steps we accidentally found another set of smaller groovings in the rock, apparently unknown before our chance discovery. Were these cut out by the same hands? Or made by Indian raiders who had designs on the horse herds of the Mormon settlers? Or hurriedly fashioned by Armíjo when he stopped the baggage train and "repaired the upgrade of the canyon, the same one which had been worked by the padres"? The questions were never answered — but the steps are there.

And the land held other wonders. Off in the lonely distance we saw a valley, silent, old, and vast, that brooded forever over the ruins and remnants of a broken world, a world of ancient sandstone buttes and pinnacles, grooved and fluted by the wind and sand, a world where Time had never wakened and the centuries and ages lay sleeping in the sun.

After leaving the Crossing of the Fathers, Armíjo and his band continued across the desert reaches of southern Utah till they came to the *"Severo"* or Virgin River and found Jedediah Smith's old route to the Colorado. The company struck the river on January 1, 1830 and proceeded downstream two days over what the diarist tersely designates as a "rugged trail."

Some eleven days' travel across the dry Nevada plains brought the caravan to the Amargosa River, heavy and white with alkali. A number of watering-places such as Cottonwood Spring, Bitter Creek, and Aqua del Tornaso, or the Lake of the Miracle, as Armíjo more picturesquely named it, enabled the company to reach the sandy bed of the Mojave River; but on the three weeks' journey from the Colorado to this fickle stream the diary frequently held the laconic entry: "A day's journey without water."

After striking the Mojave, the caravan proceeded upstream for six days, living principally on horses and mules, crossed the mountains, probably by way of Cajon Creek, to the outlying ranch of San Bernardino, and on January 31 reached the San Gabriel Mission. The Californians, though finding it hard to believe that a caravan could cross such a wide expanse of rough, unknown country, gave the strangers a cordial welcome and readily exchanged horses, mules, and other livestock for the traders' merchandise.

Some of Armíjo's men started back to New Mexico on February 24, 1830 and, "unhindered by the terrain and the mountains," nor lacking "water, firewood, or pasture," reached Santa Fe in only forty days. Other members of the party went south to Sonora. Armíjo and the remainder of the company left California on March 1 and arrived in Santa Fe two months later.

The reports in the *Registro Oficial* mentioned the Indian tribes encountered by the expedition, explained the time-consuming difficulties encountered on the outward journey by the pertinent comment: "the said Armíjo was traveling over an unknown route and found it necessary to make numerous detours to avoid impassable cañons and mountains"; and expressed the hope that a shorter route might be discovered between Santa Fe and California and that "from this discovery great usefulness will accrue to this territory and to all the Mexican nation."

Armíjo had one regret: "The *empresarios*, although they are known to be courageous, rugged, and eager to discover new lands, are lacking in instruction and literature, by means of which they would have been able to note the various products that the territory of the Mexican Republic possesses in this region; and they are able only to say that there exist suitable locations for establishing new villages and that in the hills there appear variously colored rocks or veins resembling minerals, some of the said hills having the shape of elevated *bufas* without forest or grass land, streaked with veins or rock strata."

With some modifications, the trail opened by Armíjo's pioneer venture became the one important caravan route between New Mexico and California for over twenty years. The trade was almost monopolized by New Mexicans, though from time to time Americans probably participated in it. The westbound caravans carried mostly silver, woolen goods, and blankets. On the return the traders brought back horses, mules, jennets, jacks, and small quantities of goods of Chinese or New England manufacture.

Unfortunately, the New Mexican traders as a class proved to be a reckless and disturbing element in California. Horse-stealing became more important than legitimate trade, and the California authorities often complained of the "scandalous robberies committed by individuals from New Mexico." For a time the situation grew worse instead of better. The more lawless traders, usually making use of liquor for the purpose, persuaded gentile or renegade Indians to raid the California herds and drive the stolen horses to designated locations in the unsettled country behind the mountains. The largest and most popular of these rendezvous lay in the southern end of the San Joaquin Valley.

To what extent American trappers, such as Peg-leg Smith, Jim Baker, and Old Bill Williams, associated themselves with the New Mexicans in these large-scale horse-stealing operations is a matter of speculation. The California records referred to the horse-thieves as *"Los Chaquanosos,* or adventurers of all nations"; and after one of the largest of the raids the investigating official set forth the need of a "strong and combined expedition against the Chaquanosos thieves, as it is known the greater part of them are American and English." [23]

It is difficult to say how far these charges against American and English fur traders were justified. There were great numbers of wild or half-wild horses in California (of no use to the missions or rancheros), which, in earlier years at least, had been systematically destroyed to save the grazing lands for cattle. If such animals were rounded up and driven off by the fur traders, no damage was done to the Californians and the action could be called horse-stealing only in a very technical sense.

Raids on the *caballadas* — bands of broken or "gentled" horses belonging to the rancheros — were another matter, and presumably it was against such depredations that the Californians protested. This form of horse-stealing, however, was much more extensive after American annexation, when the fur traders were almost gone, than before. By the very nature of things, the charges made against the early mountain men were based in large part upon vague or hearsay evidence; and certainly the trappers' fanciful tales of their own exploits against the Californians are not to be taken at face value. But the subject is sufficiently interesting and important to warrant at least passing mention.

Rufus Sage once camped in the Rocky Mountains with a party of Americans who were driving a large herd of

[23] The best treatment of this whole matter is found in Eleanor Lawrence's "Horse Thieves on the Spanish Trail," *Touring Topics* (*Westways*), Vol. XXIII, No. 1, pp. 22–5.

horses to the States. "Their horses had been obtained from Upper California the year previous by a band of mountaineers, under the lead of one Thompson," he wrote.

This band, numbering twenty-two in all, had made a descent upon the Mexican *ranchos* and captured between two and three thousand head of horses and mules. A corps of some sixty Mexican cavalry pursued and attacked them, but were defeated and pursued in turn, with the loss of several mules and their entire camp equipage: after which the adventurers were permitted to regain their mountain homes, without further molestation; but, in passing the cheerless desert, between the Sierra Nevada and Colorado, the heat, dust, and thirst were so intolerably oppressive, that full one half of their animals died. The remainder, however, were brought to rendezvous, and variously disposed of, to suit the wants and wishes of their captors.[24]

The most notorious of the horse-stealing mountain men, according to popular account, was Thomas L. ("Peg-leg") Smith, a Kentuckian who ran away at the age of sixteen because of the daily floggings he received both at school and from his father. After trapping for some years with Antoine Robidoux and Céran St. Vrain, Smith, or the "Bald Hornet," to use a name coined by Albert Pike, made a number of expeditions to the Grand and Green river valleys and a long excursion with one companion to the sources of the Sevier River and the country of the Navajos. His best-known feat was the amputation of his own leg, the bones of which had been shattered by a rifle ball in an Indian fight, and the fashioning of a wooden leg out of the

---

[24] *Scenes in the Rocky Mountains*, p. 27.

limb of an oak tree. This pegleg gave him both his name and a widespread reputation among the mountain men, but his exploits in raiding the California horse herds were probably colored by his vanity and imagination. He died in the county hospital of San Francisco in October 1866.[25]

Next to Peg-leg Smith, Bill Williams was said to have made away with more California horses than any other mountain man.[26] Much of this dubious fame apparently rested on an article by George D. Brewerton that appeared under the caption: "A Ride with Kit Carson," in *Harper's New Monthly Magazine* for August 1853. After speaking of the large number of horses' skeletons that marked the trail across one of the waterless stretches of the Mojave Desert, Brewerton added:

The frequent recurrence of these bleaching bones in a road so lonely, induced me to ask some explanation in regard to them of an old trapper belonging to our party. He informed me, that many years before, Billy Williams, a mountaineer almost as distinguished as Carson himself, had, in some interval of catching beaver and killing Indians, found time to gather a band of mountain men, with the view of undertaking a sort of piratical expedition to the coast of Lower California. In this enterprise he succeeded so far as to enter California, help himself to upward of fifteen hundred head of mules and horses, and regain the desert without losing a man. But from this point his troubles began. The Californians, disapproving of this summary mode of treating their property, determined to pursue and retake it by force; and to carry out their design, followed closely upon the trail of Williams's party, with nearly two hundred men. Finding him-

---

[25] *San Francisco Bulletin,* October 26, 1866.
[26] Jim Baker was a good runner-up.

self pursued, the mountaineer, whose men were not over
thirty in number, pushed on with all possible speed; and in
crossing the great jornada, lost from fatigue and over-
driving nearly one thousand head of his ill-gotten booty."

The anonymous "old trapper" then went on to tell Brewerton how Williams turned the tables on his pursuers and
even made off with the California posse's own horses and
mules. The Americans were then in turn raided by the
Indians and forfeited all the twice-stolen animals to these
other desert thieves. "Such is the story," Brewerton con-
cludes, "but beyond the dry bones in the jornada, I can
bear no witness to its truth."

Though the more lawless American fur traders probably
had no scruples against turning horse-thieves as opportunity offered, the chief quarrel of the Californians was
with the disorderly element among the New Mexicans and
with the authorities at Santa Fe and Taos who gave such
trouble-makers official licenses to trade with other Mexican
citizens. In time California officials were compelled in self-
defense to impose a number of practical restrictions and
regulations on the inter-province traffic in mules and horses.

"An act was passed by the legislative assembly," wrote
Eleanor Lawrence, "which provided that the New Mexicans
should not buy mules, mares, and horses at other than the
price set by one of the Justices of the Peace; that if they
went to ranchos that belonged to this province they must
have permission of the Alcalde; and furthermore, that the
individuals should present a document authorizing the le-
gality of their purchases. Henceforth it became the practice of the Los Angeles officials to set a place for the assem-

bling of the traders before they left for New Mexico. In this way they could inspect the herds and recover stolen animals. Stock which did not bear the brand that denoted sale was easily identified, and could be returned to the rightful owners, and the thieves punished." [27]

The government of New Mexico also sought to bring about a better organization of the California trade and co-operate with the California authorities in the suppression of lawlessness and crime. With these ends in view, the leader of a caravan was given authority to make arrests and inflict other penalties, prevent desertions, "lead the caravan with as much order as if it were in national service," and hand over any evildoers to the California authorities for punishment.[28]

---

[27] "Mexican Trade between Santa Fe and Los Angeles, 1830–1848," *California Historical Society Quarterly*, Vol. X, No. 1, p. 29.

[28] Ibid., p. 34. See also the passport or safe conduct granted by Santiago Abreu to Santiago Martin, August 13, 1832, to go to California with fifteen men. Huntington Library, RI 138.

CHAPTER 8

Joseph Reddeford Walker:

To the "Extreme End of the Great West"

W H I L E trappers and traders from Santa Fe and Taos swung south in increasing numbers to the interior provinces of Mexico and westward to the Pacific, other men of the same breed opened similar trails across the land of distance, silence, salt deserts, and brooding solitude known in that day as the Great American Desert and in this as the Great Basin. Next to Jedediah Smith, the six-foot Tennessean Joseph Reddeford Walker became the foremost trapper-explorer of the region.

Walker, for whom at least three important landmarks in the West are named,[1] was born on December 13, 1798. He was thus approximately the same age as Jedediah Smith, Ewing Young, William Wolfskill, Thomas Fitzpatrick, Peter Skene Ogden, and many other well-known mountain men. His birthplace, as recorded on the Walker tombstone in Vallejo, California, was Roane County, Tennessee; but there is some evidence to show that he was born in Virginia, just before rather than after the family's removal

---

[1] Walker Pass, California; Walker River, California and Nevada; Walker Lake, Nevada.

to the Western settlements. Like Kit Carson, Joe was only one of several brothers who won distinction in the Far West.

Walker learned the craft and skill of the backwoodsman on the Tennessee frontier; in 1819 he moved to the neighborhood of Independence, Missouri; thereafter for half a century he trapped the streams of the Rocky Mountains and found new paths, some of which in all likelihood he was the last as well as the first to travel, through the broken lands beyond. There are those indeed who say that Joe Walker knew the Southwest from Santa Fe to Los Angeles, from the Gila River to the Humboldt, as no one has known or understood it "that ever was before his time, in his time, or since his death."

Becknell's Santa Fe expedition of 1821 gave Walker his first taste of both the possibilities and the hazards of Mexican trade and introduced him to the hardships and dangers of a trapper's life. It also exposed him to the mystery and fascination of an enchanted land that held him for half a century in an unbroken spell.

For twelve years Walker hunted, trapped, and traded out of Independence. For a time he also served as sheriff of the newly created Jackson County. Then, in 1832, Benjamin Louis Eulalie de Bonneville, by birth a Frenchman, graduate of West Point, captain in the United States Army, and holder of a two years' furlough to engage in exploration and the fur trade, made Walker one of his principal lieutenants and advisers.

Bonneville's entrance into the Rocky Mountain fur business intensified the cut-throat rivalry already existing between the American Fur Company, the Rocky Mountain Fur Company, the Hudson's Bay Company, and the independent trappers. The captain's personal accomplishments, whether in the field of exploration or financial success, were inconsequential, and his contemporaries usually spoke of him with ridicule or contempt. Of his right to a place among the leaders of the mountain men, Chittenden bluntly wrote:

The adventures of Captain Bonneville in the Rocky mountains from 1832 to 1835 have attained a prominence in the history of the West to which they are not entitled. They and their hero are an apt illustration of Diedrich Knickerbocker's profound idea of the power of history to rescue men and events from the "wide-spread, insatiable maw of oblivion." Captain Bonneville, so far as his work in the Rocky mountains is concerned, is a history-made man. Irving's popular work, which in later editions bears Captain Bonneville's name, is not in reality so much a record of that officer's adventures, as it is of all the transactions of a period in which the business of the fur trade in the Rocky mountains was at its height. Scarcely a third of the work has to do exclusively with Bonneville, but around this theme as a nucleus are gathered the events of the most interesting era of the fur trade, until the central figure in the narrative is encased in a frame more costly and attractive than the picture itself.[2]

It may be added that unless Bonneville was engaged on some secret mission for the United States government in neutralizing the British advance in the Northwest — a mission hinted at but not as yet substantiated by official documents or other authentic proof — the verdict of Chittenden

---

[2] *The American Fur Trade,* Vol. I, pp. 396–7.

must stand.[3] But the army captain had a skillful flair for publicity, and the facile pen of Washington Irving magnified him into a figure of such heroic proportions that a vast, long-extinct lake, one of the world's greatest dams, and many other Western landmarks now perpetuate his pleasant-sounding name.

Backed by the money of New York capitalists headed by Alfred Seton, one of Astor's former associates, Bonneville organized an expedition of a hundred and ten men, selected Joe Walker and Michel S. Cerré to be his chief assistants, purchased an exceptionally large assortment of goods for trading-purposes, and, in addition to the usual complement of riding-horses and pack mules, provided twenty wagons drawn by mules and oxen to carry his equipment to the mountains and bring back the anticipated furs.

The expedition left Fort Osage on May 1, 1832 and followed the familiar route along the Platte (which one writer characterized as the "most magnificent and useless of rivers," and another described as "a thousand miles long and six inches deep"), into the Sweetwater Valley and on to the Green River. The company reached the Green on July 27, only to find a band of American Fur Company trappers under Lucien Fontenelle already there. Bonneville then

---

[3] Some years ago J. Neilsen Barry of Portland, Oregon, published a number of important documents relating to Captain Bonneville in the *Annals of Wyoming* (April 1932, Vol. VIII, No. 4). The documents are interesting and show rather clearly that Bonneville was commissioned by the War Department to collect all sorts of data and information on the Indian tribes of the Northwest. The documents themselves are too vague on Bonneville's Oregon mission, however, to be conclusive, and Barry's painfully brief comments and explanations do nothing to make the situation any clearer.

continued a little farther up the river and built a fortified trading post on its west bank.

Unfortunately for Bonneville's purse and reputation, the annual rendezvous had already taken the place of the permanent fort as a center for the Indian and trapper trade of the Green River Valley, and the post that bore his name proved of such little value that it came to be known as "Fort Nonsense," or "Bonneville's Folly."

W. A. Ferris, a member of the Rocky Mountain Fur Company, thus described the fort and its surroundings:

This establishment was doubtless intended for a permanent trading post, by its projector, who has, however, since changed his mind, and quite abandoned it. . . . It is situated in a fine open plain, on a rising spot of ground, about three hundred yards from Green river on the west side, commanding a view of the plains for several miles up and down that stream. On the opposite side of the fort about two miles distant, there is a fine willowed creek, called "Horse Creek," flowing parallel with Green river, and emptying into it about five miles below the fortification. The river from the fort, in one direction, is terminated by a bold hill rising to the height of several hundred feet on the opposite side of the creek, and extending in a line parallel with it. — Again on the east side of the river, an abrupt bank appears rising from the water's edge, and extending several miles above and below, till the hills, jutting in on the opposite side of the river, finally conceal it from the sight. The fort presents a square enclosure, surrounded by posts or pickets firmly set in the ground, of a foot or more in diameter, planted close to each other, and about fifteen feet in length. At two of the corners, diagonally opposite to each other, block houses of unhewn logs are so constructed and situated, as to defend the square outside of the pickets, and hinder the approach of an enemy from any quarter. The prairie in the vicinity of the fort is covered with fine grass, and the whole together seems well calculated for the security both of men and horses.[4]

Bonneville's trapping expeditions, like his fort, brought disappointing results. When he reached the mountains in 1832, the spring trapping season was far advanced and he obtained barely enough furs to pay the wages of his men. His rivals, especially the American Fur Company, got the better of him at nearly every turn; his lieutenants suffered heavy losses at the hands of the Indians; as fast as he escaped one round of troubles, either bad management or bad luck plunged him into another.

After the summer rendezvous in Green River Valley, Bonneville tried to recoup his fortunes by dividing his company into three bands. The smallest of these, under Cerré, left for St. Louis with the accumulated furs; Bonneville himself set out at the head of a much larger force for the country of the Crow Indians; and Walker was made commander of a well-equipped expedition designed to trap and explore the territory that lay in and beyond the valley of the Great Salt Lake.

By that time the Great Salt Lake, or "Big Lake," as the trappers frequently called it, was already one of the best-known and most familiar landmarks of the West; and Washington Irving's attempt (presumably at Bonneville's instigation) to change its name to Lake Bonneville was

---

[4] *Life in the Rocky Mountains,* pp. 206–7.

properly condemned.[5] Ferris spoke the mind of his fellows when he wrote:

An attempt has been recently made to change the name of this lake to Lake Bonnyville, from no other reason that I can learn, but to gratify the silly conceit of a Captain Bonnyville, whose adventures in this region at the head of a party, form the ground work of "Irving's Rocky Mountains." There is no more justice or propriety in calling the lake after that gentleman, than after any other one of the many persons who in the course of their fur hunting expeditions have passed in its vicinity. He neither discovered, nor explored it, nor has he done anything else to entitle him to the honour of giving it his name, and the foolish vanity that has been his only inducement for seeking to change the appelation by which it has been known for fifty years, to his own patronymic, can reflect no credit upon him, or the talented author who has lent himself to the service of an ambition so childish and contemptible.[6]

What was the specific mission of the Bonneville-Walker expedition? Washington Irving assumed that Bonneville was primarily interested in the exploration of the Great Salt Lake and the discovery of its scientific secrets, and that he instructed Walker "to keep along the shores of the lake, and trap in all the streams along his route," but to go no farther west.

Irving, however, apparently relied only on Bonneville's unsupported word for this interpretation, and his statement is flatly contradicted by every contemporary record that has so far come to light. Only a few years after the return

[5] Unfortunately Frémont's presumption a decade later in changing the name of "Ogden's River" to the Humboldt was more successful.

[6] Op. cit., p. 69.

of the company Zenas Leonard, Walker's official clerk, published a straightforward narrative of the expedition. In it he wrote:

"Walker was ordered to steer through an unknown country towards the Pacific and to return to the Great Salt Lake the following summer in case he failed to find beaver in the 'unknown country.'" He "was a man well calculated to undertake a business of this kind," added Leonard. "He was well hardened to the hardships of the wilderness — understood the character of the Indians very well — was kind and affable to his men, but at the same time at liberty to command without giving offense — and to explore unknown regions was his chief delight." [7] George Nidever, a seasoned trapper of known integrity, declared that he joined the Walker expedition at the rendezvous in Green River Valley because the company was bound for California and he and his companions were tired of the cold and snow of the Rocky Mountain winter and wanted to enjoy the warmer climate for which California was already widely known.[8]

If, to this direct testimony, one adds the circumstances under which Bonneville equipped the expedition, the length of time the company planned to be away, and the captain's failure to travel the few necessary miles to make his own explorations and scientific investigations of the Great Salt Lake, to which Irving declared he attached such supreme significance, it is clear that California rather than Salt Lake

[7] *Narrative of the Adventures of Zenas Leonard,* written by himself (Clearfield, Pennsylvania, 1839), p. 33.

[8] *The Life and Adventures of George Nidever,* ed. by William Henry Ellison (Berkeley, California, 1937), pp. 31–2.

was the ultimate objective of the Walker expedition; and Bonneville's statement that he instructed his lieutenant to confine his operations to the lake and its immediate vicinity simply cannot be accepted at its face value.[9]

But without arguing the matter further, whatever Bonneville's objectives or instructions, Walker moved from the Green River encampment to the valley of the Salt Lake with a well-equipped company that numbered from forty to sixty men. Each trapper was provided "with four horses, and an equal share of blankets, buffalo robes, provisions, and every article necessary for the comfort of men engaged in an expedition of this kind." Somewhere east of Salt Lake the party made an extensive buffalo hunt and converted the meat into jerky. Then, about the middle of August, Walker broke camp, skirted the northern shore of the lake, and plunged into the unexplored waste lands to the west.

Sand, rock, and thirst — thirst, sand, and rock! Such was the tale. Each day's travel reduced the company's morale and sapped the physical vitality of its members. Relief came only when they reached Ogden's River — the Humboldt River of today — which offered a passable route to the west. But a Hudson's Bay Company brigade and a band of trappers under Edward Rose and Jim Bridger had recently taken most of its beaver, so from a trapping standpoint the stream proved a disappointment.

Then, too, the banks of the stream were so completely

---

[9] Bonneville himself expressed great interest in California and mentioned it as one of the countries he "was so anxious to visit." Unable to make the journey himself, one might reasonably suppose that he would entrust the mission to one of his chief lieutenants. See J. Neilsen Barry: "Capt. Bonneville," loc. cit., p. 612.

naked of vegetation that Leonard appropriately called it "Barren River," and the flesh of its beaver was said to turn poisonous whenever the animals fed on the wild parsnips that grew along the water.

The natives of the region, at first a mere annoyance and inconvenience, finally became a source of positive danger to the trappers. Dubbed by Leonard the Root Eaters or Shuckers, they were of Shoshone stock and occupied one of the lowest levels of the cultural scale of North American Indians. They ate, literally, whatever seeds, animals, fish, birds, reptiles, or insects their undiscriminating stomachs could digest. In hunting they used bows and arrows and the common Indian throwing stick, and fished with fiber lines and crude but fairly effective bone hooks.[10]

According to Sage, the natives of the Great Basin, to which this tribe belonged, had an ingenious method of catching ants. They first spread a dampened skin or piece of fresh-peeled bark over the anthills; when the streams of ants poured out, the Indians shook the insects into a sack and left them there to die. The ants were then thoroughly dried in the sun, stored away for future use, and eaten without further preparation.[11]

The Indians who lived on the shores of the sinks near the western side of the Great Basin were skillful fishermen. They used rafts woven out of the reeds and rushes that grew in large quantities along the margins of the lakes and made fishing spears by fastening the long leg-bone of a

---

[10] According to Leonard, the Indians would trade a beaver skin worth eight or ten dollars for an awl, a fishhook, a knife, or a string of beads.
[11] Rufus Sage, op. cit., p. 179.

sand-hill crane to the end of a willow pole. "They exhibit great dexterity with this simple structure," Leonard wrote, "sometimes killing a fish with it at a great distance."

As Walker's men proceeded down the river, the Indians stole their irreplaceable beaver traps and threatened to ambush solitary hunters. At last the tension reached the breaking-point and a few of the rawer recruits, inspired in part by bravado and the perverted ambition to shoot down an Indian under any circumstances, disobeyed Walker's orders and surreptitiously killed a number of the wretched, though by no means harmless, natives.

The incident increased the Indians' hostility toward the strangers, while the hope of acquiring the trappers' horses, food, and equipment — spoils that represented incalculable riches to the miserable Diggers — doubtless intensified their determination to get revenge. So as the expedition approached the brackish water and tule marshes now known as Humboldt Sink, the Indians concentrated in large numbers along the trappers' route with the apparent intention of making an attack.

The situation finally became so threatening that Walker fortified his position against the expected outbreak. The lake protected his rear; around the rest of the camp he erected a breastwork of the baggage and equipment "as impregnable to the Indian arrows, as were the cotton bags to the British bullets at New Orleans in 1815."

After waiting some time in vain for the Indians to begin hostilities, the company broke camp and moved out across the plain; but the natives continued to follow in even larger force until there were nearly twenty Indians to every white, and their manner and actions grew steadily more alarming. Afraid of being overwhelmed by sheer numbers if he waited any longer, Walker at last reluctantly gave his men the order to attack. Leonard thus described the grim results:

We now began to be a little stern with them and gave them to understand, that if they continued to trouble us, they would do it at their own risk. In this manner we were teased until a party of 80 or 100 came forward, who appeared more saucy and bold than any others. This greatly excited Capt. Walker, who was naturally of a very cool temperament, and he gave orders for the charge, saying that there was nothing equal to a good start in such a case. This was sufficient. A number of our men had never been engaged in any fighting with the Indians, and were anxious to try their skill. When our commander gave his consent to chastise these Indians, and give them an idea of our strength, 32 of us dismounted and prepared ourselves to give a severe blow.

We tied our extra horses to some shrubs and left them with the main body of our company, and then selected each a choice steed, mounted and surrounded this party of Indians. We closed in on them and fired, leaving thirty-nine dead on the field — which was nearly the half — the remainder were overwhelmed with dismay — running into the high grass in every direction, howling in the most lamentable manner.

Capt. Walker then gave orders to some of the men to take the bows of the fallen Indians and put the wounded out of misery.[12] The severity with which we dealt with these Indians may be revolting to the heart of the philanthropist; but the circumstances of the case altogether atones for the cruelty. It must be borne in mind, that we were far removed from the

---

[12] For a similar episode, see the account of James Ohio Pattie, p. 191.

hope of any succor in case we were surrounded, and that the country we were in was swarming with hostile savages, sufficiently numerous to devour us. Our object was to strike a decisive blow. This we did — even to a greater extent than we had intended.[13]

The affair on the Humboldt was a dirty business, a victory that no one is ever likely to describe as a glorious, soul-stirring epic. As Leonard intimated, the trappers undoubtedly went further than military necessity required or their leader intended them to go, and the episode left a permanent stain, deserved or undeserved, on Walker's reputation.[14] But by treating the incident as the slaughter of the innocents and failing to take into account the Indians' hostile intentions and the risk the company ran of complete annihilation, Walker's critics were unjustifiably severe. If there was no element of the heroic in the engagement on the Humboldt, neither was there any evidence that Walker planned or condoned a wanton massacre.

Leaving the scene of the shambles, the expedition crossed the eastern end of Humboldt Sink on tule rafts, continued south to the body of water now known as Carson Sink, and from there traveled east of the base of the mountains to the present Walker Lake. Walker and his men had now crossed the Great Basin from Green River Valley to the central Sierra — the first organized company to open the great wilderness trace west of Salt Lake over which thousands and tens of thousands of emigrants found their way to Cali-

---

[13] Leonard: *Narrative,* p. 37.
[14] The trappers gave the name Battle Lakes to the modern Humboldt Sink and its marshes.

fornia during the days of the gold rush and even until the coming of the railroad.

The expedition also conclusively showed that the much-sought Buenaventura River, so long supposed to carry the waters of the Rocky Mountains into the Pacific, was only a creation of the imagination and that the huge rampart of the Sierra Nevada was nowhere divided by such a water-way. Frémont had the satisfaction of discovering the same facts all over again, however, some ten years after Leonard wrote.

By following a clear running stream that emptied into Walker Lake from the near-by mountains, the trappers reached the vicinity of what is now the town of Bridgeport. From late spring to early fall the valley is one great meadow, green, lush, and flower-strewn. Seen against its backdrop of massive mountains and sharp, snow-clad minarets, it presents a picture of faultless, long-remembered beauty. But Walker and his wandering trappers reached the valley after summer had given place to fall. The grass was burned level with the ground by frost; snow clung in deep, ice-coated patches to the mountainsides; rough granite peaks rose stark and bleak above the timber line; and a cold, harsh wind, the courier of winter, swept sullenly across the naked ridges and roared ominously down the wooded slopes.

The route by which Walker led his men to the crest of "the dark and deathlike wall" of the Sierra is, and probably always must remain, a matter of speculation; but Farquhar, the best authority on the subject, tentatively concluded that the party ascended the eastern flank of the

Sierra by one of the southern tributaries of the East Walker River, became entangled in the lakes and mountains near Virginia Cañon, crossed over to the Tuolumne River and Lake Tenaya, and followed the general course of the present Tioga road to the edge of the Yosemite.[15]

As the trappers stood on the top of the gaunt Sierra range, by whatever route they reached its summit, the view to the west was at once magnificent and appalling. Trained to interpret every obstacle or advantage offered by forest, waterway, pass, or ridge, their appraising eyes looked out across a chaos of mountains, cañons, lakes, and splintered granite peaks. They had given themselves as hostages to the mountains, and their lives were forfeit unless they succeeded in crossing that forbidding, solitary land. Through it no trail of animal or man offered an escape. Walker and his ragged band must go where none had ever gone before.

As the trappers slowly fought their way across the mountains, the food supply grew perilously low. There were nights when the spits and the cooking pots were almost empty, and days when the men "had nothing to eat worth mentioning." Finally Walker fell back on his last reserve and gave the trappers leave to kill a horse from time to time to keep the hunger from getting out of hand; but the meat was black, tough, and lean — fit only "for a dog to feast on."

Worn down by the long months of travel from the Green River rendezvous, exhausted by the constant effort to break a path through rocks, snow, brush, and fallen timber, tor-

---

[15] Francis P. Farquhar: *Exploration of the Sierra Nevada* (San Francisco, 1925), pp. 6–7.

mented by the belly-pinch of hunger, dreaming, awake or asleep, of the ribs, steaks, and humps of the buffalo country, a number of the men grew mutinous and threatened to turn back over the long trail to Salt Lake. But that was suicide. The trappers must either cross the mountains or ultimately die. There was no alternative.

So Walker fed his men on horse meat and encouragement and kept steadily, if slowly, on.[16]

The trail, along the watershed between the Merced and Tuolumne rivers, ran through a region where "the high hills are fashioned of the rubble and refuse from off the knees of the mountains," and the majesty and grandeur of the Sierra find few counterparts. But cold, weariness, and hunger leave scant room for wonder or appreciation. So the chronicler of the expedition gave little time to panegyric or glowing picture. But once, for a brief moment, Leonard's reticence broke down. After long days of travel, as he notes, the company found itself in a region of rapid, snow-born streams that ran a little way through deep rock chasms, suddenly plunged headlong over the rim of a sheer-walled canyon, and lost themselves in spray and mist a mile below.

In this fashion a fur trader recorded civilized man's first impressions of the Yosemite Valley — that enchanted land of massive domes and shining water, of changeless but ever changing beauty of forest, sky, and stream. When Walker died, half a century later, he asked to have the discovery of the valley inscribed on his tombstone. Accord-

---

[16] Seventeen horses were killed for food and seven others died along the way.

ing to common report, that was his one request. What else would not seem trivial by comparison?

A few days after leaving the rim of the Yosemite, the party found itself in a different world. The snow had disappeared, the mountains were more friendly, a grove of immense trees, "16 to 18 fathom round the trunk at the height of a man's head from the ground," excited the amazement of even the wonder-hardened trappers; [17] and, best of all, the hunters brought in more deer and bear than their half-starved associates could eat. It was good again to be alive.

The San Joaquin Valley, with its wealth of grass and game and its level trail to the coast, offered a striking contrast to the cold and hunger of the mountains; but despite the country's inexhaustible supply of wild fowl, antelope, elk, and deer, some of the trappers characteristically forgot the starving time in the Sierra and grumbled because they found no buffalo.

The great meteor shower of the night of November 12–13, 1833, which terrorized thousands of people even in the thickly populated parts of the United States and convinced the credulous multitude that the end of the world had come, found Walker's company camped in the lonely expanse of the San Joaquin Valley, and for hours "the air appeared to be completely thickened with meteors falling toward the earth." Some of the meteors exploded in the air and others were dashed to pieces on the ground. Frightened by the noise and dazzling light, the horses tried re-

[17] The Tuolumne or Merced grove of *Sequoia gigantea*, according to Farquhar.

peatedly to stampede; and until Walker explained the nature of the phenomenon, some of the superstitious trappers
were probably as panic-stricken as the frantic horses.

The morning after the meteor display the company broke
camp and traveled on till it came to an arm of San Francisco
Bay. A day and a half later the party crossed the Coast
Range Mountains and reached the shores of the Pacific. In
Leonard's simple words, "they had come to the extreme end
of the great West." Some of the trappers were deeply
stirred by the experience and found in it compensation for
all the long journey's hardships and privations, not merely
because it represented a personal achievement that might
live in the memory of many generations but also because
they believed it had significant national implications. It
was the latter feeling that moved Leonard to write:

Most of this vast waste of territory belongs to the Republic of the United States. What a theme to contemplate
its settlement and civilization. Will the jurisdiction of the
federal government ever succeed in civilizing the thousands
of savages now roaming over these plains, and her hardy
freeborn population here plant their homes, build their towns
and cities, and say here shall the arts and sciences of civilization take root and flourish? yes, here, even in this remote
part of the great west before many years, will these hills and
valleys be greeted with the enlivening sound, of the workman's hammer, and the merry whistle of the ploughboy. But
this is left undone by the government, and will only be seen
when too late to apply the remedy. The Spaniards are making inroads on the South — the Russians are encroaching
with impunity along the sea shore to the North, and further
North-east the British are pushing their stations into the
very heart of our territory, which, even at this day, more

resemble military forts to resist invasion, than trading stations. Our government should be vigilant. She should assert her claim by taking possession of the whole territory as soon as possible — for we have good reason to suppose that the territory *west* of the mountain will some day be equally as important to the nation as that on the *east*.[18]

Some forty miles below San Francisco the trappers, still keeping close to the sea, attracted the attention of the captain and crew of the *Lagoda,* a New England vessel engaged in a sea-otter hunt under command of Captain John Bradshaw, and at Bradshaw's invitation Walker and his men came aboard and enjoyed the ship's hospitality. The wandering landsmen feasted on bread, butter, cheese, and other delicacies they had not tasted for two years, and, with the aid of several casks of cognac, prolonged the celebration until daylight. Captain Bradshaw and his crew then went ashore with the trappers, "to taper off on the harder fare" of the mountain men.

Obtaining a rough idea of California's geography and physical characteristics from Captain Bradshaw, Walker started overland for Monterey. Two or three days' travel through an almost uninhabited region brought the company to the home of John Gilroy, a former English or Scotch sailor, who had married a member of the Ortega family and lived on the Rancho San Isidro. The next night the trappers camped at the nearby Mission of San Juan Bautista.

Like Harrison Rogers and James Ohio Pattie, Zenas Leonard, the observant chronicler of the expedition, re-

[18] Leonard: *Narrative,* pp. 49–50.

corded many details of California life in his absorbing journal. He wrote of the Mission of San Juan as follows:

This station much resembled a fort or garrison. The part which is called the Church, forms one side or end. The other three sides are divided into different departments like cells, each cell sheltering so many Indians, and covers near half an acre of ground, with the door of each cell opening to the inside. These buildings are the same as if they were under one roof, with the exception of a gate at each corner of the square. The buildings are constructed of brick. For rafters they use poles tolerably well shaped, and for lathing they make use of poles of a smaller size. The roof is generally composed of a kind of cane grass which is carefully laid on the rafters and then covered with earth; for which purpose they generally have the roof nearly flat in order to hold the earth. But the church, or principal building, is built of handsome brick, and is well finished, being covered with tile. For the instruction of these Indians there is four hours of each day devoted to education and prayer, and the balance of the day is occupied in teaching them the rudiments of agriculture and the mechanical arts. The females are carefully instructed in the art of sewing, and other accomplishments of housewifery. Every thing in this station is under the control & management of the Priests, who exercise the authority of Governor, Judge, &c., being privileged to try and condemn all criminal acts.[19]

With Governor Echeandía's treatment of Smith and the Patties possibly in mind, Walker left his men at the iso-

---

[19] Ibid., p. 52. For a comparable account of the Mission San Gabriel, see the journal of Harrison G. Rogers in Dale: *The Ashley-Smith Expedition,* pp. 194–224. The Secularization Act that brought about the ruin of the California missions had not been put into effect at the time of Walker's visit.

lated mission while he and Leonard went to Monterey to spy out the land and make their peace with the civil authorities. José Figueroa, one of the most liberal of Mexican-appointed officials, was then Governor of California, and Walker had no difficulty in obtaining permission to winter in the country. The Governor also allowed the trappers to supply themselves with game and to trade as they pleased with the Spanish population; at the same time he forbade all traffic with the Indians or license to trap in their territory.

The company remained at San Juan until February. During that interval Walker made two excursions to Monterey, both to see the country and to exchange the company's modest catch of furs for Captain Bradshaw's sugar, coffee, tea, and other supplies on the *Lagoda.* There were no beaver to trap along the coast, but other game was plentiful and the men spent much of their leisure time in hunting. On one occasion a bear reversed the usual order of things and nearly killed one of the hunters. "It appeared that Philips [the man in question] had been out hunting deer," wrote Leonard,

and having killed one, took out the insides and hung it upon a tree, and started to the camp to get a horse to bring it home. After travelling a mile or so, whilst ascending a hill, he came suddenly upon an old bear and two cubs. — The bear immediately on seeing Philips, as is their custom, reared on her hind feet, and being very close, commenced growling most furiously. This our hero could not brook, and fearing the consequences if he should shoot and wound her, lost his presence of mind, and started to run. — The bear immediately pursued and caught him. He now found it quite useless to attempt to get loose, and only saved his life by sinking to the ground and affecting to be dead. The bear then left him, but not without wounding him to such a degree that it was a long time before he could collect strength enough to raise to his feet. It was late at night when he reached the camp, and was so far gone, from hunger & loss of blood, that his life was despaired of at first. One of his arms was broke & his body most shockingly cut and mangled.[20]

According to Washington Irving, the trappers threw off all discipline and generally went to the devil during their stay in California. "They attended bull fights and horse races," he wrote, "forgot all the purposes of their expedition; squandered away freely the property that did not belong to them; and, in a word, revelled in a perfect fool's paradise." Irving's charge may be true; but present-day historians can find no better foundation for it than Captain Bonneville's unsupported word and his evident desire to make Walker the scapegoat for his own failures and financial debacle.

Affidavits from two of Walker's trappers, Nathan Daily and George W. Frazier, indicate that their leader was in good standing with Governor Figueroa, and that the latter had no complaint against the Americans. Daily declared that he was originally employed by Captain Bonneville, "who had passports from the United States to enter any part of the Mexican dominions," and came with him to the Rocky Mountains. He then continued: "My time being expired, I bought animals and entered the company of Capt. Walker, who was a-trapping Beaver in the service of Capt. Bonnival, under whose passports we entered California

[20] Leonard: *Narrative*, p. 57.

297

in the year 1833. Wishing to stop in the country, Capt. Walker gave me letters of recommendation to General Figaror. I presented them to the General, who told me I was welcome to stop in the country as long as I liked." [21]

For the most part, the trappers were on friendly terms with the local inhabitants as well as with Governor Figueroa. But when a band of Californians "borrowed" some of the trappers' horses — a common and accepted practice in the California of that day — Walker quietly broke camp and moved leisurely across the mountains to a new location, about forty miles east of Mission San José, in the San Joaquin Valley. "Our encampment," wrote Leonard, "is beautifully located on a rising piece of ground, with a handsome river gliding smoothly along immediately in front, an extensive oat plain stretching out as far as the eye will reach to the rear. . . . The banks of this river are most delightfully shaded with timber, principally oak and elm. The soil in the plain is very strong and deep, producing heavy crops of wild oats and grass — affording excellent pasture for horses, at this season of the year." [22]

The region was full of game — elk, deer, bear, and wild horses by the thousand — and the trappers laid in a huge supply of dried meat for future use. While they were thus occupied, a force of Californians, looking for a "party of

---

[21] Frazier's statement is almost identical with that of Daily. The two men were among the large number of American and English residents of California seized by Governor Juan B. Alvarado in the so-called "Graham affair" of 1840 and sent in irons to Mexico. The affidavits are datelined U. S. Legation, Mexico. Dispatch No. 26, July 2, 1840. Huntington Library Photostats L 16 I 71.

[22] Leonard: *Narrative*, p. 60.

Indians who had eloped from the St. Juan Missionary station, and taken with them 300 head of horses," rode into camp. The troops stopped overnight with the trappers, and the following morning some of the Americans accepted an invitation to join the expedition.

When the pursuers reached the raiders' village, they found that all the warriors had fled to the higher mountains and left behind only a few decrepit old men, a helpless body of women and children, and most of the stolen horses, "well-butchered and partially dried." Then, according to Leonard, the Californians ran amuck, massacred the helpless natives in a fit of sadistic fury, and wound up by cutting off the ears of their mutilated victims to "show the Priests and Alcaldes that they had used every effort to regain the stolen property."

Shortly after this incident Walker went to Monterey to purchase the last of the necessary supplies for his return to Salt Lake. "Today," wrote Leonard, "Capt. Walker returned from the settlements well supplied with such articles as we were in need of — bringing with him 100 horses, 47 cow cattle, and 30 or 35 dogs, together with some flour, corn, beans, &c., suitable for our subsistance in the long journey, for which every man was now busily engaged in making preparation."

On February 14, according to Leonard's reckoning, the expedition started on its long homeward journey. The trail was unmarked, the general course of the route only hazily known, the way necessarily encompassed by danger and hardship. Six members of the original company chose to stay in California, but new recruits were found to take their places.[23] All in all, the company made an impressive showing. In addition to some fifty-two mounted men, the cavalcade included nearly fifty head of cattle, over three hundred horses, and a mobile food reserve of at least thirty dogs.

On the evening of the second day two deserting California soldiers, "bringing with them 25 of very fine horses," rode into camp and begged to be allowed to accompany the trappers back to the Rocky Mountains. "They informed us," Leonard explained, "that they had deserted from the Spanish army, and that as it was the second time, if taken now, according to the Spanish military discipline, their punishment would be certain death." The plea was probably far-fetched, but the trappers agreeably welcomed the runaways and bought the horses.

Making no attempt to retrace the trail he had opened over the Sierra into California the preceding fall, Walker pursued his leisurely way up the San Joaquin Valley, probably intending to cross what we now know as the Tehachapi Mountains into the Mojave Desert and eventually strike the Wolfskill or Spanish trail to the Sevier and Green river valleys. At the Kern River, near the southern end of the San Joaquin plains, however, he learned of a pass through the Sierra that promised a much shorter and more direct route to the Salt Lake basin. So, with two Spanish-speaking Indians to serve as guides, he turned up the Kern and fol-

[23] George Nidever, John Price, Nathan Daily, and George W. Frazier were certainly among the six. An article in the *Santa Cruz Sentinel* of June 14, 1873 adds the names of Francisco Lajueness, "Sandy" John Hoarde, Thomas Bond, Capt. Merritt (or old "Stuttering" Merritt, as he was called), and Billy Ware, to the original members of Walker's party.

lowed that stream to a clearly defined gap in the mountain wall that gave access to a sandy plain, almost devoid of grass or other vegetation.

Through this gap, appropriately known today as Walker Pass, the cavalcade poured down the south slope of the Sierra Nevada Mountains and out on the level floor of the Mojave Desert. Here massive, naked peaks stood guard between the wooded mountains and the gray desert sand and furnished an unforgettable landmark, which later trappers appropriately named Point of Mountain or Point of Rocks. Walker's first camp after striking the Mojave Desert was presumably at the site now known as Indian Wells — a few miles from today's large Naval Ordnance Test Station of Inyo-Kern.[24]

Here Walker had two choices: he could cross the desert toward the Mojave River, strike the "Old Spanish Trail" that ran from Los Angeles to Santa Fe, and follow that fairly well-known route to the Sevier River in southern Utah; or he could travel northward along the eastern base of the Sierra, eventually intersect his earlier trail from "Battle Lakes" to Walker River, retrace his steps along the Humboldt, and cross the Utah plains to the Bear River Valley or Salt Lake. Walker elected to take the latter route.

By that time, however, many of the company were already trail-weary, badly afflicted with the mountain man's

---

[24] Joe Meek's fantastic version of Walker's return, by way of the Mojave villages, the Gila, Moqui land, etc. may be dismissed without serious consideration. His whole account of the California expedition is equally unreliable. Frances Fuller Victor: *The River of the West* (Hartford, Conn., 1870), pp. 152–3.

peculiar brand of homesickness, and desperately hungry for the companionship, excitement, and dissipation of the rendezvous. So, as the company made its way up through the present Owens Valley, a narrow depression between the Sierra Nevada on the west and the tortured, sun-scorched Inyo-White Mountain ranges on the east, the malcontents grumbled over the trail, sometimes because of the long stretches of rock and sand, sometimes because of the many ice-cold streams they were obliged to ford.

To anyone familiar with the Owens Valley, Leonard's description of the route — the only account available — is hopelessly confusing and confused. He notes twice, for example, that a level plain or desert ran directly from the base of the "Calafornia mountains" as far as the eye could reach toward the east — a statement that obviously ignores the previously mentioned wall of mountains on the eastern side of the Owens Valley, almost as high and rugged as the Sierra Nevada range itself. His full account of the passage up the valley ran as follows:

The country we found to be very poor, and almost entirely destitute of grass. We continued through this poor country travelling a few miles every day, or as far as the weakened state of our dumb brutes would admit of. The weather was mostly clear and otherwise beautiful, but we had quite a cold wind most all the time. Travelling along the eastern base of this (Calafornia) mountain, we crossed many small rivers flowing towards the east, but emptying into lakes scattered through the plain, or desert, where the water sinks and is exhausted in the earth. This plain extends from here to the Rocky mountains, being almost uninterrupted level, the surface of which is covered with dry, loose sand.

In this manner we travelled along, passing such scenes as are described above, until at length we arrived at some springs which presented a really remarkable appearance, and may be called boiling, or more properly Steam Springs, situated near the base of the mountain, on or near the banks of a small river. These springs are three in number, and rise within a short distance of each other, one being much larger than the other two. The water constantly boils as if it was in a kettle over a fire, and is so hot that if a piece of meat is put under the water at the fountain-head, it will cook in few minutes, emitting a strong sulphurous smell — the water also tastes of sulphur. In a clear morning the steam or smoke rising from these springs may be seen a great distance as it hangs in the air over the springs, similar to a dense sheet of fog. There is not a spear of vegetation growing within several rods of the spot, and the surface of the ground presents the appearance of one solid piece of crust, or hard baked mud. When the water empties in and mixes with the river water, it leaves an oily substance floating on the surface similar to tar or greace of any kind.

About the 25th of May, we again continued our journey, but our difficulties had been multiplying for some time, until now we found them quite formidable. — The principal part of our present difficulties arose from the scarcity of pasture for our horses and cattle. After travelling the best way we could, for a few days towards the North, we arrived at another beautiful sandy plain, or desert, stretching out to the east far beyond the reach of the eye, as level as the becalmed surface of a lake. We occasionally found the traces of Indians, but as yet, we have not been able to gain an audience with any of them, as they flee to the mountain as soon as we approach. Game being very scarce, and our cattle poor, gives us very indifferent living.[25]

---

[25] Leonard: *Narrative*, pp. 66–7.

Both the men and their leader, feeling that they "had been travelling many days without getting any nearer," were anxious to take a more direct route to the valley of the Salt Lake. So, presumably in the vicinity of what is now known as Benton's Crossing, the band left the Owens Valley and started off on a course running slightly east of north.[26] The move was ill-timed. The route up the Owens River actually led by easy stages into the region now known as Mono Basin, and that watershed in turn afforded ready access to the Walker River and the original outbound trail from Salt Lake, which the trappers wished to strike.

But without an intimate knowledge of the topography of the upper Owens Valley and the Mono Basin, Walker's choice was sensible enough; and almost every man in the company, anxious to get back to the Rocky Mountain rendezvous and trapping-grounds, enthusiastically welcomed the change of course.

Disappointment, suffering, and near-disaster, however, waited on the new trail. Almost as soon as they left the long grassy meadows of the upper Owens, the trappers found themselves in a region of complete and perilous desolation. There was no water; there was no grass; there was no escape from the rock, sand, and ancient lava beds that bruised the feet of the horses and cut the hoofs of the suffering cattle to the quick. Dust and heat added to the misery of men and animals alike; thirst turned men's lips and throats to ashes and their blood to fire. At the end of

---

[26] An old road crosses the Owens River in this vicinity and intersects U. S. Highway No. 6, a few miles to the east. The latter highway then crosses the White Mountains through Montgomery Pass, the only gap in the range for many miles, and runs on to Tonopah.

two days a majority of the company, against their leader's counsel, voted to leave the plains and attempt to return to the grass and water of the mountains.

The decision was made at midnight; an hour after sunrise the desert was furnace-hot. Horses, dogs, and cattle began to fall and die along the trail, and the trappers were forced to make moccasins from the hides of the dead cattle to protect the feet of the surviving animals. Leonard thus described the forlorn state of the expedition:

When night came we halted for a short time in order to collect the men and animals together, which were scattered in every direction for a mile in width, lest we should get separated at night, as we intended to travel on without ceasing until we would find water or arrive at the mountain.

When our forces collected together, we presented a really forlorn spectacle. At no time, either while crossing the Rocky or Calafornia mountains, did our situation appear so desperate. We had to keep our dumb brutes constantly moving about on their feet, for if they would once lay down it would be impossible to get them up again, and we would then be compelled to leave them. Nor were the men in a much better condition. It is true, we had food, but our thirst far exceeded any description. At last it became so intense, that whenever one of our cattle or horses would die the men would immediately catch the blood and greedily swallow it down.[27]

When night came, somewhat revived by the cooler air, the company continued its journey toward the mountains. About midnight the half-frantic horses, catching the scent of water, became unmanageable and veered sharply to the north. A few minutes later the company reached a clear,

[27] Leonard: *Narrative,* pp. 68–9.

cold stream flowing out of the mountains across the plain. The discovery marked the end of the harrowing desert march. The trappers were again in a region of water, wood, and grass.

Early in June, according to Leonard's journal, Walker struck his former trail from Salt Lake and rested a day or two before starting out to retrace his steps to the Rocky Mountains. In contrast to their recent experience, the trappers looked on the return journey as something of a holiday excursion. The horses and cattle found plenty of grass and quickly regained their strength; while the men themselves, their imagination already enflamed by the prospect of the coming rendezvous, rose early and traveled late.

Only one incident remained to mar the homeward march. As the expedition approached Humboldt Sink, bands of hostile-looking Indians began to appear along the trappers' route. Following his usual custom, Walker sought to win their confidence and friendship; but either the memory of the trappers' former bloody onslaught at Battle Lakes led them to suspect his overtures, or the prospect of loot proved stronger than any wish for peace. So Walker's efforts failed, and the tragedy of the preceding year was re-enacted. A second time the mounted trappers rode down the howling Indians and fell upon their wretched victims in the "wildest and most ferocious manner." Walker, fully aware of the ease with which the skirmish might get out of hand and degenerate into an orgy of murder, watched the attack with deep concern and ordered his men to end the slaughter as soon as the savages were in full retreat. The engagement resulted in the death of fourteen Indians and the wounding of many others. Three trappers were slightly hurt.

Leaving the scene of the encounter, Walker traveled along the Humboldt or Barren River until rapidly dwindling supplies forced him to turn north to the Snake River in southern Idaho. There the trappers found plenty of game and laid in a supply of fresh elk, deer, beaver, and bear meat.

The company then headed for the buffalo country farther east and celebrated the Fourth of July with a feast of steaks, ribs, and humps. Walker found a small quantity "of good old brandy for the occasion," wrote Leonard, "a highly welcome addition which we drank in a few moments, deeply regretting that we did not have a small portion of what was that day destroyed by the millions of freemen in the States." The rest of National Independence Day was spent in the typical manner of the mountain men — singing, shooting, speech-making, running, jumping, and attempting to imitate the feats of roping and horsemanship of the two fun-loving California vaqueros who had joined the company in the San Joaquin Valley.

About a week after this celebration the company reached Captain Bonneville's encampment on the Bear River and came again under his immediate command.

The subsequent activities of the expedition lie outside our sphere of interest; neither is Walker's later career as trapper, guide, miner, and landowner properly a part of the present narrative. The expedition to California established his fame as an explorer and made him one of the historic pathfinders of the Great West. His trail ran from

Salt Lake down the Humboldt River, across the Sierra Nevada Mountains to the coast, from the San Joaquin Valley by way of Walker Pass to the Mojave-Colorado basin, up the unknown Owens Valley almost to its source, and back again to the Humboldt.

Irving, relying wholly upon biased and unsupported charges, spoke of Walker's history-making exploits as "this disgraceful expedition," whose failure (God save the mark!) struck a cruel blow at both the pride and the purse of Captain Bonneville (incompetent at least as a fur trader), squandered the latter's funds and peltries, made it impossible for him to explore the mysteries of the Great Salt Lake, and brought his entire Western enterprise to the verge of ruin.

Walker's California expedition was also branded in later years as a typical horse-stealing venture of the American mountain men. The notorious Joe Meek, a man inclined to become "intoxicated with the ferment of his imagination," declared that the company was much more concerned with obtaining California horses than taking beaver skins; and William Craig, a mountain man of dubious past, made the unfounded statement that Walker's company left California with 500 or 600 horses, which they traded to the Indians on the way back to the Rocky Mountains.[28]

A recent writer referred to "Captain Joe Walker who with his forty land pirates" had first gone through Walker Pass with "horses appropriated from the Californians." [29]

---

[28] LeRoy Hafen: "Mountain Men," *Colorado Magazine*, Vol. XI, No. 5, p. 174.
[29] Favour: *Old Bill Williams*, p. 99.

And even the benevolent De Voto spoke of "later raids by Joe Walker, who took to trading in California horses when the fur trade petered out." [30]

These references are clear-cut and positive, but the historical evidence on which presumably they rest is extremely tenuous. At one time or another nearly every American trapper coming into California, Jedediah Smith and Ewing Young included, was charged with stealing horses. Old Joe suffered from this general, carelessly bandied accusation; but apparently the California officials themselves never made such charges.

As a mountain man Walker differed widely from the type to which Old Bill Williams, Jim Beckwourth, and Peg-leg Smith belonged. His standing with the California rancheros was apparently never called into question, and such men as Abel Stearns and Don Juan Bandini were accustomed to do business with him.

In my opinion, Walker was the victim both of careless and unverified assumptions and of a confusing identity of names. One of the most famous leaders of the Indian horse-thieves during the latter years of the fur trade was a Ute chief named Walkara. The whites anglicized his name to Walker and often called him "Chief Joseph."

Walkara spoke Spanish fluently and could also make himself understood in English. He carried on an extensive business with the Mexican traders from Santa Fe and Taos, including those bound for California, and year after year led his raiders, often in large bands, against the ranches of southern California.

---

[30] Bernard De Voto: *Across the Wide Missouri* (Boston, 1947), p. 433.

Walkara was reputedly joined in these raids by Bill Williams, Peg-leg Smith, and other trappers of similar reputation but there is no evidence to show that Joe Walker, the American, was ever a partner of his Indian namesake. The similarity of names, however, understandably made Joseph Reddeford Walker, the white, a scapegoat for the raids of "Chief Joseph" Walkara, the Ute — perhaps the greatest horse-thief the Far West ever knew.

But whatever his relation to the horse herds of the Californians, Joseph Reddeford Walker stands as a figure of heroic proportions in the history of the West, a man of integrity, courage, and simplicity, "one of the bravest and most skillful of the mountain men," a servant of destiny, "worthy to be grouped with Jedediah Strong Smith and Ewing Young as the trilogy responsible for the march of this nation to the shores of the Pacific; the true Pathfinders." [31]

[31] Douglas Watson: *West Wind, the Life Story of Joseph Reddeford Walker* (Los Angeles, 1934), p. 76.

CHAPTER 9

Partisans versus Mountain Men

THE FUR traders' invasion of the Southwest, as the Prologue explained, started either from the valley of the Salt Lake, the Spanish settlements of New Mexico, or the lower reaches of the Columbia River. American trappers dominated the first two of these approaches; the Hudson's Bay Company, old, experienced, indefatigable, monopolized the third.

Fort Vancouver, the original outpost of John Jacob Astor's dream of empire and the fur trade, served as the center of the company's Western operations. Expeditions from this post, which stood across the Columbia River from the site of the present city of Portland, penetrated the trapping-grounds of British Columbia in the north, the Yellowstone and Snake river country in the east, the wilderness of Oregon and Idaho, the San Joaquin and Sacramento valleys of California, the Humboldt basin of Nevada, and even the delta region of the lower Colorado.

For years the presiding genius of the fort was Dr. John McLoughlin, the "White-Headed Eagle," the warder of the Western marches, the benevolent despot of the old Northwest. McLoughlin, doctor of medicine, a man of culture and strong religious bent, made his "rude castle on the great river" an oasis of letters and civilization in the wilderness. Most of his fellow officers were well-educated men, many of them graduates of Oxford and Edinburgh. They were predominantly of Scottish birth, hardy, vigorous, canny, strong-willed. In their leisure they read history, biography, books on travel and agriculture, poetry, the classics, and the London *Times*. Morning prayers and Sunday worship were as much a part of the life of the post as trade with the Indians or the traffic in skins. "The keynote of life at Fort Vancouver," wrote Skinner, "was work. On the Sabbath men rested — and worshipped." Envious rivals also said that John McLoughlin's henchmen "kept the Sabbath — and everything else as well."

When Thomas Jefferson Farnham, the observant if garrulous American traveler, visited Vancouver in the early forties, he described the fort as

an oblong square 250 yards in length, by 150 in breadth, enclosed by pickets 20 feet in hight. The area within is divided into two courts, around which are arranged 35 wooden buildings, used as officers' dwelling, lodging apartments for clerks, storehouses for furs, goods and grains; and as workshops for carpenters, blacksmiths, coopers, tinners, wheelwrights, &c. One building near the rear gate is occupied as a school house; and a brick structure as a powder magazine. The wooden buildings are constructed in the following manner. Posts are raised at convenient intervals, with grooves in the facing sides. In these grooves plank are inserted horizontally; and the walls are complete. Rafters raised upon plates in the usual way, and covered with boards, form the roofs.

"Six hundred yards below the fort, and on the bank of the

river, is a village of 53 wooden houses, generally constructed like those within the pickets. In these live the company's servants. — Among them is a hospital, in which those of them who become diseased are humanely treated. — Back and a little east of the fort, is a barn containing a mammoth threshing machine; and near this are a number of long sheds, used for storing grain in the sheaf.[1]

William A. Slacum, an officer in the Navy, who, on occasion, gathered confidential information for the government, made a report to the President on the Oregon territory as he found it in 1836–7. Slacum estimated that the total population of Vancouver, including Sandwich Islanders, Indians, half-breeds, and slaves, was between 750 and 800. The fort had about 3,000 acres under cultivation and operated a small sawmill. The settlement was policed as strictly as a well-regulated military garrison.[2]

The Hudson's Bay Company differed in certain important particulars in both organization and operations from its American rivals. The fortified trading post was common to both systems; the rendezvous was peculiarly an American institution; the company's trapping brigade contained several important elements that were foreign to the typical American trapping party. The usual American fur-trading expedition, for example, consisted almost exclusively of men; a Hudson's Bay Company brigade contained fifteen or twenty whites, fifty or more French-Canadian, Indian,

---

[1] T. J. Farnham: *Travels in the Great Western Prairies* (New York, 1843), p. 103.

[2] Slacum's report is found in Sen. Ex. Doc. 25th Cong., 2d Sess., Vol. I, Doc. 24. The text, with a brief foreword, appears in the *Oregon Historical Society Quarterly,* Vol. XIII, pp. 175–224.

or half-breed trappers, and a multitude of women and children.

This large and heterogeneous personnel necessitated the use of much larger supply trains and many more horses than the American system required; so that a fur brigade, bound for a distant hunt of eighteen months' or two years' duration, resembled a small-scale tribal migration. The women of the brigade did the work of the camp, dressed the pelts, tanned the skins for shirts and moccasins, and relieved the men of innumerable other essential details. They and the children became a liability only when the brigade suffered major disaster, such as epidemic, serious shortage of food, or defeat at the hands of hostile Indians.

The brigade leader, known in Canadian terminology as the partisan, was one of the ablest and most responsible of the company's employees. The list of partisans at Fort Vancouver included Tom McKay, Alexander McLeod, Michel Laframboise, John Work, and Peter Skene Ogden, men of much the same temperament, ability, and training as their American contemporaries Jedediah Smith, Ewing Young, and Joseph Walker.

"The leader of the fur brigade," wrote Herbert E. Bolton, "had to be a man of parts. Not only was he a dictator, the sole law and authority, but he was military commander in case of attack by hostile Indians. He was physician in case of illness, linguist with a knowledge of many native tongues, and diplomat to negotiate with Spaniards, Russians, and Americans, his rivals for the harvest of furs. Above all he must be a highly competent trapper and trader, in order that he might return to headquarters with

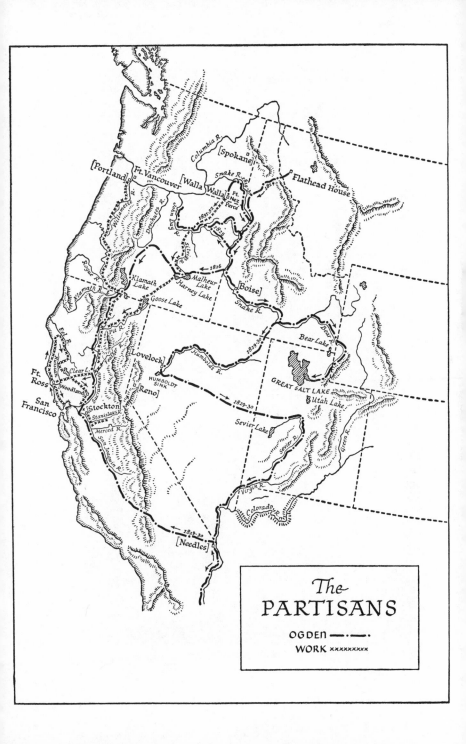

The
PARTISANS

OGDEN —·—·—
WORK ×××××××××

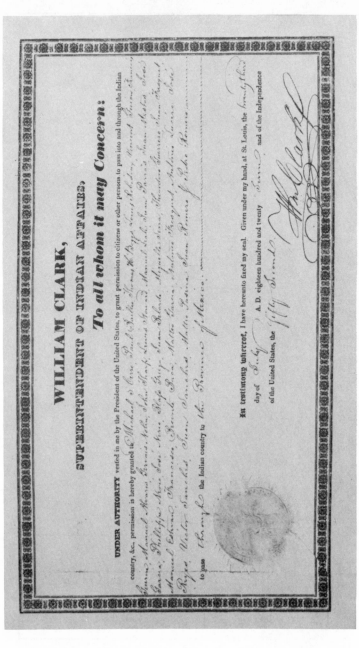

Traders' and Trappers' Permit

a satisfactory yield of beaver and other skins for shipment to the London market of his employers." [3]

It does not lie within our province, except incidentally, to describe the activities of the Hudson's Bay Company in the disputed and prolific trapping-grounds now included in the states of Idaho, Wyoming, and Montana; this chapter deals primarily with the less familiar expeditions that explored the territory lying south and west of the imaginary line, drawn from Fort Vancouver to the Great Salt Lake, that defined the northern limit of the territory covered by the present volume. The region included the Great Basin, eastern and southern Oregon, and California.

Of all the chief traders who led their motley companies from Fort Vancouver to the east and south, Peter Skene Ogden was probably the ablest and certainly the most far-ranging. Ogden's father was a graduate of King's College of New York (later Columbia University), a Tory who left New Jersey for conscience' sake, a competent lawyer who became one of the judges of the King's Admiralty Court in the province of Quebec.

Ogden, "short, dark, and exceedingly tough," entered the service of the Northwest Fur Company when he was about twenty years of age and transferred to the Hudson's Bay Company with the historic merger of the two organizations in 1821. Thereafter he became one of the most significant pathfinders of the West beyond the Rocky Mountains. The second largest city of Utah is appropriately named for him because of his primary explorations of the

---

[3] *Fur Brigade to the Bonaventura*, ed. by Alice Bay Maloney (San Francisco, 1945), p. v. Reprinted by permission of the publishers, the California Historical Society, San Francisco.

valley of the Salt Lake and the possible discovery of the great lake itself. He was the man "who first explored the region of the Humboldt river, who first recorded the name of Mount Shasta, who first explored the central and southern Oregon country . . . the man who hastened up the Columbia immediately after the massacre of the white people at the Wai-i-lat-pu Mission in 1847 and ransomed the fifty or more women and children held in captivity there by the Cayuse Indians." [4]

In 1824 Ogden was given command of the annual Snake River brigade, "the most dangerous and arduous expedition of the Columbia River district," and set out for his new trapping-grounds from Flathead House, near the present town of Thompson Falls, Montana, with "25 lodges, two gentlemen, two interpreters, 71 men and lads, 80 guns, 364 traps, and 372 horses." The territory assigned to the brigade extended east as far as the Grand Tetons and south to Salt Lake and the Humboldt.

Under Ogden's leadership successive brigades brought back thousands of beaver skins to the company's posts; but the loss of life was so great on these expeditions that in 1829 only one member of the company that had originally entered the Snake River country ten years before remained alive. In addition to its high mortality rate, the Snake River service also had a black reputation for suffering and hardship. "This life makes a young man sixty in a few years. A convict at Botany Bay is a gentleman at ease compared to my trappers," Ogden wrote; and his comment, as

---

[4] T. C. Elliott: "The Earliest Travelers on the Oregon Trail," *Oregon Historical Society Quarterly*, Vol. XIII, p. 80.

the story of nearly every brigade reveals, was, in fact, a gross understatement.[5]

Few details of Ogden's first extended expedition are available; his second venture, like his first, carried him into the rich beaver country through which the long, inconstant Snake, now turbulent, now leisurely, loops and winds and cuts its way. On the Bear River, a tributary of the Great Salt Lake, he came into contact with a band of Ashley's American trappers and suffered one of the most costly and galling experiences of his career. The incident, mentioned with little comment in an earlier chapter, may be described to better advantage here.

In 1824 Alexander Ross, then in command of the Snake River expedition, permitted Jedediah Smith and six of his destitute fellow-American trappers to accompany the Hudson's Bay brigade from Bear River in Utah to Flathead House in northwestern Montana. According to Ogden, he and his company paid heavily for this generous but foolish act on the part of his predecessor. The journey to Flathead House, through country as yet unvisited by American trappers, gave Smith and his companions a knowledge of the country's great potential wealth in furs. This meant the end of the Hudson's Bay Company's undisturbed monopoly of the resources of the region. The war for furs in the Snake River country had begun.

The visit also hurt the company's interests almost as seriously in another way. Prior to that time it had enjoyed exclusive control of the free trappers and Indians of the Northwest. It set its standard of prices and wages without

---

[5] T. C. Elliott, loc. cit., p. 390.

competition. Its agents sold dearly and bought cheaply; the victims had no redress.

The coming of the Americans changed this entire picture. Smith and his associates let it be widely known that Ashley paid his men at least twice as much per pound for beaver skins as the company allowed and sold his goods at half the price the latter charged. These reports caused widespread dissatisfaction among the company's trappers and seriously affected their morale.

Ogden left Flathead House for the Snake River country on December 20, 1824, taking Jedediah Smith and the other mischief-making Americans back to their own country with him. At the bend of Bear River, about a hundred miles north of the Great Salt Lake, the Americans left the brigade and started up the river to join a band of Ashley's men, under command of a certain John Gardner, who were wintering in the region. Ogden continued down the river to its outlet in the Great Salt Lake and thereby, along with Jim Bridger and Etienne Provost, became one of the three possible discoverers of the historic inland sea.

After visiting the lake, Ogden established camp some distance up the Bear and made preparations for a long, hazardous expedition in search of the headwaters of the Umpqua River, which supposedly lay somewhere in the unexplored country to the west.

While Ogden was thus engaged, a party of fifteen French Canadians and eight Mexicans, led by Etienne Provost, one of Ashley's men, and François, an Iroquois chief who had deserted from the company two years before, appeared at the camp. The unwelcome visitors said that they were from

Taos, fifteen days distant by pack train, and had an assortment of goods that had reached the New Mexican settlements by wagon train from St. Louis. This invasion of the Snake River country by traders from Santa Fe offered another threat to the company's once secure monopoly.

A head-on collision with the Americans now occurred. "We were well repaid for our trouble," wrote Ogden in describing his visit to the lake,

and were averaging 80 Beaver per diem until the 20th May when we met with a worse [disaster:] that damn'd all cursed day that Mr. Ross consented to bring the 7 Americans with him to the Flat heads: on this day we met with a party of 25 Men, Canadians, Americans and Spanjards, and in the evening they were joined by another party of Americans 30 in number with the American colors, headed by one Gardner, they encamped within 100 yards of our encampment *he*, Gardner lost no time informing all *hands* that they were in the United States Territorys and that they were all free, engaged or indebted, and to add to this they would pay $3\frac{1}{2}$ dollars for Beaver and Goods cheap in proportion. The ensuing morning Gardner came to my Tent, and after a few words of no import, he questioned me as follows: do you know in what Country you are? to this I replied I did not as it was not settled between Great Britain and America to whom it belonged, to which he made answer that it was, that it had been ceeded to the latter, and as I had no licence to trade or trap to return from whence I came without loss of time, to this I replied when we receive orders from our own Government then we shall obey, then he replied remain at your peril, he then left me, and on seeing him go into an Iroquois (John Gray) Tent, I followed him, on entering this Villain Gray said I must now tell you that all the Iroquois as well as myself have long wished for an opportunity to join the Americans, and if we did not sooner it was entirely owing to our bad luck in our not meeting with them, but this year we had taken our precautions, alluding to the 7 Americans who had wintered and left us in April and again joined here, but now we go and all you can say or do cannot or will not prevent us from going. Gardner now said, you have had these poor Men already too long in your service and have most shamefully imposed on them, selling them Goods at most extravagant rates and giving them nothing for their Skins.[6]

Ashley's version of the historic controversy presented the incident in a somewhat different light. In a communication to the *Missouri Observer and St. Louis Advertiser* he wrote that "Mr. Jedediah Smith, a very intelligent and confidential young man," had crossed from the headwaters of the Rio Colorado to the Snake River in the fall of 1824, followed that stream approximately a hundred miles, and then turned north to Clark's Fork of the Columbia. There he found a trading establishment of the Hudson's Bay Company with a complement of eighty men who, trapping on both sides of the Rocky Mountains, had taken out about 160,000 pounds of beaver furs in four years. Ashley then continued:

The circumstances which produced this visit had nearly led to serious consequences. Messrs. Jedediah S. Smith, Wm. L. Sublette and several others of the American party, intelligent young men, of strict veracity, had visited the

---

[6] Ogden's version of this affair was given in a long dispatch to the "Governor Chief Factors and Chief Traders Hms. Hudson's Bay Company N. dist. York Factory," *The Letters of John McLoughlin. . . .* First Series, 1825–38, ed. by E. E. Rich (Toronto, 1941), Appendix A, pp. 296–7. See also Frederick Merk: "Snake Country Expedition, 1824–25," *Oregon Historical Society Quarterly,* Vol. XXXV, No. 2, pp. 93–122.

British camp and reported to their comrades that the British flag had been repeatedly hoisted during their stay there. The Americans, indignant at such impertinence and understanding, too, that the British camp was within eight miles of them, resolved to proceed to the place and tear down the flag, even at the risk of their lives. Twenty-two of them, with the American flag hoisted, advanced to the spot but no British flag was to be seen. They made known their business to Mr. Ogden and protested in threatening language against a recurrence of the same insult offered them; they also required of Mr. Ogden to move his party from that vicinity without delay.

The incident had both temporary and lasting repercussions. Ogden felt its immediate effects in the loss of at least twenty-three trappers, the necessity of writing off the substantial debts the deserters owed the company, and the diversion of some three thousand pounds of beaver fur to his American rivals. The defection of his men also forced him to abandon his proposed expedition to the sources of the Umpqua, damaged the company's prestige with the trappers and Indians of the Northwest, added materially to Ashley's catch of furs, and ushered in a persistent battle for supremacy on the western slopes of the Rockies between the long-established company interests and the American interlopers.

On the other hand, as a result of the victory of the Americans, Ogden was able to persuade the company to increase the price of beaver fur paid to the trappers and lower the cost of goods, thereby removing the principal incentive for the free trappers to desert. He also advocated a concentration of the company's activities in what he called the

"Claminitt," or Klamath country, roughly the region south of the Columbia and west of the Great Salt Lake, to forestall any American rivalry in that sector.[7]

Ogden advanced both economic and political reasons for the adoption of this latter policy. First, he pointed out that it would require much less time for a brigade to reach the new trapping-grounds than to make the journey to the Snake River and its tributary regions. Second, he argued that if the company moved at once, it could forestall its rivals and trap out the beaver so thoroughly that the Americans would have no cause to invade the region either for furs or for settlement, and thus enable England to gain permanent possession of the land.

As Sir George Simpson wrote Dr. McLoughlin, some two years later: "The greatest and best protection we can have from opposition is keeping the country closely hunted as the first step that the American Government will take towards Colonization is through their Indian Traders and if the country becomes exhausted in Fur bearing animals they can have no inducement to proceed thither. We therefore entreat that no exertions be spared to explore and Trap every part of the country and as the service is both dangerous and laborious we wish our people to be treated with kindness and liberality." [8] More than a decade later Slacum testified to the company's continued adherence to this policy and its success in the ruthless exploitation of the beaver.

[7] Frederick Merk: *Fur Trade and Empire* (Cambridge and London, 1931), pp. 274 *et seq.*; *Publications of the Champlain Society* (Toronto, 1940), Vol. III, pp. lxvi–lxix.
[8] Ibid., Vol. III, p. lxviii.

In the spring of 1825 Ogden was again on the shores of the Great Lake and a few months later led his long-delayed expedition into the rugged country of eastern Oregon, where the John Day River finds its source. Crossing the mountains to the Powder or Burnt River in the dead of winter, under the most damnable conditions, the brigade nearly perished. A few brief entries in Ogden's journal tell the story: "Many in the camp are starving. For the last ten days only one meal every two days." Again, "A horse this day killed; on examining his feet, the hoof entirely worn away and only raw stump." A few days later, "A more gloomy country I never saw." Finally, "Two of the men could not advance from weakness. We have been on short allowance almost too long and resemble so many skeletons." [9]

It may be said in passing that the diaries of the company's partisans were often curious and fascinating objects. "No one who has not seen the original of one of the Journals used by the trappers and traders when in the field can appreciate the difficulty in reading their contents," wrote T. C. Elliott.

They were made of small sheets of beaver skin often indifferently cured and tied with a thong; and the writing was done with a quill often under very uncertain conditions of weather or comfort. Unless conversant with the French language and with the names and terms common to the country and trade, it is practically impossible to decipher the writing at times, which covers margins and outside as well as inside of the sheets. The wonder is that these journals are so well

[9] T. C. Elliott: "The Earliest Travelers on the Oregon Trail," *Oregon Historical Society Quarterly,* Vol. XIII, pp. 81–2.

preserved as to be deciphered at all, and blunders in the copying may well be overlooked, as it is quite often a question of interpretation, especially with proper names.[10]

In the fall of 1826 Ogden visited Malheur and Harney lakes, later ascended the Des Chutes River, crossed the divide to the Klamath, looked on the white glory of Mount Shasta, and trapped the river that still bears the name of that majestic mountain.[11] Two years later Ogden penetrated an unexplored region that lay south of the Snake River country into which he had led his earlier brigades, and found there a stream that meandered to the southwest, across a land of loneliness and waste. He named the river the Unknown, but his men more appropriately christened it the Ogden. Seventeen years later John Charles Frémont, the follower of other men's trails, gratuitously dropped the name Ogden and called the river the Humboldt.

Ogden's excursions out of Fort Vancouver were supplemented by similar expeditions of his fellow partisans into the Great Basin, southern Oregon, and northern California. The arrival of Jedediah Smith and his companion refugees at Fort Vancouver after the Umpqua massacre in 1828 gave added impetus to these activities and opened a new field in the company's operations.

It is evident, in fact, that Smith's account of the wealth of beaver skins in the San Joaquin and Sacramento valleys and the fur possibilities of the lower Colorado aroused the fever of speculation among the partisans and trappers at

[10] "The Peter Skene Ogden Journals," ed. by T. C. Elliott, loc. cit., Vol. XI, pp. 359–60.
[11] It was known to Ogden as the Sasta.

the fort in much the same way that the report of a new bonanza affects the prospectors in a mining camp. Immediately after Smith's arrival, as we have already seen, McLoughlin sent a brigade under McLeod with orders first to recover the property lost by the Americans and then to explore the country drained by the Buenaventura (or Sacramento) River.[12]

Part of this region was already known. McLeod had gone as far south as the Klamath River the year before; and John Turner, one of the four survivors of the Umpqua massacre, accompanied the brigade to act as guide through the rough country that lay beyond. The expedition successfully trapped the Sacramento and its tributaries and ranged almost as far east as the present town of Sonora and perhaps as far south as the city of Stockton.

On his return, however, McLeod encountered a succession of misfortunes. Floods and heavy winter snows overtook him on Ogden's "Sasta" River, played havoc with the horses, threatened the brigade with starvation, and finally forced him to cache his furs (many of which he lost in trying to ford the river), and started him back to Fort Vancouver in a grim race against cold and hunger to save the lives of his people. The unlucky leader, whom Sir George Simpson, governor of the company, described as "illiterate, self-sufficient, and arrogant," was severely criticized for his management of the enterprise and transferred a year later to the Mackenzie River district.

---

[12] Louis Pickette, a trapper for the Hudson's Bay Company, is said to have visited California in 1820–1. Maloney: *Fur Brigade to the Bonaventura,* p. 89.

While McLeod was engaged in trapping the tributaries of the Sacramento and searching for the western outlet of the imaginary Buenaventura, Ogden undertook what was probably the longest expedition of his adventurous career. Ostensibly charged with the examination of the territory between the Columbia River and California and furnished by Jedediah Smith with a detailed account of the American explorer's Western explorations, Ogden extended his operations far beyond the limits set by any of his predecessors.

From Fort Nez Percés, near the mouth of the Snake, he made his way to the sink of the Humboldt, between the present towns of Fulton and Lovelock, traveled for a month across the sterile wastes of the Great Basin that lie west and south of the great lake, and found the Indians of the country, like those whom Smith had encountered a year and a half before in the same region, unspeakably filthy and degraded. The brigade had little trouble with the natives, though early one morning some of the half-starved wretches, in a futile effort to capture a few horses for food, made a desultory attack on Ogden's camp. The Indians lost one of their number, and the trappers had three horses more or less badly wounded in the foray.

In a "country as barren as ever Christians traversed," the brigade lost many of its horses from thirst and exhaustion and barely escaped a major catastrophe before it reached the Sevier River. Crossing to the Virgin, Ogden finally came to the country of an Indian tribe that bordered the waters of the Rio Colorado. "These Indians," he added, "I strongly suspected to be the same who, the year preceding, had massacred the men attached to the party of

Mr. Smith, an American adventurer;" [13] and the members of the brigade proposed to fall on the Mojaves and avenge the massacre of Smith's trappers. Ogden, however, was not sure enough of the identity of the Indians to warrant such bloody retaliation and forbade the attack.

But when he tried to establish friendly relations with the Mojaves, they grew more and more insolent and finally started a small-scale demonstration. Anticipating such a move, Ogden had armed his men with short spears to supplement their firearms, and after a short but bloody melee the Indians hastily fled. In the trapper's strikingly vivid phrase, now grown trite and flavorless by overuse, twenty-six of the Mojaves were " made to lick the dust."

Ogden's own narrative unfortunately ends with a brief account of this incident. Fragmentary references in other documents indicate that he trapped on down the Colorado with indifferent success to the head of the gulf, returned to the Yuma and Mojave villages, and made his way from there into the San Joaquin Valley.[14] Somewhere in the valley he encountered Ewing Young and his party of American trappers from New Mexico, and the two bands kept amicable company up the Sacramento River until they

---

[13] *Traits of American Indian Life & Character* (San Francisco, 1933), pp. 5–6.

[14] See "Ogden's Report of his 1829–1830 Expedition," ed. by John Scaglione, *California Historical Society Quarterly,* Vol. XXVIII, No. 2, pp. 117–24.

Ogden may have taken Smith's old route to the San Bernardino Mountains, as J. J. Warner suggests, and followed the base of that range to one of the passes across the Tehachapi Range into the San Joaquin; or he may have turned back up the Colorado and broken a new trail across the desert to the present Walker Pass.

came to the abandoned camp sites of Ogden's fellow trapper Alexander McLeod.

There Young turned back empty-handed; while Ogden, with a thousand beaver skins in his possession, returned to Fort Nez Percés and the Columbia. He then unfortunately abandoned the overland trail and attempted to complete his journey by water. But the boat, a crazy, poorly built affair, capsized in a whirlpool below The Dalles and drowned nine members of the party. Ogden himself had "a most narrow escape" and lost all of his precious journals and note books.[15]

For the better part of a decade after the McLeod and Ogden expeditions the Hudson's Bay Company sent its annual trapping brigades to California "to drain the country of its Riches." The account of one of these parties must here serve to tell the story for the rest.

In 1832 Michel Laframboise, a participant in the American Fur Company's Astorian misadventure and one of the most colorful of the Hudson's Bay Company's Western traders, entered the Sacramento Valley by the trail that Alexander McLeod had opened four years earlier from the Columbia. Laframboise reached San Francisco Bay on October 15, visited the missions at San José, Sonoma, and San Rafael, and trapped the sloughs and estuaries of San Francisco Bay so successfully that he described the region as the richest hunting-grounds south of the Columbia.

In the fall of 1832, before Laframboise had begun to

---

[15] See Alice Bay Maloney: "Peter Skene Ogden's Trapping Expedition to the Gulf of California, 1829–30," *California Historical Society Quarterly*, Vol. XIX, pp. 308–16.

exploit the waters of the Great Bay, a second brigade left the Columbia on a long, roundabout trail for the California trapping-grounds. John Work, a conspicuous figure for many years in the fur trade of the Northwest, was in command. Born in 1792 near Londonderry, Ireland, Work entered the employ of the Hudson's Bay Company in his early twenties and served the interests of that company, loyally and successfully, for over forty years. He died in Victoria, British Columbia, in 1861.

Work's wife, Josette Legace, the daughter of a French trapper and a Nez Percés Indian girl, was known for her beauty, courage, physical endurance, and strength of character. She was her husband's unfailing companion, both when he directed the affairs of the Company's post and when he marched at the head of a brigade, and neither hunger, danger, plague, nor battle could induce her to remain in the safe environs of the fort when her husband set out on a trapping venture.

Work badly needed his wife's good cheer and companionship on such expeditions, for he was afflicted with chronic self-pity and had a tendency to magnify his trials and misfortunes under every circumstance. He undertook his California expedition, which consisted of about a hundred persons — twenty-eight men, twenty-two women, forty-four children, and six Indians — with characteristic pessimism and saw little prospect of success with such "ragamuffin freemen" as he had in his command. The company left Fort Vancouver by boat in August 1832 and began the overland journey at Fort Nez Percés, or Walla Walla, early in September.

Work first proposed to cross the northern segment of the Great Basin to Ogden's River, follow that stream to its sink, thence make his way across the mountains to the San Joaquin River, which he called the south branch of the Bonaventura or Sacramento, and travel up the San Joaquin Valley to San Francisco Bay.[16] But a severe epidemic, characterized by the fever and complete prostration of influenza, swept through the brigade in the early stages of the march and so greatly delayed the company's progress that Work abandoned his original plan and sought to find a more direct route to California.

The new trail led almost due south, by way of Silvies River, to Malheur and Harney lakes in central Oregon, and thence southwest to Goose Lake on the border of Oregon and California. Crossing to the Pit River, Work followed that stream down to the Sacramento. Though the brigade suffered more than its share of cold, rain, snow, and sickness after reaching California, the long marches across the dry plains of western Oregon were even worse. Thus on October 11, 1832 Work set down the following entry in his journal:

We have this day made two usual days journey, in consequence of not finding water at the first station where the people used to find it when they passed this way twice before but earlier in the season than at present. On proceeding on to this place a small stony ravine, a former encampment, we have the mortification to find the spring dried up. Our situation is rather gloomy, the more so as a number of the men have become quite discouraged and talk of turning back lest

[16] Work's trail under this plan would have paralleled or crossed that of the American trapper Joseph Reddeford Walker.

themselves & horses die of thirst. They have taken it into their heads that the lake at the next usual station is also dried up & that the horses will not be able to go on to the next station where they also doubt whether there is any water at this season. None of them thought of giving me this information before I left our last station. L. Kanota, on whose information I can place most reliance assures me I will find water tomorrow, I am therefore determined to proceed. Some of the people took the precaution to bring some water from our last station. A small hole is dug where some of the people obtain a small quantity of muddy water taken up in spoonfuls. Two horses gave up on the way and were left behind. Two of the men . . . who had recovered of the fever relapsed today & were very ill, the long day's journeys with the thirst & dust to which they are exposed is very hard upon them.[17]

The country provided a few beaver streams, but the catch was small, Indians proved annoying, and the epidemic, which for a time had been quiescent, now reappeared, though fortunately in somewhat milder form. Near the mouth of Hat Creek, a tributary of the upper Sacramento, Work found traces of another trapping party that had evidently visited the region the preceding spring, and the discovery gave him new causes for pessimism and concern. A little later his discouragement increased.

Early in December two couriers, whom Laframboise had dispatched with letters to Fort Vancouver from his headquarters near San Francisco Bay, stumbled upon Work's camp on the "Big River," or Sacramento. These messengers told him that Laframboise, abandoning his original plan to hunt along the California coast, had turned inland to

[17] Maloney: *Fur Brigade to the Bonaventura,* p. 9.

trap the Sacramento. They brought the further unwelcome information that the tracks which the brigade had so recently encountered were those of a party of American trappers led by Ewing Young.

Work was badly upset by both reports, especially by the word that Laframboise had left the untrapped waters of the coast to trespass on the inland streams on which his own brigade had planned to make its major hunt. But since there was no help for the situation, the disgruntled leader hastened south to join his colleague. The march down the Sacramento added little brightness to the general gloom. Trapping was poor, the winter floods had turned the floor of the valley into a great lake, and the company suffered severely from cold and lack of meat.

Meanwhile, Laframboise had broken camp and started up the Sacramento to join forces with Work's brigade. His company also had a rugged time. Food was scarce, and flooded streams, newly formed lakes, and miles of mud and marsh blocked the trail. Despite these obstacles, however, the two brigades met on January 16, 1833, on the north side of a sizable tributary of the Feather River named the Bear.[18]

The combined party, now under Work's command, numbered 163 persons. It crossed the principal branch of the Feather River above the present site of Marysville and found an immense number of elk on the adjacent plains.

---

[18] Some time before the reunion John Turner, who had been with the Hudson's Bay Company since his escape from the Umpqua massacre, left Laframboise to join Ewing Young; but Work testified that the errant American "paid his debt & delivered up his traps and horses before he went off."

The main body of the expedition remained a month in this vicinity while Laframboise and a few scouts undertook, unsuccessfully, to locate the rival American trappers under Ewing Young.

During that time high water brought trapping to a standstill, but for a month the hunters had a field day, killing 395 elk, 148 deer, 17 bear, and 8 antelope — a slaughter so far in excess of the actual needs of the company that Work regretfully remarked: "when the most of the people have ammunition and see animals they must needs fire upon them let them be wanted or not." [19]

Still of the belief that his men would find it profitable to trap the streams along the coast, Work at last succeeded in crossing the flooded Sacramento and turned southwest toward the ocean. At Putah Creek, in the vicinity of Clear Lake, one of the Indian hunters "got himself badly torn by a bear" and narrowly escaped being killed. There, too, Work again came across the cold trail of Ewing Young and sent a detachment to track down the elusive American. At the same time he dispatched a small party under Laframboise to Sonoma to obtain ammunition from the Mission of San Francisco Solano for the spring and summer hunt.

Though courteous enough to the strangers, the Californians had neither powder nor lead to place at their disposal, so the trappers went on to the Russian settlement at Fort Ross. This was an imposing establishment, and Laframboise and his associates must have found more than passing interest in comparing it, in construction, resources,

---

[19] *Fur Brigade to the Bonaventura,* p. 31.

and fortifications, with Fort Vancouver and the other posts of the Hudson's Bay Company with which they were familiar.

Begun in the spring of 1812, the Russian fort stood on a bluff a hundred feet and more above the ocean. Its outer defense was a redwood stockade, twelve feet high, three hundred feet long, two hundred and eighty feet wide, well provided with loopholes, and surmounted by iron spikes or wooden palings. A two-story bastion, twenty-five feet in diameter, protected the northwest corner, and a somewhat larger bastion stood diagonally opposite.

The space within the stockade contained warehouse, barracks, the commandant's house, a chapel, a kitchen, and a jail. Beyond the stockade there were nearly fifty buildings, including blacksmith shop, tannery, flour mill, dairy house, stables, corrals, kitchens, bathhouses, and cabins. At the time of Laframboise's visit the total population of Ross was about two hundred and sixty, including fifty Aleuts and thirty-nine baptized Indians.

At Ross, as at Sonoma, Work's emissaries received a hospitable welcome; but the Russians, like the Californians, were short of supplies themselves, and the trappers had to be satisfied, at the cost of seven beaver skins, with only ten pounds of powder, a like weight of tobacco, and thirty pounds of lead. For good measure, however, the Russians added the unwelcome information that the route along the coast was difficult, the Indians troublesome, and beaver extremely scarce.

Laframboise's return to the base camp almost empty-handed increased Work's already jaundiced outlook, and his pessimism grew worse when the scouting party came back from its search for Ewing Young with the discouraging report that it had neither found the Yankee, learned anything of his whereabouts, nor taken any skins. He dismissed the report of the scarcity of beaver as merely a Russian device to keep the English from invading the coastal trapping-grounds and laid the blame for the failure of the party to "the old man who was at their head," who listened "too much to the babbling among the people." [20]

With nothing further to gain by remaining where he was, Work raised camp and moved down to one of the northern arms of San Francisco Bay. Here he was visited by a friendly group of California officials from Governor Figueroa, and two Americans, possibly J. J. Warner and Moses Carson, who had left Young's employ some time before.

According to these trappers, Young had found few beaver north of the Russian settlements, and the party had experienced great difficulty in crossing the mountains that paralleled the coast. But Work looked on the Yankees as virtual deserters and refused to put any credence in information derived from such untrustworthy "runaways."

In the meantime dwindling supplies and an even more

---

[20] About this time a small party, including Moses Carson and George Yount, former members of Ewing Young's company, brought a drove of horses to Work's camp and sold some of the animals to the trappers for a reserve food supply on the long return to Fort Vancouver. But the two Americans, much to Work's disappointment, knew nothing of Young's whereabouts.

critical shortage of ammunition were adding to Work's anxieties. On hearing the report that a foreign ship, with a quantity of powder in its cargo, was lying at anchor in San Francisco Bay, he hurried Laframboise off to the harbor; but the ship had sailed the day before the party reached Yerba Buena. Living as usual on a hand-to-mouth basis, the presidio itself came to the rescue with only twenty-four pounds of powder, forty pounds of ball, and a bottle of rum.[21] Thereafter disappointments and misfortunes multiplied. A flock of sheep stampeded the brigade's horses, one of the hunters died from wounds inflicted by a bear, and the dread epidemic that had first appeared on the Columbia broke out again as virulent as before. The rains continued late, moreover, and high water seriously interfered with trapping and almost immobilized the expedition.

About the middle of April, however, Work finally broke camp and started up the coast, still firm in his belief that the men would find good trapping above the Russian settlements. But presently he discovered to his sorrow that the reports of the scarcity of beaver, which he had so cavalierly discounted as the work of rivals or scoundrels, were understatements rather than exaggerations. The route, too, against which Work had vainly been warned, proved a nightmare of toils and tribulations. Horses rolled off the trail or were swept into the sea by raging floods. Barrancas, cañons, heavy undergrowth, dense fogs, and swollen rivers taxed the endurance of man and beast alike. The plague

---

[21] Work regarded the price for the powder, lead, and rum as exorbitant and called the Californians "a set of mean scoundrels."

reappeared and gave grim warning of the evil days and nights that lay ahead. [22]

Near the Mattole River, a stream that falls into the Pacific a few miles south of Cape Mendocino, even Work became convinced of the futility of looking further for profitable beaver streams along the coast and divided the company into its two original brigades. Laframboise, with thirty men and their complement of wives and children, was instructed to continue northward till he came to Jedediah Smith's old trail along the coast and to follow that into the Willamette Valley. Work, with the remainder of the company, undertook to cross the mountains and trap the Sacramento.

The parties separated on May 13, 1833. After traveling as far north as the Eel River, Work turned southeast and followed that stream through rough, exhausting, heavily wooded country, almost to its source. Later he came to one of the upper branches of the Russian River and reached the large body of water known today as Clear Lake. Still looking in vain for beaver, the brigade pushed across the Coast Range Mountains, while the truculence of the Indians kept the men under constant tension and the rocky trail played havoc with the horses' feet. [23]

The brigade reached the Sacramento Valley, near the present town of Woodland, on May 29. The river still ran

---

[22] The trail finally led to the site of one of Ewing Young's old camps, but the camp told nothing except that the Americans had made an extended stay and then gone farther north.

[23] Under such conditions American trappers usually prepared rawhide moccasins for the suffering animals, but Work apparently made no effort to use this simple device.

high, and the floor of the valley was full of lakes, pools, marsh, and mud. Under such conditions the usual methods of taking beaver were almost useless, so Work put his trappers in dugout canoes and sent them down the river while he and the rest of the brigade floundered along overland as best they could.

To add to the brigade's troubles, spring suddenly gave way to summer and the weather turned almost unbearably hot and sultry. Swarms of "Muscatoes," as Work wrote, tormented the company throughout the day and made sleep impossible at night. In addition, the Indians became more threatening and finally a party of ten or twelve, including one who spoke some Spanish, under pretense of a friendly visit to the camp attempted to steal some of the brigade's horses. But the plot was discovered in time and the trappers killed two of the would-be thieves and wounded several others. The survivors fled into the tules and escaped. Work himself had a narrow escape in the melee. One of the raiders was about to shoot him in the back when a woman attached to the brigade attacked the Indian with an ax and put him to flight. The Indians kept the men on the alert during the night, but just before dawn they gave their war-whoop, fired a heavy flight of arrows into the camp, and silently made off.[24]

After this incident the expedition continued along the San Joaquin until eventually it reached the Stanislaus River, one of the tributaries on which Jedediah Smith had camped five years before. The water continued high, the season was growing late, and the catch of beaver skins had

---

[24] Maloney: *Fur Brigade to the Bonaventura*, pp. 64–5.

fallen far short of expectations. Finally, and most impera-
tive of all, the critical shortage of ammunition made it necessary for the brigade to face about and begin its return
to Fort Vancouver without additional delay.[25]

The homeward journey started badly. The Indians were
becoming more and more troublesome and the trappers
found it necessary to be constantly on guard. In retaliation
for numerous hostilities Work's men finally burned two
native villages, killed many of the occupants, and recovered fifteen or twenty horses. Before starting up the "Big
River," the brigade camped for several days on or near
the present site of Sacramento while the hunters killed and
dried a quantity of meat for the journey homeward.

But there was now a threat of death in the air. The heat,
almost unbearable by day, gave place at night to a cold,
heavy dew that saturated clothing and blankets and chilled
the sleeping camp. As soon as the sun came up, the heat
and stagnant air created a constant, intolerable thirst, and
the people drank excessively of the bad, unpalatable water
that seems to have constituted their only available supply.
The mosquitoes grew worse and made life a torment to
man, woman, and papoose. Then the chills and fever returned and the plague stalked unhindered through the
camp.

The Indian villages, too, were almost depopulated. Variously identified as malaria, cholera, typhus, measles, a
contagious fever aggravated by syphilis, but more prob-

---

[25] Between June 11 and July 24 the brigade took a total of 249 beaver
and 85 otter — a poor return for the six weeks' effort of the number of
men engaged.

ably a virulent form of influenza, the epidemic swept through the region like a devastating fire.[26] In the vicinity of the Feather River it carried off the natives in such numbers that the bodies of the dead remained unburied, a prey to the wolves, buzzards, and coyotes; and the survivors, reduced to skin and bones, lay in the huts and bushes too weak to move.[27] One trapper declared that he saw only six or eight living Indians between "the head of the Sacramento and the great bend and slough of the San Joaquin."

As the summer heat increased, the sickness among Work's own people reached alarming proportions; and before the end of August sixty-one members of the brigade alternately suffered from what their leader realistically called "shaking fits" and "hot fits." "Our condition is really deplorable," Work wrote on August 20, "so many of the people taken ill and no medicines, fortunately not many of the men are yet ill, but it is to be apprehended they will soon fall and that we will soon become so weak that we will not be able to raise camp, and I am afraid to stop lest we die like the Indians . . . the most of the people completely disheartened, and indeed well they may be." [28]

A few days later the number of sick had risen to seventy-two and the situation became so alarming that Work was afraid the company would never see Fort Vancouver's friendly walls again. "Indeed we are in a most deplorable condition and all my efforts can scarcely keep up the men's

[26] This was the same epidemic that Young had encountered. See p. 239.
[27] See Dr. Edward W. Twitchell: "The California Pandemic of 1833," *California and Western Medicine*, Vol. XXIII, pp. 592–93.
[28] *Fur Brigade to the Bonaventura*, p. 72.

spirits," he wrote on August 24. "A long road it is," he added as he thought of the barriers of mountain and forest, the slow march of the caravan, and the hostile Indians ahead, "but we must push on as it is our only means of safety."

Rain and cold greeted the suffering brigade as it crossed the mountains at the head of the Sacramento Valley; and the Indians killed and wounded so many horses that even the sick, half-dead trappers were forced to undergo the extra burden of keeping nightly guard. Work himself suffered a severe attack of the sickness; but though he shook at times like the leaves of the quaking asp and had no more strength than a little child, the rugged old partisan refused to lessen his activities or transfer the burden of his responsibilities to another's shoulders.

After leaving the "Big River," or Sacramento, the trail ran from the Pit to the McLeod, from the McLeod through the valley of the Shasta to the Klamath, from the Klamath across the high Siskiyou mountains, with their raw, penetrating cold, to the Rogue. Here and there along the route the brigade found traces of Ewing Young's expedition and more recent evidence of the presence of Laframboise and their fellow trappers of his brigade; but the tracks were old and their discovery did nothing to relieve the deepening gloom. Storm, rain, threatened Indian attack, and the ever present sickness made the journey a nightmare of suffering and apprehension.

One of the victims of the epidemic died of a relapse, leaving a widow and five children. An Indian and two children also succumbed. Work was "reduced to a perfect skeleton" and became so ill that he could scarcely walk. With increasing difficulty and more frequent delays because of the sick and afflicted, the brigade continued its forlorn advance until by good fortune it met Laframboise, returning at the head of a small party from Fort Vancouver to the Umpqua, and obtained from him a small quantity of fresh supplies. Rain and cold still continued to harass the sick, but the epidemic was dying out; and on October 29, 1833, after an absence of almost fourteen months, Work and a small advance party reached Fort Vancouver. Two days later the rest of the company was welcomed at the post.

The expedition returned slightly over a thousand beaver and otter skins, and thus proved a financial disappointment; but Work brought back a knowledge of the country and its potential fur resources that was worth many times the cost of the venture. For an additional ten years the Hudson's Bay Company trapped the long reaches of San Francisco Bay and the streams of the Sacramento and San Joaquin valleys.[29]

In 1841, by that time presumably influenced more by

[29] Even as late as the season of 1837–8, a brigade under Laframboise, who had returned from California to Fort Vancouver the preceding July "with fair hunts," made its headquarters at the junction of the Feather and Sacramento rivers and reported a catch of 2,700 skins. This interesting and important expedition is described in a letter of October 18, 1838 to the "Governor, Deputy Governor and Committee, Hon. Hudsons Bay Comy," by James Douglas. *McLoughlin's Fort Vancouver Letters,* First Series (Publications of the Champlain Society, Toronto, 1941), pp. 252–3, 279, 289–90.

See also Laframboise to Mariano G. Vallejo, September 29, October 9, 1838, and John McLoughlin to Vallejo, January 10, 1838, Vallejo *Documentos,* Bancroft Library.

political than economic motives, the company established William Glen Rae, McLoughlin's son-in-law, as resident agent in San Francisco. Domestic and financial difficulties led Rae to commit suicide four years later; but the presence of such a representative in San Francisco during the critical years before the Mexican War gave color to the report that Great Britain was using the Hudson's Bay Company as a stalking-horse to gain control of California, and aroused some resentment among American residents and a few of the more loyal Californians.[30]

As leaders, adventurers, explorers, whom many followed but none preceded, these partisans of the "Great Company" — Peter Skene Ogden, John Work, Michel Laframboise, "the Captain of the California Trail" — were cast in the same mold and made of the same stuff as Jedediah Smith, Ewing Young, and Joseph Walker, the best of the American mountain men.

[30] For a detailed account of this venture, see Anson S. Blake: "The Hudson's Bay Company in San Francisco," *California Historical Society Quarterly,* Vol. XXVIII, Nos 2, 3.

EPILOGUE

THE COURSE of history is unpredictable. It responds
as often to seemingly insignificant factors as to those that
command the attention of the world. It is sensitive alike to
the death of kings, the words of unknown prophets, the
outcome of devastating wars, the discoveries of obscure
scientists, the triumph or failure of revolutions, and even
ephemeral changes in manners, styles, and social customs.

For generations most of the beaver fur of North America
was used in the manufacture of men's hats. As long as that
demand continued, the trappers' market was assured. But
British and New England ships were expanding their trade
with China and bringing back increasing cargoes of silks,
teas, and similar rare commodities. So between 1830 and
1835, when the opening of the Five Treaty Ports was only
about a decade off, fashion joined forces with the merchants and decreed that men's hats should be made of silk
instead of fur. That decision closed the chapter of the
Western fur trade and concluded the era of the mountain
men.

Other factors worked toward the same end. Even before
the extensive use of silk, hat-makers had begun to substitute seal, South American nutria, and even rabbit fur for
beaver. Heavy, unrestricted trapping depleted most of the
beaver streams and in places depopulated them altogether.
The large-scale migration of settlers over the trappers'
routes to Oregon and California, even before the Mexican

War, the occupation of Utah by the Mormons, or the gold rush to California, robbed the fur trader of his monopoly of the Western streams.

The trapping industry reached its height in 1830 or 1832. The average price of beaver fur in the mountains was then from four to six dollars a pound and a good trapper, with luck, could take four or five hundred pounds a year. By 1840 the price had fallen to one or two dollars a pound and a trapper's annual catch seldom ran above a hundred and fifty pounds.

Overtaken by such adversity, the industry, at least as the mountain men had known it since the days of Colter, Hobach, Henry, Pilcher, and Manuel Lisa, inevitably died out. The American Fur Company held the last of the trappers' rendezvous on Green River in 1840. The fur traders' forts became military posts, fell into melancholy ruins, or degenerated into stopping-places and supply centers for westward-moving emigrants.

The mountain men, even by the close of 1845, were thus a fast-disappearing race. Death had already come to Ashley, Smith, Jackson, the two Sublettes, Ewing Young, and many others who had figured so prominently in the history of the Southwest. The mulatto Jim Beckwourth, long a chief among the Crows, had died of poison administered by his people, with his precious amulet — a perforated bullet and two large oblong beads — around his neck.

The fate of Peg-leg Smith, James Ohio Pattie, and Old Bill Williams has already been described. William Wolfskill, Benjamin D. Wilson, George Nidever, James Clyman, George Yount, and a few others would end their days as useful and prosperous citizens of California. Pauline Weaver was to become one of the creators of the modern Arizona. Kit Carson, Joe Walker, Thomas Fitzpatrick, and Jim Bridger were soon to establish Frémont's reputation as an explorer and later serve as emigrant guides, army scouts, or government representatives among the Indians. Antoine Robidoux was predestined to spend his final years as pensioner of the government, feeble and half-blind. Death likewise loitered too long along the trail for old Jim Bridger — poor, suffering, nearly sightless, and sometimes bitter against the world.

So life dealt kindly or harshly with the mountain men, as it deals with everyone. They were a tough, reckless, none too gentle breed. But they lived their lives, did their work, served their day and generation, and went up to possess the land. And when they passed over, all the trumpets must have sounded for them on the other side.

BIBLIOGRAPHY

THE *following bibliography includes only those sources that have actually been consulted in the preparation of this study. Though the list relates primarily to the fur trade of the Southwest, it necessarily contains many items that are not confined exclusively to that region but cover the fur trade of the entire trans-Mississippi West.*

In addition to the valuable and often extensive references that appear in many works on the fur trade, three separately issued bibliographies deserve special mention: Henry R. Wagner's The Plains and the Rockies (*San Francisco, 1921*); *Library of Congress: "List of References on the Fur Trade in the United States" (typescript, 1914: supplement, 1937); and St. Louis Public Library: "Furs and Fur Bearers of the United States and Canada, a List of Books and Articles . . ."* Bulletin, *April 1929.*

MANUSCRIPT COLLECTIONS

Chouteau Collections. A great body of letters and documents relating to the Santa Fe trade and the activities of Pierre and Auguste Chouteau beyond the mountains. *Missouri Historical Society.*

Clark Papers. Correspondence and official documents of General William P. Clark. *Missouri Historical Society.*

Coe Collection of Western American History. The letters of George Bent to George E. Hyde, relating to Bent's Fort and members of the Bent family, are especially useful. *Yale University Library.*

Floyd [W. P.?]: Diary of a Trip with Beale's Expedition, September 27, 1858 to May 1, 1859. *Huntington Library, San Marino, California.*

347

Fort Sutter Papers. Correspondence and other papers, chiefly of Edward M. and Richard H. Kern. *Huntington Library.*

John Parish Papers. Selections from the Sublette Papers and other documents in the Missouri Historical Society Collection. *Library of the University of California, Los Angeles.*

Letters of Francis Ermatinger, 1823–53. The Hudson's Bay Company's activities. (Typescript) *Huntington Library.*

Mexico, General Archives, Department of State, Expediente No. 2721 (1827). Official Documents relating to Ewing Young, Milton Sublette, and other American trappers in New Mexico. *Huntington Library Microfilm.*

——: Secretariat of Government, Expediente No. 45. Papers relating especially to Ramón Vigil. *Huntington Library Microfilm.*

National Archives. Chiefly documents of the State and War departments. Especially valuable for background material and official government activities in territory bordering on the provinces of Mexico. Washington, D. C.

New Mexico State Museum Documents, including New Mexican Archive Manuscript Material. Microfilms of selections from these manuscripts in the Huntington Library relate to the activities of American trappers and traders in Santa Fe and occasional controversies with New Mexican officials or inhabitants.

Ritch Collection. This very extensive collection of manuscripts contains a number of official documents, customs declarations, books of passports, court proceedings, and government decrees relating to Americans in New Mexico and Chihuahua and the trade and trapping industry of the Southwest. *Huntington Library*.

St. Vrain, Céran, to "Messrs. B. Pratte & Co." (September 28, 1828) and "Declaration of the Party of Engages, Taos, N. M., September 1, 1829." *Missouri Historical Society*.

Santa Fe Envelope. Miscellaneous collection of manuscripts relating to the traders and trappers in New Mexico. *Missouri Historical Society*.

Sibley Papers. An extensive collection of documents and manuscripts relating to the activities of George C. Sibley, the early Santa Fe trade, and the construction of the road to Santa Fe. *Missouri Historical Society*.

Stearns, Abel, Papers. *Huntington Library*.

Sublette Papers. These include an original diary of William L. Sublette from March 25 through June 3, 1825, and numerous business papers and correspondence relating to the firm of Smith, Jackson, & Sublette. *Missouri Historical Society*.

United States Legation, Mexico. Dispatch #26, July 2, 1840. Affidavits of Nathan Daily and George W. Frazier, members of Joseph Reddeford Walker's expedition of 1833–4. *Huntington Library Photostat (original in the State Department Archives, Washington, D. C.)*.

Vallejo, Mariano Guadalupe: *Documentos Para la Historia de California*, 1713–1851. Chiefly useful because of the official correspondence relating to the expeditions of Jedediah Smith and the activities of the Hudson's Bay Company in California. *Bancroft Library, University of California, Berkeley*.

Walker Collection. Petition of Ewing Young to Governor Juan B. Alvarado, March 10, 1837, for the removal of cattle to the Willamette Valley. *Huntington Library*.

William Henry Ashley Manuscripts. Drafts of Ashley's

letters, business accounts, etc. Of unusual value for any study of the Western fur trade. *Missouri Historical Society.*

NEWSPAPERS AND PERIODICALS

The Alta California (July 2, 1856).

ATHERTON, LEWIS E.: "Business Techniques in the Santa Fe Trade," *Missouri Historical Review* (April 1940), Vol. XXXIV, No. 3.

AUERBACH, HUBERT S.: "Father Escalante's Journal and Related Documents," *Utah Historical Quarterly*, Vol. XI, Nos. 1–4 (January, April, July, and October 1943).

BARRY, J. NEILSEN: "Capt. Bonneville," *Annals of Wyoming* (April 1932), Vol. VIII, No. 4.

BLAKE, ANSON S.: "The Hudson's Bay Company in San Francisco," *California Historical Society Quarterly* (June and September 1949), Vol. XXVIII, Nos. 2 and 3.

BREWERTON, GEORGE D.: "A Ride with Kit Carson," *Harper's New Monthly Magazine* (August 1853), Vol. VII.

CAMP, CHARLES L., ed.: "The Chronicles of George C. Yount," *California Historical Society Quarterly* (April 1923), Vol. II, No. 1.

CAMP, CHARLES L., ed.: "James Clyman, His Diaries and Reminiscences," *California Historical Society Quarterly* (June 1925), Vol. IV, No. 2.

COX, ISAAC JOSLIN: "Opening of the Santa Fe Trail," *Missouri Historical Review* (October 1930), Vol. XXV, No. 1.

DYE, JOB F.: "Recollections of a Pioneer of California," *Santa Cruz Sentinel* (May 15, 1869).

EDWARDS, P. L.: "Rocky Mountain Correspondence," from

the *Missouri Enquirer* (Liberty, Mo.), in *Niles Register* (October 11, 1834), vol. XLVII.

ELLIOTT, T. C.: "The Earliest Travelers on the Oregon Trail," *The Oregon Historical Society Quarterly* (May 1912), Vol. XIII, No. 1.

—— ed.: "The Peter Skene Ogden Journals," *The Oregon Historical Society Quarterly* (June 1910), Vol. XI, No. 2.

FLYNN, ARTHUR J.: "Furs and Forts of the Rocky Mountain West," *The Colorado Magazine* (March 1932), Vol. IX, No. 2.

FROST, DONALD MCKAY: "Notes on General Ashley, the Overland Trail, and South Pass," *Proceedings of the American Antiquarian Society* (October 1944).

GRINNELL, GEORGE BIRD: "Bent's Old Fort and Its Builders," *Collections of the Kansas State Historical Society* (1919–22), Vol. XV.

HAFEN, LEROY R.: "Armíjo's Journal," *Huntington Library Quarterly* (November 1947), Vol. XI, No. 1.

——: "Mountain Men — Andrew W. Sublette," *Colorado Magazine* (September 1933), Vol. XI, No. 5.

——: "Mountain Men — Louis Vasquez," *Colorado Magazine* (January 1933), Vol. X, No. 1.

Harper's New Monthly Magazine (January 1856), "Fur Hunting in Oregon," Vol. XII.

HARVEY, CHARLES M.: "Fur Traders as Empire Builders," *Atlantic Monthly* (March–April 1909), Vol. CIII.

HILL, JOSEPH J.: "Antoine Robidoux, Kingpin in the Colorado River Fur Trade 1824–44," *The Colorado Magazine* (July 1930), Vol. VII, No. 4. *Touring Topics* (*Westways*) (December 1928), Vol. XX, No. 12.

——: "Ewing Young in the Fur Trade of the Far Southwest 1822–1834," *Oregon Historical Society Quarterly* (March 1923), Vol. XXIV, No. 1.

——: "The Fur Trade in the Far Southwest," *Touring*

Topics (September and October 1928), Vol. XX, Nos. 9 and 10.

———: "Spanish and Mexican Exploration and Trade Northwest from New Mexico into the Great Basin, 1765–1853," *Utah Historical Quarterly* (January 1930), Vol. III, No. 1.

———: "Free Trapper, the Story of Old Bill Williams," *Touring Topics* (March 1930), Vol. XXII, No. 3.

KELLY, CHARLES: "The 'Mysterious D. Julien,'" *Utah Historical Quarterly* (July 1933), Vol. VI, No. 3.

LANMAN, J. H.: "The American Fur Trade," *Hunt's Merchants' Magazine* (September 1840), Vol. III.

LAWRENCE, ELEANOR: "Horse Thieves on the Spanish Trail," *Touring Topics* (January 1931), Vol. XXIII, No. 1.

———: "Mexican Trade between Santa Fe and Los Angeles, 1830–1848," *California Historical Society Quarterly*, Vol. X, No. 1 (March 1931).

MALONEY, ALICE BAY: "Peter Skene Ogden's Trapping Expedition to the Gulf of California, 1829–30," *California Historical Society Quarterly*, Vol. XIX, No. 4 (December 1940).

MARMADUKE, M. M.: "Journal from Franklin to Santa Fe in 1824," *Missouri Historical Review* (October 1911), Vol. VI, No. 1.

MARSHALL, THOMAS MAITLAND: "St. Vrain's Expedition to the Gila in 1826," *Southwestern Historical Quarterly* (January 1916), Vol. XIX, No. 3.

MERK, FREDERICK: "Snake Country Expedition, 1824–25," *The Oregon Historical Society Quarterly* (June 1934), Vol. XXXV, No. 2.

Missouri Advocate and St. Louis Enquirer (October 29, 1825).

Missouri Republican (March 22, 1822 and October 25, 1827).

POLLARD, LANCASTER: "Site of the Smith Massacre of July 14, 1828," *Oregon Historical Quarterly* (June 1944) Vol. XLV, No. 2.

RUSSELL, CARL P.: *Picture Books of the Fur Trade History,* reprint from the *Missouri Historical Society Bulletin* (April 1948), Vol. IV, No. 3.

————: "Trapper Trails to the Sisk-ke-dee," *Annals of Wyoming* (July 1945), Vol. XVII, No. 2.

San Francisco Bulletin (October 26, 1866).

Santa Cruz Sentinel (June 14, 1873).

STEPHENS, F. F.: "Missouri and the Santa Fe Trade," *Missouri Historical Review* (April and July 1917), Vol. XI, Nos. 3 and 4.

THOMAS, CHAUNCEY: "Frontier Firearms," *Colorado Magazine* (May 1930) Vol. VII, No. 3.

TWITCHELL, DR. EDWARD W.: "The California Pandemic of 1833," *California and Western Medicine,* Vol. XXIII.

VARNEY, EDITH, comp. by: *Furs and Fur Bearers of the United States and Canada,* a list of books and articles on the technology and romance of the subject, reprinted from the St. Louis Public Library monthly *Bulletin,* Vol. XXVII, No. 4 (April 1929).

VOELKER, FREDERIC E.: "The Mountain Men and Their Part in the Opening of the West," *Bulletin of the Missouri Historical Society* (August 1947), Vol. III, No. 4.

WALDO, WILLIAM: "Recollections of a Septuagenarian," *Missouri Historical Society, Glimpses of the Past,* Vol. V, Nos. 4–6 (January–March 1938).

WARNER, J. J.: "Reminiscenses of Early California, 1831–1846," *Annual Publications of the Historical Society of Southern California, 1907–8,* Vol. VII.

WESLEY, EDGAR B.: "The Government Factory System

among the Indians, 1795–1882," *Journal of Economic and Business History,* Vol. IV (1931–2).

Wilmington Journal, Wilmington, Calif., October 20, 1866.

WOODBURY, A. M.: "The Route of Jedediah S. Smith . . ." *Utah Historical Quarterly* (April 1931), Vol. IV, No. 2.

WORCESTER, D. E.: "The Weapons of American Indians," *New Mexico Historical Review* (July 1945), Vol. XX, No. 3.

YOUNG, F. G.: "Ewing Young and His Estate," *Oregon Historical Quarterly,* Vol. XXI, No. 3 (September 1920).

YOUNT, GEORGE C.: "Sketches of the Early Settlers of California," *The Hesperian* (March 1859), Vol. II, No. 1.

BOOKS AND PRINTED DOCUMENTS

ALTER, J. CECIL: *James Bridger* (Salt Lake City, 1925).

Annual Report of the American Historical Association for the year 1944, Vol. II, Part I, and Vol. III, Part II; Calendar of the American Fur Company's Papers.

BANCROFT, H. H.: *Works,* 39 vols. (San Francisco, 1882–91).

BEALE, E. F.: *Wagon Road from Fort Smith to the Colorado River* [1860] 36th Cong., 1st Sess., House Ex. Doc. 42.

BENTON, THOMAS H.: Report to the Senate relative to conditions of the fur trade within the limits of the United States, February 9, 1829, 20th Cong., 2nd Sess., Sen. Ex. Doc. 67.

BOLTON, HERBERT EUGENE: *Athanase de Mézières and the Louisiana-Texas Frontier, 1768–1780* (Cleveland, 1914).

BONNER, T. D.: *Life and Adventures of James P. Beckwourth* (New York and London, 1856).

BROWN, MRS. JENNIE BROUGHTON: *Fort Hall on the Oregon Trail* . . . (Caldwell, Idaho, 1932).

BUREAU OF AMERICAN ETHNOLOGY: *Journal of Rudolph Friederich Kurz*, Bulletin 115 (Washington, 1937).

BURTON, RICHARD F.: *The City of the Saints* (London, 1861).

CAMP, CHARLES L., ed.: *James Clyman, American Frontiersman* (San Francisco, 1928).

CARVALHO, S. N.: *Incidents of Travel and Adventure in the Far West* (New York and London, 1856).

CHITTENDEN, HIRAM MARTIN: *The History of the American Fur Trade of the Far West*, 3 vols. (New York, 1902).

CLARKE, S. A.: *Pioneer Days of Oregon History*, 2 vols. (Portland, 1905).

CLELAND, ROBERT G.: *The Cattle on a Thousand Hills* (San Marino, Calif., 1941).

———: *Pathfinders* (Los Angeles, 1929).

COMAN, KATHERINE: *Economic Beginnings of the Far West* . . . , 2 vols. (New York, 1912).

CONRAD, HOWARD LOUIS: *Uncle Dick Wootton* (Chicago, 1890).

COUES, ELLIOTT: *Journal of Jacob Fowler* (New York, 1898).

COX, ROSS: *Adventures on the Columbia River* . . . (New York, 1832).

COYNER, DAVID H.: *The Lost Trappers* (Cincinnati, 1847).

CRONISE, T. F.: *The Natural Wealth of California* (San Francisco, 1868).

DALE, HARRISON CLIFFORD: *The Ashley-Smith Explorations and the Discovery of a Central Route to the Pacific 1822–1829* (Glendale, Calif., 1941).

DELLENBAUGH, F. S.: *Breaking the Wilderness* (New York, 1905).

DE VOTO, BERNARD: *Across the Wide Missouri* (Cambridge, Mass., 1947).

DILLIN, JOHN G. W.: *The Kentucky Rifle* (New York, 1946).

DUFFUS, R. L.: *The Santa Fe Trail* (New York, 1930).

ELLISON, WILLIAM HENRY, ed.: *The Life and Adventures of George Nidever* (Berkeley, 1937).

EMORY, LT. COL. W. H.: "Notes on a Military Reconnaissance from Fort Leavenworth in Missouri to San Diego in California," House Ex. Doc. No. 41, 30th Cong., 1st Sess.

FARNHAM, THOMAS JEFFERSON: *Travels in the Great Western Prairies* (Poughkeepsie, 1843).

——: *Travels in the Californias, and Scenes in the Pacific Ocean* (New York, 1844).

FARQUHAR, FRANCIS P.: *Exploration of the Sierra Nevada* (San Francisco, 1925).

——: *Yosemite, the Big Trees, and the High Sierra* (Berkeley, 1948).

FAVOUR, ALPHEUS H.: *Old Bill Williams* (Chapel Hill, N. C., 1936).

FERRIS, WARREN A.: *Life in the Rocky Mountains* (Denver, 1940).

FLEMING, HARVEY, ed.: *Minutes of Council Northern Department . . . 1821–31* (Champlain Society, Toronto, 1940).

FLINT, TIMOTHY, ed.: *The Personal Narrative of James Ohio Pattie of Kentucky* (Cincinnati, 1831).

GARRARD, LEWIS H.: *Wah-To-Yah and the Taos Trail* (Cincinnati and New York, 1850).

GIBSON, W. H.: *Complete American Trapper* (New York, 1876).

GRANT, BLANCHE C., ed.: *Kit Carson's Own Story of His Life* (Taos, 1926).

GREENE, J. EVARTS: *The Santa Fe Trade: Its Route and Character* (Worcester, Mass., 1893).

GREGG, JOSIAH: *The Commerce of the Prairies*, 2 vols. (New York, 1844).

GRINNELL, GEORGE B.: *Beyond the Old Frontier . . .* (New York, 1913).

GRINNELL, JOSEPH, DIXON, J. S., and LINSDALE, J. M.: *Fur-Bearing Mammals of California*, 2 vols. (Berkeley, 1937).

HAFEN, LEROY R., and GHENT, W. J.: *Broken Hand, the Life Story of Thomas Fitzpatrick, Chief of the Mountain Men* (Denver, 1931).

HALL, SHARLOT M.: *Pauline Weaver, Trapper and Mountain Man* (Arizona, 1929).

HAMILTON, WILLIAM THOMAS: *My Sixty Years on the Plains* (New York, 1905).

Handbook of American Indians North of Mexico, edited by Frederick Webb Hodge. Bureau of American Ethnology, Bulletin No. 30, Part 2 (Washington, 1907–10).

HILL, JOSEPH J.: *The History of Warner's Ranch and Its Environs* (Los Angeles, 1927).

HOBBS, JAMES: *Wild Life in the Far West* (Hartford, 1872).

HUNTER, JOHN D.: *Manners and Customs of the Western Indians* (Philadelphia, 1823).

INMAN, HENRY: *Old Santa Fe Trail* (New York, 1898).

IRVING, WASHINGTON: *Adventures of Captain Bonneville* (Vol. X of *Works of Washington Irving*, new edition, revised, New York, 1861).

———: *Astoria, or Anecdotes of an Enterprise beyond the Rocky Mountains*. Caxton Edition (New York, n.d.; first published in 1841, two vols., Philadelphia).

JAMES, EDWIN: *Account of an Expedition from Pittsburg to the Rocky Mountains*, 2 vols. (Philadelphia, 1823).

JAMES, THOMAS: *Three Years among the Indians and Mexicans* (St. Louis, 1916).

JOHNSON, ROBERT C.: *John McLoughlin, Patriarch of the Northwest* (Portland, Oregon, 1935).

KELLY, CHARLES: *Old Greenwood* (Salt Lake City, 1926).

LARPENTEUR, CHARLES: *Forty Years a Fur Trader on the Upper Missouri . . .* , ed. by Elliott Coues, 2 vols. (New York, 1898).

LAUT, AGNES CHRISTINA: *The Fur Trade of America* (New York, 1921).

LEONARD, ZENAS: *Narrative of the Adventures of Zenas Leonard* (Clearfield, Pa., 1839).

[McDONALD, MRS. CATHERINE:] *An Indian Girl's Story of a Trading Expedition to the Southwest about 1841*, ed. by Winona Adams (reprinted from the *Frontier*, State University of Montana, Missoula, Vol. X, No. 4, May 1930).

MALONEY, ALICE BAY, ed.: *Fur Brigade to the Bonaventura* (San Francisco, 1945).

MARSH, J. B.: *Four Years in the Rockies, or The Adventures of Isaac P. Rose* (New Castle, Pa., 1884).

MERK, FREDERICK: *Fur Trade and Empire* (Cambridge and London, 1931).

Message from the President of the United States Concerning the Fur Trade, and Inland Trade to Mexico, 22nd Cong., 1st Sess., Sen. Ex. Doc. 90 (Washington, 1832).

Message from the President of the United States Relative to the Arrest and Imprisonment of Certain American Citizens at Santa Fe . . . (Washington, 1818).

Message from the President of the United States Relative to the British Establishments on the Columbia, and the State of the Fur Trade, 21st Cong., 2nd Sess., Sen. Ex. Doc. 39 (Washington, 1831).

MONTGOMERY, RICHARD G.: *The White-Headed Eagle,*

John McLoughlin, Builder of an Empire (New York, 1934).

MORGAN, LEWIS H.: *The American Beaver and His Works* (Philadelphia, 1868).

[OGDEN, PETER SKENE:] *Traits of American-Indian Life & Character* (San Francisco, 1933).

PARKER, SAMUEL: *Journal of an Exploring Tour beyond the Rocky Mountains* . . . (New York, 1838).

PARKMAN, FRANCIS: *The California and Oregon Trail* (New York, 1849).

PETERS, DEWITT CLINTON: *Pioneer Life and Frontier Adventures* (Boston, 1884).

——: *The Life and Adventures of Kit Carson* . . . (Boston, 1858).

PIKE, ALBERT: *Prose Sketches and Poems* (Boston, 1834).

PIKE, ZEBULON M.: *Exploratory Travels through the Western Territories of North America* (London, 1811).

PORTER, KENNETH W.: *John Jacob Astor, Business Man*, 2 vols. (Cambridge, Mass., 1931).

Report of the Secretary of War Conveying a List of Licenses to Trade with the Indians as issued during the quarter ending September 30, 1826. House Ex. Doc. No. 86. 19th Cong., 2nd Sess. (Washington, 1827).

RICH, E. ed.: *The Letters of John McLoughlin from Fort Vancouver to the Governor and Committee, 1825–38*, first series (Toronto: Champlain Society; 1941); Second Series *1839–44* (1943).

RICKARD, T. A.: *A History of American Mining* (New York, 1932).

ROSS, ALEXANDER: *Adventures of the First Settlers on the Oregon or Columbia River* . . . (London, 1849).

——: *The Fur Hunters of the Far West* . . . , 2 vols. (London, 1855).

RUSSELL, OSBORNE: *Journal of a Trapper* (Boise, Idaho, 1921).

RUXTON, GEORGE FREDERICK: *Adventures in Mexico and the Rocky Mountains* (New York, 1848).

———: *Life in the Far West* (New York, 1859).

SABIN, EDWIN L.: *Kit Carson Days* (*1809–1868*), (Chicago, 1914).

SAGE, RUFUS: *Scenes in the Rocky Mountains* (Philadelphia, 1846).

———: *Rocky Mountain Life* (Boston, 1858).

SCHARF, JOHN T.: *History of Saint Louis City and County* . . . , 2 vols. (Philadelphia, 1883).

SIMPSON, SIR GEORGE: *Narrative of a Journey round the World, during the Years 1841 and 1842*, 2 vols. (London, 1849).

SITGREAVES, L.: *Report of an Expedition down the Zuñi and Colorado Rivers* [1851]. 32nd Cong., 2nd Sess., Sen. Ex. Doc. 59.

SKINNER, CONSTANCE L.: *Adventurers of Oregon* (New Haven, 1920).

SLACUM, WILLIAM A.: *Report to accompany Senate Bill No. 206*. 25th Cong. 2nd Sess., Sen. Ex. Doc. 470. (A memorial of Slacum to the Senate and House of Representatives, Dec. 18, 1837, appears in Sen. Ex. Doc. 24 of the same Cong. This memorial is reprinted in the *Oregon Historical Society Quarterly*, Vol. XIII).

STANSBURY, HOWARD: *An Expedition to the Valley of the Great Salt Lake of Utah* . . . (Philadelphia, 1852).

STEWART, WILLIAM GEORGE DRUMMOND: *Edward Warren* (London, 1854).

———: *Altowan; or, Incidents of Life and Adventure in the Rocky Mountains*, ed. by Watson Webb, 2 vols. (New York, 1846).

STORRS, AUGUSTUS: *Answers to Certain Queries* . . . , 18th Cong., 2nd Sess., Sen. Doc. 7 (reprinted in *Niles Weekly Register*, January 15, 1825).

SULLIVAN, MAURICE S.: *The Travels of Jedediah Smith* (Santa Ana, Calif., 1934).

U. S. Congress: *American State Papers*, 38 vols. (Washington, 1832–61).

VESTAL, STANLEY: *Mountain Men* (Boston, 1937).

VICTOR, FRANCES FULLER: *The River of the West* (Hartford, 1870).

WAGNER, HENRY R.: *The Plains and the Rockies* (San Francisco, 1921), revised and extended by Charles L. Camp (San Francisco, 1937).

WATSON, DOUGLAS: *West Wind, the Life Story of Joseph Reddeford Walker* (Los Angeles, 1934).

WELLS, FRANK EVARTS: *Story of Old Bill Williams*. A collection of stories about Old Bill printed and sold at Williams, Arizona, in pamphlet form.

WHITMAN, DR. MARCUS: *Journal of an Exploring Tour beyond the Rocky Mountains* (Ithaca, N. Y., 1840).

WILKES, LIEUTENANT CHARLES: *Narrative of the United States Exploring Expedition, during the Years 1838, 1839, 1840, 1841, 1842*, 5 vols. (Philadelphia, 1845).

WILLIAMS, CHAUNCEY P.: *Lone Elk* (Denver, 1935).

WISLIZENUS, ADOLPHUS: *A Journey to the Rocky Mountains in the Year 1839* (St. Louis, 1912).

INDEX

Abreu, Don Santiago, 221; issues a passport to Santiago Martin, 275 n
Across the Wide Missouri, see De Voto, Bernard
Adams River, *see* Virgin River
Adventurers of Oregon, see Skinner, Constance L.
Adventures in Mexico and the Rocky Mountains, see Ruxton, George Frederick
Alta California, 194
Alvarado, Juan B., Governor of California, 243, 298 n
American Fur Company: importance of, 17; practices of, 17 n; toll of fatalities in, 34; blamed for use of liquor, 36; rivalry with other companies, 278; holds last rendezvous, 345
American Fur Trade of the Far West, The, see Chittenden, Hiram Martin
American River, 80, 80 n, 102, 102 n, 239 f
Ammuchaba Indians, *see* Mojave Indians
Annals of Wyoming, 235 n, 279 n
Antelope Hills, 60
"Antoine Robidoux in the Colorado Fur Trade," *see* Hill, Joseph J.
Apache Indians, 38, 40, 143, 154, 167, 178 f, 193, 225, 227–8
Appelamminy River, *see* Stanislaus River
Aragón, Dr. Juan Estevan, 219
Arkansas River, 10, 123 f, 127, 139, 144 f, 164, 187
Arapahoe Indians, 154
Arikara Indians, 38, 58, 164

Armíjo, Antonio: expedition from New Mexico to California, 141; unofficial account of, *quoted,* 265–6; route of, 266–8; reaches San Gabriel Mission, 268; report of, in *Registro Oficial, quoted,* 269–70; importance of venture, 270
Armíjo, Manuel, Governor of New Mexico: denounces Bent's Fort, 158; measures against American trappers, 213; confiscates Young's furs, 218; official report and proceedings, *quoted,* 219–20; measures against Young and Sublette, 219–24; 234
Ashley, General William H., 18; introduces the rendezvous, 23; 38; advertises for trappers, *quoted,* 56; erects trading post on Yellowstone, 57; Ashley-Henry company, personnel and size of, 57–8; his men encounter Ogden's brigade, 61; explores Green River, 61, 61 n; rendezvous on Henry's Fork, 62; returns to St. Louis, 62; success of expedition, 62; last journey to Rockies, 63; sells interests to Smith, Jackson & Sublette, 63; 63 n; letter to Pratte & Company, *quoted,* 63–5; Ashley MSS., 65 n; agreement with Smith, Jackson & Sublette, 65–6; Smith names modern Sevier River in honor of, 68; takes wheeled cannon to rendezvous, 85 n, 132; Ogden's encounter with Ashley's trappers on Bear River, 317–21; version of incident, *quoted,* 319–21; death of, 345

ii